# SELINA TODD

Selina Todd is Professor of Modern History at Oxford University. She grew up in Newcastle-upon-Tyne and was educated at Heaton Manor Comprehensive School and the Universities of Warwick and Sussex. She writes about class, inequality, working-class history, feminism and women's lives in modern Britain. Her book *The People: The Rise and Fall of the Working Class 1910–2010* was a *Sunday Times* bestseller and was described by the *Observer* as 'A book we badly need'. Based on the voices of working-class people themselves, it charted the history of ordinary workers, housewives, children and pensioners over the turbulent twentieth century.

ALSO BY SELINA TODD

*The People: The Rise and Fall of the Working Class*
*1910–2010*

*Young Women, Work and Family in England*
*1918–1950*

SELINA TODD

# Tastes of Honey

The Making of Shelagh Delaney and a
Cultural Revolution

**VINTAGE**

1 3 5 7 9 10 8 6 4 2

Vintage is part of the Penguin Random House
group of companies whose addresses can be found at
global.penguinrandomhouse.com

Penguin
Random House
UK

Copyright © Selina Todd 2019

Selina Todd has asserted her right to be identified as the
author of this Work in accordance with the Copyright,
Designs and Patents Act 1988

First published in Vintage in 2021
First published in hardback by Chatto & Windus in 2019

penguin.co.uk/vintage

A CIP catalogue record for this book is available from the
British Library

ISBN 9781784703486

Printed and bound in Great Britain by Clays Ltd, Elcograf S.p.A.

The authorised representative in the EEA is Penguin Random House
Ireland, Morrison Chambers, 32 Nassau Street, Dublin D02 YH68.

Penguin Random House is committed to a sustainable future for our
business, our readers and our planet. This book is made from Forest
Stewardship Council® certified paper.

MIX
Paper from
responsible sources
FSC® C018179

*For Charlotte Delaney*
*and Senia Paseta*

# Contents

# 1

# Curtain Up

In April 1958, nineteen-year-old Sheila Delaney, the daughter
of a Salford bus driver, sent a manuscript to Joan Littlewood,
the director of London's avant-garde Theatre Workshop. Her
covering note explained to 'Miss Littlewood' that this bundle
of thin, closely typed sheets of paper was her first play – *A Taste
of Honey*. 'A fortnight ago I didn't know the theatre existed,'
she claimed. But then, 'a young man, anxious to improve my
mind, took me to the Opera House in Manchester and I came
away after the performance having suddenly realized that at
last, after nineteen years of life, I had discovered something
that meant more to me than myself'. The next day she 'borrowed
an unbelievable typewriter' and 'set to and produced this little
epic – don't ask me why – I'm quite unqualified for anything
like this'.[1]

The story Sheila Delaney told to Joan Littlewood was only
partly true – her letter was a typically shrewd attempt to appeal
to her audience, in this case by presenting herself as a naive,
northern ingénue. Even her signature was embellished. She
called herself 'Shelagh Delaney' – the name she will be known
by for the rest of this book – in a deliberate rejection of the
identity of plain Sheila from Salford and the future laid out for

1

her. 'Shelagh' Delaney was a young woman ambitious to escape the life she'd been born into. But she was also determined to tell the stories of the women she left behind. *A Taste of Honey* was her first attempt, and arguably her best. Shelagh's play focuses on Jo, a working-class teenager who lives in Salford with her single mother, Helen, and who becomes a single mother herself as the result of a brief affair with a black sailor. Jo rages against her fate, but finds solace in her friendship with Geof, a gay art student, who is keen to make a home for her and the baby. The play ends when Helen returns from a brief, failed marriage to find Jo's labour pains beginning.

*A Taste of Honey* grabbed Joan Littlewood's attention. Working-class people, if they appeared at all in books, films or plays in the fifties, were – as the *Listener* magazine said – 'comic or loyal, or more frequently both'.[2] For most audiences, these appearances provided the only glimpses of working-class life they got. 'They weren't people one knew … they were people you saw from the tops of buses,' said Stephen Frears, a seventeen-year-old public schoolboy in 1958, destined for Cambridge and a film career.[3]

This situation was slowly changing. John Osborne's play *Look Back in Anger*, staged at the Royal Court in London in 1956, was the ripple that quickly turned into a 'new wave' of novels, plays and films about a restless generation of young working-class upstarts. But the protagonists who wanted adventure – Joe Lampton in John Braine's novel *Room at the Top* (1957), or Arthur Seaton in Alan Sillitoe's *Saturday Night and Sunday Morning* (1958) – were men. Women often held them back. One kiss and they were envisaging marriage; pregnancy turned them into dutiful replicas of their mothers. Their biology determined they could do nothing else.

Shelagh Delaney was the first post-war playwright to suggest that these women had minds and desires of their own, a radical proposal in the fifties. 'Motherhood is supposed to come natural to women,' says Geof, voicing the standard medical opinion of the time – pregnancy was meant to render women docile, maternity to fulfil them.[4] Advertisers, educators, policymakers and psychologists told women that they were luckier than their mothers – the post-war welfare state, and affluence brought about by full employment, rendered their lives both easier and more fulfilling. Clad in New Look dresses they could spend their lives making happy homes for their hard-working husbands and their healthy children – the citizens of Britain's brave new future. But this was a life that Shelagh showed was beyond thousands of women who, like Jo and Helen, continued to live in overcrowded slums. Even more radically, she suggested it was a life that they did not want. More than a decade before the Women's Liberation Movement emerged in Britain, Shelagh Delaney created characters who challenged the assumption that women found fulfilment in marriage and motherhood. Neither Jo nor Helen is satisfied by being a wife or mother. For Helen, motherhood and marriage present at least as many burdens as joys. Jo, meanwhile, rages against her body and her fate. In a world that told working-class women they should be grateful for anything they got, Jo and Helen openly longed for a taste of honey, craving love, creativity, adventure and escape.

In a telegram to her new protégée, Joan Littlewood announced that her company would stage *A Taste of Honey* as their next production at the Theatre Royal, Stratford East. Shelagh was present for the premiere on 27 May 1958. Theatre Workshop had a reputation for courting controversy, but neither Joan nor Gerry Raffles, her theatre manager, had any idea how Shelagh's play would be received. Raffles warned Frances Cuka and Murray Melvin – the actors playing Jo and Geof – to 'be ready to run' from the stage if the audience turned abusive when they took their curtain call.[5]

When the curtain fell on that Tuesday evening, there was a moment's stunned silence – and then the audience roared their approval. Within days *Honey* was a hit and Shelagh the most famous teenager in Britain. Over the next three weeks, hundreds of people flocked to Stratford East to watch an extraordinary episode in British theatre history. A story of slums, sexual politics and race relations, *A Taste of Honey* caught Britain on the cusp of change. At a time when Conservative Prime Minister Harold Macmillan was claiming people 'had never had it so good', reactions to the play exposed a deep social chasm. Almost all the press condemned *Honey* as tasteless muck. Even those reviewers who enjoyed it betrayed their amazement 'that such apparently moronic people can be so moving', as Denis Constanduros, sent from the BBC drama department to see what all the fuss was about, put it.[6] But theatregoers from working-class Stratford did not agree. Norman Rimmell, who worked at the local Co-op, thought 'it groundbreaking ... but it wasn't particularly controversial';[7] Shelagh depicted a life with which he and his wife were familiar. Builders, labourers and office workers told a BBC news crew that *Honey* was 'about people like us, isn't it? Real life.'[8]

*Honey* turned Shelagh into a celebrity. The burning question posed by journalists, fans and most of the arts establishment was how a working-class teenage girl from Salford could write such a shattering play. For Shelagh came from the place she wrote about, much to the horror – and prurient fascination – of her critics. The *Spectator* declared that *Honey's* only redeeming feature was that 'it is not scholarly anthropology observed from the outside through pince-nez, but the inside story of a savage culture observed by a genuine cannibal'.[9] By the late 1950s there were quite a lot of outsiders peering at the working class, but Shelagh was different. She wasn't, as some critics would imply, a single mother or a prostitute, but she'd grown up in an area where women were independent; many worked for a living; some were widowed or had been deserted by their husbands; some sold their bodies and some babies were black. In fact, the north as she presented it looked a lot more eclectic than supposedly bohemian Bloomsbury.

Her working-class background set her apart from the few other women playwrights emerging in the late fifties. Ann Jellicoe had seen her play, *The Sport of My Mad Mother*, premiere at the Royal Court just weeks before *Honey's* debut. The story of a juvenile gang, the play explored relations between young men and women growing up with little hope for the future. But Jellicoe's work was grounded in improvisation – she saw herself as a director as well as a writer – and hers was an outsider's view of working-class life. She had had a boarding school education before training at the Central School of Speech and Drama, and *The Sport of My Mad Mother* has a narrator who is detached from the juvenile gang he observes. By the

5

time *Honey* became a film in 1961, a group of women writers were beginning to explore the frustrations and desires of highly educated girls of Shelagh's generation. But most of these writers, like their protagonists, were middle class. In asserting that working-class women deserved their own voice in the theatre, as playwrights and as the subjects of plays, *A Taste of Honey* was unique.

This book is about how and why Shelagh Delaney became a writer, and about what happened next. It is also about how this might change the way we regard the recent past – particularly the 1950s, and the history of feminism. Shelagh's work as a playwright and a screenwriter for television and film repeatedly returned to the fifties, and to the stories of women and children. We can only understand why she did so by scrutinising her own early life. Her story begins at a time when a moribund conservative elite, shaken by a war that had handed a landslide election victory to a Labour Party that established a welfare state, used the new threat of nuclear war to try to revive an imperial past, in which 'British values' meant those of the white privileged men who held the reins of power. Yet this was also a period when some women and working-class people grasped new opportunities to claim broader horizons for themselves. Shelagh's work shows that the demands made by the Women's Liberation Movement of the 1970s were alive in the 1950s. Her childhood and youth reveal that her ideas sprang from her experience of growing up as a working-class girl in Salford. A desire to lead a different sort of life from your mother's wasn't new to Shelagh's generation, but their opportunities to do so were unique, thanks to a welfare state, council housing, education and full employment. Shelagh and her contemporaries grew up able to imagine taking unprecedented risks, knowing that failure would not mean hunger and poverty.

But Shelagh was provoked to write by the unimaginative manner in which politicians planned these gains, and the grudging delivery of them by those in authority. The rationing of education; the bleak out-of-town estates without libraries or cinemas; the assumption that working-class women only needed a part-time factory job, a fridge and an indoor toilet to be content; the neglect of ordinary people's lives by the theatre and the BBC – these were the post-war facts of life that Shelagh hoped both to escape and to expose through her writing.

She had a crucial and unusual vantage point. A series of events meant that she directly experienced both the positive and the negative effects of the major transitions brought about by war and the welfare state. She spent the Second World War living in an inner-city area called a 'slum' by outsiders, her mother, like many women in the area, struggling single-handedly to keep her family while her husband fought overseas. Afterwards, they moved to a new council estate, where housing was better but friends and entertainment were in short supply. When Shelagh fell seriously ill in the late 1940s she was treated by the new National Health Service; but her care was in the hands of authoritarian nuns whose power to tyrannise their working-class charges hadn't yet been stripped away. After failing the eleven-plus exam she attended a secondary modern school meant to produce the next generation of factory workers – but, exceptionally, she was transferred to a grammar school in her mid-teens. After leaving school she worked as an usherette and a shop assistant before becoming a playwright at the age of nineteen. She often found that she preferred the option meant to be second-best: the slum, the secondary modern, the factory; but she was no romantic about working-class life – her experiences made her determined to flee the fate that the post-war state had in store for her.

Her story belongs in the history of feminism, though not to the history as it's usually told, which assumes middle-class women were the sole agents of change. In that story, the women's movement of the 1970s was precipitated by those who, warned by the example of educated mothers forced to be full-time housewives in the servantless fifties, demanded more from life.[10] Many of them attribute their sense of entitlement to the 1944 Education Act. This Act introduced free and compulsory secondary education for eleven- to fifteen-year-olds; but the kind of academic education that gave you opportunities beyond the factory gates was strictly limited to the top 15 or 20 per cent of performers in the eleven-plus examination. These grammar school pupils were 'picked out *on account* of how they were extra-bright', said one of them, the writer Angela Carter. 'And were they grateful? Were they, hell ... We'd the full force of the [1945 Labour] Attlee administration behind us, too, and all that it stood for, that lingered on after the Tories got back in. All that free milk and orange juice and cod-liver oil made us big and strong and glossy-eyed and cocky and we simply took what was due to us whilst reserving the right to ask questions.'[11] When, in the late 1960s and 70s, these women entered employment, or marriage, or motherhood, and found their opportunities were not as rich as they expected, it was this sense of entitlement that gave them the impetus to challenge the barriers they confronted.

But most of these women, like Carter, came from middle-class homes. They had grown up learning of their difference not only from their brothers – men – but also from the uncivilised rabble of their working-class peers, relegated by the eleven-plus (which social scientists had recognised by the late 1950s tested social class and little else)[12] to secondary moderns and a future of factory work. 'We seemed to stand, isolated and alone, in a hostile environment, in which the natives might at any time engulf us in a tide of split infinitives and generally dissolute behaviour,' recalled Mary Evans of her middle-class upbringing in the Home Counties. Misbehave, she was warned, and she'd end up 'working in Woolworths'.[13] In the early 1960s, Sheila Rowbotham, educated in the even more socially elite world of a girls' boarding school, agonised at Oxford University over whether 'I could be a socialist because I didn't love the working class'.[14] In the turbulence of the late 1960s, many, including Rowbotham and Evans, would reject the contempt of working-class people with which they had been brought up. But these middle-class women take centre stage in histories of feminism, while working-class women are shunted into the wings, their stories unheard. 'It was tough, in the fifties,' wrote Carter. 'Girls wore white gloves.'[15] Not in Salford they didn't.

Shelagh wrote not in spite of her working-class upbringing but because of it. In 1957, Richard Hoggart's bestselling, semi-autobiographical account of working-class life, *The Uses of Literacy*, declared that the 'cardinal sin' in working class communities was conceiving a child out of wedlock. He claimed many girls 'retain ... an ignorance about the facts of sex'; marriage was their dream and most wished to walk up the aisle 'quite untouched'.[16] Shelagh, twenty years Hoggart's junior, and a woman, disagreed. The builders, cleaners and clerks who watched *Honey* had a better idea about its wider appeal than those established authorities who declared it a disaster. Like Shelagh, many of them lived in neighbourhoods where some women found work as prostitutes; where many struggled to make ends meet as single mothers; and where 'flitting' between decrepit lodgings was common in an era when slum landlords reigned supreme.

*A Taste of Honey* proved to have enduring appeal. In 1959 the play transferred to London's West End; in 1960 the cast enjoyed a Broadway run; in 1961 Shelagh helped to adapt it into a film. Through the 1960s it was staged and screened across the world, finding fans on both sides of the Iron Curtain. By the 1970s it had become a set text in Britain's new comprehensive schools, and would remain so for the next forty years. In the 1980s Shelagh's words were immortalised by singer-songwriter Morrissey when his band the Smiths swept to international fame with hits that cherry-picked her lines. Performed by repertory and community theatre groups in the UK and abroad, in 2014 *Honey* returned to London with a sell-out run at the National Theatre. In the same year, her home town, Salford, launched an annual Shelagh Delaney Day to celebrate her achievements. The survival of *A Taste of Honey* testifies to a fascination with the post-war world that it evokes – one of conservative morality and ideals, certainly, but also a world where these were never quite as monolithic as they could appear. It speaks, too, to the contemporaneity of her subjects: her work showed that mixed-race relationships, teenage pregnancy, lone motherhood and homosexuality were not marginal or abnormal aspects of life, but experiences that many shared or were touched by, a truth that became more evident in later decades. But the timelessness of *A Taste of Honey* is also due to Shelagh's affirmation that the search for love is both innately human and a hopeful quest. By showing that everyone, no matter their circumstances, is capable of loving and being loved, Shelagh offered an optimistic vision for the future, one that survived all the political and economic turbulence she was to live through.

She went on writing about women who challenged the conventions in which they found themselves through her long career. From as early as 1963, journalists asked: 'whatever happened to Shelagh Delaney?'[17] When she died in 2011 most obituaries concurred that she'd 'quietly petered out', as Jeanette Winterson put it, unable to live up to her first play.[18] In fact she enjoyed a career as a screenwriter in television and film, working on pioneering realist dramas like *Z Cars*, bringing surrealism into British film with productions like *Charlie Bubbles*, and finding a new audience with her 1985 screenplay for *Dance with a Stranger*, the story of Ruth Ellis, the last woman in Britain to be hanged (in 1955). Shelagh wrote television plays which made marriage the focus of family drama rather than the backdrop to the action, and scripted radio plays that placed older women at the centre of the storyline.

Why was her subsequent work ignored, or greeted with luke-warm praise? In part, as we shall see, this was due to her reliance on instinct and insight to refute the political 'common sense' of her times. Against post-war representations of women and work-ing-class people as stereotypes: the immoral single mother or the juvenile delinquent – or as ideals: the angel of the house, the cheeky chappie or the socialist hero, Shelagh explored ambiv-alence and uncertainty. She never sought to present a coherent alternative to capitalism or male dominance, as some socialist and feminist theatres of the 1970s and 80s did. While her work often focused on women chafing against marriage and mother-hood, or who had escaped these institutions altogether, her explorations of women's desires – for children but also freedom; for lust but also love; for independence but also dependence on a man – could be contradictory. She created characters who, like their author, were influenced more by emotion than by formal education or political ideology. The results could be sensitive and compelling, but also frustrating: fragmentary characters, incoherent or circular plots, and ambiguous endings.

But her work, at its worst as well as at its best, illuminates a current of thought, and a way of being, that deserves to be taken seriously. Her insights may not have amounted to a coherent vision of society, but they were interrelated. They sprang from her conviction that experience – including one's inheritance from one's family and community, and encom-passing emotional as well as material life – required more serious consideration than abstract ideas and theories. This way of thinking and of writing enabled her to give a voice to work-ing-class women who lacked the political platform or the educa-tion or professions of many middle-class feminists. But it also distinguished women from the notion – so prevalent in medical and political thought in the 1950s – that they were governed by their biology. Shelagh showed that people acted and felt within contexts they had not chosen. In doing so she suggested that love, desire, motherhood, marriage – the experiences of womanhood, in fact – were shaped by historical circumstances, and that they could change.

Despite the flaws in her work Shelagh had a very successful career as a writer; she was a pioneer in getting women's lives onto stage and screen. That her achievements have been overlooked is due to the condescending belief that a working-class woman has only a limited amount to say. During the 1960s and 70s it became more acceptable for working-class men, and, to a lesser extent, women, to create art from their experiences. But many of the artistic establishment remained incredulous that they might be able to write about subjects that strayed beyond the autobiographical. And working-class writers were, and are, granted a national platform only when they produce absolutely exceptional work. Shelagh's second play, *The Lion in Love* (1960), is regarded as a failure that forced her ignominious retreat into obscurity. In fact it enjoyed a reasonably successful run at the Royal Court before being staged in New York. When middle-class writers or playwrights achieve a small audience, they are talked of as having a niche following, or a distinctive appeal. Shelagh, however, was dismissed as uneducated, *A Taste of Honey* as a fluke or the work of Joan Littlewood. Yet in the expanding world of 1960s television, both her plays were successful enough to provoke the BBC to plead with Shelagh to join its drama department.

She refused that invitation; and her desire to go her own way is another reason why she has been ignored. Disillusioned by the critics' hostility towards her and impatient with journalists who only wanted to ask about her sex life, she chose to retreat from the limelight. When, in 1964, she became a single mother, the prurient press attention made her eschew further media attention. She gave only a handful of interviews during the rest of her life.

This book is called *Tastes of Honey* because Shelagh constantly pursued the fun, excitement, love, sexual adventure, artistic fulfilment, fame and fortune that working-class women had been denied. Still in her teens, she asserted that women had every right to express desire, but showed that they paid a heavy price for doing so. Shelagh herself took advantage of every door of opportunity that lay ajar and forced others open, often provoking loud cries of disapproval from the press and the artistic establishment. She rejected every category into which they tried to pigeonhole her. She wasn't a starving artist in a garret, but nor did she retreat into a celebrity marriage as journalists anticipated she would. She wrote for a living, and liked spending much of her time on that living which, she said, was essential for a writer. She relished the benefits that fame and wealth conferred, delighting in telling friends that 'I earned a lot of money, I spent it all. I loved the parties, I loved the cocktails.'[19] Being brought up in a family where everyone had to work hard and watch the pennies made her appreciate not having to do so. She established herself as an independent woman at a time when single women found it hard to get a mortgage or even open a bank account. She created her own family as a single mother, in a household that included close female friends as well as relatives. And she kept on writing.

This is a hopeful story. Not just because Shelagh Delaney's work and life helped to change the way working-class women are treated and represented in Britain, but because she is a reminder that dissent is more widespread than we might think. While in their everyday lives people may act primarily in the bread-and-butter interests of themselves and their loved ones – after all, everyone needs a roof over their heads and food to eat – it doesn't stop them imagining a more hopeful and expansive future. Clothes, cosmetics, music, storytelling, romance, comics, novels, films and plays are the tools by which working-class women can fashion those different futures. Rarely do they find a national stage and an audience. This is the story of one who did.

# 2

# Becoming Shelagh

'Shelagh' Delaney came alive in April 1958, the product of her own pen. Born Sheila Mary Delaney on 25 November 1938, she thought 'Shelagh' exotic, a hint that she wanted to stand out rather than fit in.

She chose it thinking, erroneously, that Shelagh was the Irish spelling of her Christian name. That was important – a link with her father's Irish heritage of which she was proud, and a sign of her adoration for him. Joseph Delaney was twenty-four when Shelagh, his first child, was born. His own father was an illegitimate coal-carter whose mother hailed from southern Ireland; his mother was a Dubliner who came to Manchester in search of work in the 1900s. Shelagh admired her paternal grandfather, 'a Socialist ... of the Kier Hardie tradition'.[1] Politics in the 1950s seemed to her, as to her contemporary Sheila Rowbotham, a game of 'power and ambition' played by a few men in Parliament.[2] But Shelagh's imagination was caught by the rebellious ideals her grandfather had espoused.

Shelagh knew her father as 'a great storyteller and reader',[3] but most of his reading was done after he'd left school at the age of fourteen. There was no thought of staying on for Joseph Delaney; his family were too poor to consider it. For the same reason he couldn't try for one of the engineering apprenticeships that many Salford lads hankered after; these were a passport to a skilled job, but apprentices earned a pittance until the age of twenty-one.

Joseph, quietly spoken and well mannered, managed to get a job as a bus conductor, which proved to be a better post than an apprenticeship. When the economic slump came in the early 1930s, engineering was decimated, but Joseph's job was safe. By 1936, he'd become a bus driver, with enough money in his pocket to frequent Salford's cinemas and dance halls. Tall, olive-skinned and with thick, unruly black hair – physical traits he'd pass on to his daughter – Joe caught the admiring glance of many young women. Gregarious and witty under his quiet demeanour, he wanted a girl who was pert as well as pretty. He found her in Elsie Twemlow.

Joseph Delaney was a good catch for Elsie. She was one of seven children; her father, John Twemlow, was a cotton worker from Manchester; her mother, Mary Ann Doyle, from Liverpool, had also worked in the mills. Elsie didn't tell stories like Joseph did, but she had a turn of phrase that Shelagh found compelling, and in the 1970s she asked her mother to write down her childhood memories. Born in 1915, Elsie could just recollect the Armistice, particularly 'my uncle coming home from the war – he had a leg amputated but there was [*sic*] so many people in our house to welcome him that I believe someone sat on me'. This uncle moved into the Twemlows' already crowded home until he married in the early 1920s. Nearby lived her grandmother and 'two old-fashioned old maid aunts' who she visited each week – 'we used to love going because we used to get half a crown each'.

Growing up in a crowd meant Elsie had to shout to be heard. She had plenty to say for herself and she was also a joker. At school her swift repartee won her plenty of friends, but she wasn't sorry to leave in 1929 because she found lessons dull. She 'loved' her first job at a small woodwork firm where she quickly knew everyone. If she was late in the mornings she could 'sneak in a side door', confident that no one would give her away, and when she and her workmates were bored, 'we used to run out and buy things' from local shops.[4] She was part of a generation of young working-class women intent on fashioning the future. They spent their days manufacturing the new consumer goods – wirelesses, fashionable clothes, ready-made furniture and cosmetics – that they aspired to own themselves. Elsie spent her evenings practising the latest dances with her sisters, before launching herself on Salford's dance halls every weekend with a carefully waved bob and a touch of lipstick to show off her confident smile.

But when she met Joe, Elsie was ready to settle down. In 1936 her father died suddenly of a heart attack. Life was precarious, particularly for a widow with a family to keep, like Mary Ann Twemlow. Her youngest boy was only fourteen, so Joe's wage was welcome. In 1937 Elsie and Joe were married and settled into Elsie's childhood home, helping Mrs Twemlow to pay the rent.

By the time Shelagh was born, Elsie and Joseph were renting their own house. Her first home was a two-up two-down in New Thomas Street in Pendleton, the working-class district of Salford made famous by Walter Greenwood's 1934 novel *Love on the Dole*. The house backed onto Pendleton Railway Station;

horse-drawn carts clattered past the front door day and night to collect coal from Harry Ainscough's coal yard next door. Their neighbourhood was badly polluted, a place where poverty robbed children of their health. In the 1930s Salfordians were more likely to die of tuberculosis than the residents of any other British town or city.[5] Between 1931 and 1935, of every thousand babies born in England and Wales, 62 died before their first birthday. But in the working-class districts of Manchester and Salford, this was true of more than 140 babies in every thousand.[6]

Shelagh had no memories of New Thomas Street. By her second birthday she and Elsie and Elsie's mother had moved to Hartington Street in Ordsall, Salford's dockland neighbourhood. Shelagh's father had effectively disappeared from her life. As a bus driver, Joseph was under no obligation to join up when war was declared in September 1939, but he immediately enlisted in the army. In a semi-autobiographical short story written in her early twenties, Shelagh described a man who 'ought never to have been a soldier, according to his wife, but he insisted'.[7] On his daughter's first birthday in November 1939, he was training with the Lancashire Fusiliers at 'an unknown location'.[8]

Ordsall was 'a little community that was all on its own', a triangle of closely packed terraced streets bordered by Trafford Road and the docks, busy Regent Road heading into Manchester, and the River Irwell.[9] It was not an idyllic place to live. In 1930, a group of young volunteers from middle-class Manchester homes decided to 'discover for ourselves what life is like in the slums', and chose Ordsall as their destination. They discovered that 'factory buildings pollute the air with smoke and block out sunshine and light, so that many householders have to burn gas all day'. Residents lived in overcrowded homes that were 'grimy with soot', pervaded with damp, and 'infested with vermin'. The investigators were at first shaken and disconcerted by what they saw; then they became angry that people were forced to live in this manner, just a few miles from their own prosperous suburbs. 'We have,' they concluded in this report, 'discovered conditions the existence of which did not seem possible in a Christian community.'[10] Nothing had changed by the 1940s.

Despite these problems, Ordsall was Shelagh's home, a place where her family and their neighbours worked hard to create a life for themselves. In 1957, Richard Hoggart's *The Uses of Literacy* described his upbringing in Hunslet, a working-class district of Leeds that was similar to Ordsall. Hoggart's vivid account of his childhood, and his assertion that his community had values and a culture worth celebrating, appealed to thousands of readers. *The Uses of Literacy* helped to create a popular image of northern England as a vista of endless terraced streets, populated by parochial communities sustained by working-class mothers scrubbing the steps of their two-up two-down houses.[11] It was a picture of life that Shelagh would recognise. 'There's a terrific life force,' she said of Salford. 'You can go all over these parts and you put your hand down on the ground and you can feel its heart beating.'[12]

Ordsall's sense of community sprang from the men's work at the docks, but also from the mutual support of the women who lived there. Dorothy Green grew up a few streets away from Shelagh. 'If your mum wasn't in it wasn't a problem,' she said. 'You'd just go in someone else's house and get a jam butty and a drink.'[13] Hoggart spoke of working-class mothers as 'devoted to the family and beyond proud self-regard'.[14] Certainly Elsie proved determined to keep her family together, refusing to allow Shelagh to be evacuated in 1939.

Yet in other ways Shelagh Delaney's Ordsall differed markedly from Richard Hoggart's Hunslet. For Shelagh, Salford 'means one thing – restlessness'. The city, as viewed from Ordsall, was in constant flux. 'Running right through the city is a great roadway, like a sort of main artery,' she said. 'All the blood rushes along here. And great carts and cars and everything.' It was a community defined by work. 'The docks were alive!' recalled one of Shelagh's contemporaries. 'There was always something going on, something loud and noisy and a bit on the dirty side to look at.'[15] Trafford Road, the dock road, was lined with pubs catering for sailors from ports across the world, factory workers employed at the vast Trafford Park industrial estate, dockers and, on match days, the crowds of football fans who surged down to Manchester United's ground at Old Trafford. 'We called it the Barbary Coast,' recalled one man, 'all these different nationalities you could pass, and the prostitutes – they was all sort of painted up to glory.'[16] It was a side of life that Richard Hoggart preferred to gloss over.[17] But to Shelagh it was home.

Hoggart described the world from a male vantage point. Shelagh knew life for women was harder than he suggested. In Ordsall, girls learned about sex early. Eight-year-old Shelagh, playing alone in a back alley, was approached by a sailor who made to grab her; a neighbour quickly intervened and the man ran away.[18] She learned that men seeking sex, not the prostitutes trying to earn a living, were a danger to her. And while the women recounted by Richard Hoggart were parochial and insular – 'She leaves the outer world of politics and even of the "news" to her husband'[19] – that wasn't true of Elsie and her friends. In wartime Ordsall many women worked – including Elsie, who had grown up with a working mother and sisters and to whom factory work was nothing new. After Shelagh's brother, Joe, was born in 1941 – 'under a table in an air raid' as Elsie was fond of telling people[20] – her mother took a factory job in Trafford Park to make ends meet. And when the Fusiliers were caught up in a big battle, everyone in Ordsall knew about it, children included. Sue Lane's father served in North Africa with Joseph Delaney. She recalled that the Siege of Tobruk in December 1941 'was followed closely by everyone back home because no one thought the British troops could get out alive (Dad included)'.[21] Between 1941 and 1943, as the war raged in North Africa and then Italy, the Fusiliers were very often on the front line.

Shelagh witnessed her mother's hard work and worry. She later wrote that 'Children understand far more, much earlier, than their parents are ever willing to give them credit for'.[22] She came to understand in the 1940s a truth that would become central to the Women's Liberation Movement thirty years later: that marriage and motherhood caused women stress and exhaustion as well as joy. This was particularly true of working-class wives and mothers who had to struggle to make ends meet. Shelagh would never romanticise their lives as Richard Hoggart did.

Shelagh had two great escapes – reading and the cinema. She loved the *Just William* books, including *William Does His Bit*, in which William and his gang of Outlaws make fools of pompous Home Guard officers and invade soldiers' canteens; and she liked the sound of his well-heeled home with its endless supplies of cream buns and pocket money.[23] Even better were Saturday-morning matinees at the local picture house: 'that was the week's climax for us and we had a roaring time … we used to take part in it, laugh and shout'.[24] Later, she'd aim to foster that enjoyment among her audiences and readers – and to recapture her childhood sense that no division existed between the action up front and the rowdy spectators. Westerns were her favourite films; Saturday afternoons were spent re-enacting them by cantering up and down the street. Some girls hoped to marry a cowboy,[25] but Shelagh wanted to be one of the heroes, not yet realising there were no vacancies for women.

In 1943 she started school, probably at Nashville Street Infants School which most children living on Hartington Street attended. One memory of that first year stayed with her. 'Every school in Salford has to its credit a Lowry painting, and every child in the city grows up, as I grew up, with that artist's vision of their own particular world before them.' L. S. Lowry's painting *Coming From the Mill* hung 'on our classroom wall just left of the blackboard and the teacher's desk'.[26] These paintings were the brainchild of Salford Education Committee, whose members hoped that the pictures would acquaint Salford's children, 'in however limited a way, with a form of cultural expression without which their education would lack a vitality and a developed aesthetic sense'.[27] In Shelagh's case they succeeded.

*Coming From the Mill* – which Lowry called his 'most characteristic mill scene' – depicts red-brick terraced houses, factory chimneys and the entrance to a mill, set along a street brought to life by the people who trudge along it. In the foreground, on a scrubby patch of grass, a group of children play with a dog. The painting asserted that the people of Salford – children and women, as well as men – were worthy of artistic exploration. Lowry captured the vital role that ordinary working people played in a world where their needs and desires were often ignored. 'They know each other, recognize each other,' wrote John Berger of Lowry's characters, 'they are fellow travellers through a life which is impervious to most of their choices.'[28] They were not masters of their own fate – but neither were they simply victims. How to convey this was a question that was to shape all Shelagh's writing.

Shelagh was six years old when the war ended. Huge celebrations in Manchester city centre greeted VE Day in May 1945. On 26 July, Clement Attlee's Labour Party won the first general election held since 1935 by a landslide, provoking more outdoor parties. By this time cinema newsreels were full of returning servicemen being rapturously reunited with their loved ones. But many families found themselves out of step with the public mood: for them these months were ones of grief, sadness and uncertainty. Shelagh knew she was lucky – her father had survived the war. But he had been badly wounded while fighting in Italy, and when he returned to Britain he spent months in hospital. When Elsie took Shelagh to meet her father for the first time since she was two, he was a stranger to her. All her life Shelagh remembered her visit to the hospital ward and her disbelief that this 'man lying in bed with long hair who looked old and frail' was married to her youthful mother.[29] Joe would remain in poor health for the rest of his life. Jean Whur, a school friend of Shelagh's, remembered that 'he looked really ill ... yellow, with sunken eyes ... I was aware that he'd had a bad war.'[30]

In January 1947 Shelagh left her first school when the Delaneys moved out of Ordsall and into 77 Duchy Road. This was a painful uprooting for Shelagh. Her new home was a council house on a suburban housing estate several miles from Ordsall. When Salford Council had begun building the Duchy estate in the 1930s it had caught the attention of the local press for its houses were spacious and of excellent quality.[31] Now the council was extending the estate, and the Delaneys were allocated a sought-after three-bedroom house on a corner plot, prized because it gave them a particularly large garden in which to grow vegetables and hang washing.[32] Shelagh's family got such a nice house because Joseph was both an invalid and a valued public sector worker. He was unable to return to bus driving, but Salford Council offered him a job as a bus inspector, helping to coordinate the new routes urgently required to connect the city's growing council estates with its workplaces.[33]

Shelagh's life, which had been full of noise and companionship in Ordsall, was now quiet and lonely. 'We didn't know a soul,' she said later, and reckoned it took 'years' before they felt at home.[34] For the first time, she felt herself to be an outsider. She was a stranger at her new school and on the new estate. The Delaneys' new home was one of the gains Attlee's Labour government pledged to protect and extend: a council house, in a peaceful suburb, where families could recuperate after six years of war. But to Shelagh, the disadvantages of Duchy Road were initially more apparent than the benefits. There were few shops, no cinemas, and little street life. Much of the estate was still a building site, and a lack of street lights didn't encourage people to leave their homes after dark, even when the wartime blackout was lifted. When Jean Whur visited Shelagh's home, she thought Duchy Road 'very bleak ... bombsites and scrubland'.[35]

The move to Duchy Road made clear to eight-year-old Shelagh how tough women's lives could be. She witnessed how her mother and her neighbours had to work hard to turn their half-finished housing estate into a community. She also watched her mother act as her father's carer; the experience left a strong impression. Hoggart praised the 'steady and self-forgetful routine' of the 'working-class mother'. But Shelagh knew there was no sharp division between these 'good' women and those Hoggart condemned as 'shiftless' or 'bitten-in' by resentment.[36] Elsie sought to create a loving home and Joseph was a kind and gentle father. But Shelagh would later tell her own daughter, Charlotte, about 'watching her mother come home from work at a local factory or shop and then nurse Joe, make the tea, make sure he was OK before she even sat down'.[37] A decade before sociologists began to write of women's 'double burden' of paid and unpaid work, Shelagh witnessed this in her own home and learned from her mother's exhaustion.[38] By her mid-teens she would regularly declare that she did not want to get married.[39]

Every change in her life that was meant to make her happy – the coming of peace, her new home, a family reunited – made

Shelagh miserable. As a young woman, Elsie Delaney had aspired to the security that marriage to a wage-earner could bring, and dreamed of a home of her own. Shelagh, however, saw how the post-war changes that were meant to make women's lives easier – new housing, housewives' shifts in the factories and families reunited – relied on women's hard work. She did not want to be the kind of woman the post-war world seemed to desire. As Carolyn Steedman – born in 1947 to a working-class family in south London – observed, 'a sense of dislocation can provide a sharp critical faculty in a child'.[40] The teachers at Shelagh's new school found her inclined to 'sullenness'.[41] She had thick black hair that her mother vainly tried to tease into ringlets; a photograph of her visiting friends in Ordsall shows a solemn girl sulking under frizzy black bunches. And she stooped, for she was growing tall – five feet five inches at the age of nine, at a time when the average adult woman was just over five feet and tall women were thought unattractive – and thin, when being 'a long streak of nothing'[42] suggested maternal neglect. Post-war children were meant to be filled with suet pudding and wholesome stews. Unbiddable, sulky and silent, Shelagh was neither the quiet, obedient helpmeet of a daughter, who had been valued in large families before the war, nor the pert and pretty Shirley Temple type, whose mothers could clothe them in the dreams and dresses that poverty had denied their own girlhood.

At the age of ten, Shelagh suddenly left home again – this time without her family. She had contracted osteomyelitis, a painful and life-threatening bone infection, 'after knocking her leg against a table'.[43] By the late 1940s doctors could treat it with penicillin if caught early enough, but late diagnosis was common because the condition was rare.[44] One sufferer, hospitalised with osteomyelitis as a child in the 1950s, described 'being so racked with pain and feeling so ill that death was quite a decent option'. Shelagh's doctors pinned their hopes on the tried and tested cures of 'cleaning and draining the wound and rest'.[45] She was sent to a children's convalescent home in the genteel seaside resort of Lytham St Anne's – a two-hour train ride from Salford – where she remained for several months.

'I'm still afraid of the dark, I still don't like to be alone,' she'd tell a journalist in 1960,[46] fears that likely stemmed from her months at Lytham. The home was run along strict lines by nuns, and Shelagh rarely saw her parents. In 1947 the government launched an investigation into children's convalescent homes; the new National Health Service would be inaugurated the following year, so clinics found themselves subject to a generally unwelcome scrutiny. Investigators found that most homes had short visiting hours, often between 2 and 4 p.m. – a very inconvenient time for working parents or those who travelled a long distance. Life for the inmates was bleak. Many homes had 'a bare institutional look' and 'long minatory lists of rules which take no account of the real welfare of the patient'. Those 'run by religious orders' – like the one in which Shelagh was placed – were among the most forbidding.[47] In the early 1950s Annette Kuhn 'spent what seemed to me a very long time away from home' when she, too, was sent to convalesce after a serious illness. 'I received no visitors and some unaccustomedly rough treatment at the hands of the nuns who ran the place.'[48] Children, particularly working-class children paid for by local authorities, were meant to be grateful for whatever they received. But too often the new fruits of the welfare state were given grudgingly or with patronising disregard. '[T]hey say I need building up but I get fed better at home than I do here,' says the ten-year-old narrator of Shelagh's semi-autobiographical short story 'Sweetly Sings the Donkey', of her convalescent home in Blackpool. 'I am frightened being here in this place,' she confesses.[49]

Already acutely conscious of being tall, thin and sulky, Shelagh experienced her time at Lytham as a banishment for failing to fit into a post-war world where conformity was both valued and narrowly defined: 'we were all either too thin or too fat, too tall or too short'.[50] Shelagh disliked being treated as one of an undifferentiated mass: 'nothing more or less than a statistic'.[51] 'Many a time I felt like screaming,' the narrator of her story remarks, 'but the only time I ever did I was treated as if there was something wrong with me ... you're not allowed to let it out – if I screamed out loud every time I felt like it I'd be put in a home for mental defectives.'[52]

But Lytham also taught Shelagh how to defy such strictures. Some women writers have described how childhood illnesses fostered their love of reading, because, bedbound, they had nothing else to do; they achieved a space of their own, if not a full room.[53] For Shelagh, though, her *lack* of opportunities to read and write at Lytham were more significant. She was tantalised by 'a big library full of books that look interesting but we are not allowed to read them'; infuriated by the rule that 'IT IS FORBIDDEN to buy comics'.[54] Sulking gave way to answering back. 'I've never liked being told what to do,' she would warn Gerry Raffles, manager of Theatre Workshop, in 1959.[55] Being a good girl only resulted in boredom and being forgotten; you were, Shelagh realised, as likely to die whether or not you behaved well. Shelagh fought to live; she read the forbidden books and tried to run away. Far from this behaviour resulting in some sort of celestial punishment, she eventually returned home cured.[56]

She came back with a profound scepticism towards authority, and a new self-reliance. She never talked openly about her time in Lytham. In her twenties she made a day trip to Blackpool with her friend Harold Riley 'and we passed it. But she didn't want to talk about it, so we never did.'[57] Instead, she wrote about her experience in short stories and later in radio plays. Other writers have described how a sense of detachment from their environment – the 'insider/outsider' status claimed by Richard Hoggart, a 'scholarship boy' whose education removed him from his working-class origins, or the 'perpetual alienation from where [we] happened to be' that Sheila Rowbotham experienced in her 1950s youth, spent between a suburban home in Leeds and a girls' boarding school – could offer a useful perspective.[58] Shelagh's separation from Ordsall, and then her long convalescence at Lytham, induced an independence of spirit. Her experiences strengthened her affection for Salford and the people she knew there, but also made her more aware of the world beyond its boundaries.

In the months following her return home, she became an even more avid reader, revelling in her ability to choose and read library books in peace. Her father became her closest companion. She loved listening to his war stories, as well as his Irish legends: 'true stories about his experiences in … North Africa, Monte Cassino'.[59] The stories she read and heard were pointers to a different sort of life from the one she had been told to expect.

That she wanted something different to marriage and motherhood is evident from the vivid dreams described by the narrator of 'Sweetly Sings the Donkey'. These show that imagination is dangerous, precisely because it can affect the real world: '[T]he contents of my head will soon be like a rubbish tip,' the girl thinks, 'and some rubbish tips I've known have festered first then burst into flames.'[60] She imagines a woman who has had visions and then 'set fire to herself and ran away down Deansgate [in Manchester] screaming'.[61]

Other girls of Shelagh's generation had nightmares between the ages of about seven and ten – that time in a child's life when she is becoming conscious of the world around her and her place within it. Filled with fire and blood, these dreams drew on the trauma of war. They sprang, however, from women's paradoxical position in the post-war world. At seven, Carolyn Steedman imagined her mother with 'thin wounds across her breasts pouring forth blood, not milk'.[62] Steedman thought that this image sprang from her guilt about her mother's struggle to provide for her children, and her own awareness of the resentment and pain that this provoked.[63] In 1947, ten-year-old Margaret Forster endured weeks of nightmares, 'waking up and screaming in the middle of torrents of running blood', as she waited for the results of her eleven-plus examination – the passport, she thought, to escaping her mother's fate as a working-class wife and mother.[64] These were the fantasies of girls who wanted more than their mothers had, but who feared that fulfilling their desires would inflict untold hardship and pain. Ten-year-old Shelagh already knew that women were meant to sacrifice themselves for others, but she was beginning to envisage a future very different from this feminine ideal.

# 3
# Borderline Girl

When she returned from Lytham in 1948, Shelagh enrolled at her third school, St John's Primary in Broughton. Her two years there were devoted to preparing for the eleven-plus, the test that determined which children entered Britain's grammar schools. Since the passing of the 1944 Education Act, secondary education had become free and compulsory for all eleven- to fifteen-year-olds. The lucky few Salford children considered 'intelligent' enough to benefit from an academic education would attend Salford Grammar School or Salford Technical School if they were boys, Broughton or Pendleton High Schools if they were girls. But the vast majority of Shelagh's classmates would go to Broughton Secondary Modern School, where they would stay until fifteen when, if they were lucky, they'd get an engineering apprenticeship or an office job.

Shelagh sat the exam in February 1950 and, a few weeks later, filed into assembly to hear the results. She had failed. 'I didn't care, quite honestly, when I was eleven whether I passed the scholarship or not,' she later said. (The eleven-plus exam was still commonly called 'the scholarship', a reminder of pre-1944 Education Act days.) 'And I don't think many children do.'[1] Jean Whur, who did pass, thought 'the scholarship ... was awful

... they would read the results out ... it broke up friendships, and there was no pleasure in it'.[2]

But Shelagh's teachers were surprised and her father very disappointed. Working-class parents were often accused of harbouring 'low aspirations' for their children, but a nationwide survey of parents' views on the 1944 Education Act showed that most wanted their children to get the best education they could, and stay at school for as long as possible.[3] Joseph Delaney, bolder than most, 'rang up the town hall', Shelagh recalled. The clerk he spoke to in the Education Department 'told him that I had the marks for grammar school, but there was no place available'.[4] This made a mockery of the claim that the eleven-plus scientifically selected children for grammar school; clearly availability of places was a huge factor. Shelagh's failure to get a grammar school place also fuelled her growing suspicion that life was harder for girls and women. In Salford, as Jean Whur's mother, a teacher, told her daughter, 'it was very hard to get a grammar school place if you were a girl, because there were fewer places than for boys'.[5]

Shelagh was what quickly became known as 'a borderline child'[6] – hard to categorise and tidy away into the neat, statistical boxes on which the administration of the post-war welfare state relied. She was told that she had excelled in her English paper, but did less well in maths and 'intelligence'.[7] 'Bright' children, writes Annette Kuhn – who did pass the eleven-plus – were characterised by 'a meticulous approach to the task at hand rather than a passionate engagement in it'. Passion was 'untidy, unpredictable and above all, unladylike'.[8] It was also politically dangerous. This was the age of the so-called post-war political 'consensus', in which Labour and Conservative politicians created new boundaries of acceptable political debate – the welfare state was sacrosanct, but so too was capitalism, and the nuclear weapons to defend the capitalist states against the totalitarian Eastern bloc. The radical socialist historian E. P. Thompson wrote of the 'reduction of political idealism to suspect motive' – anyone opposed to capitalism or nuclear power could be labelled a Communist. Stepping beyond the boundaries of 'acceptable' behaviour was considered to be 'maladjusted': women who found buying a fridge or television didn't bring them happiness were classified as 'neurotic', while gay men could be ordered by the courts to undergo medical castration.[9] All this may seem far distant from Shelagh Delaney's life in Salford, but the eleven-plus was an early means of shaping children into the kinds of citizens they were meant to become, with the 'intelligent' defined as obedient and conformist, rather than innovative and creative.[10]

In September 1950 Shelagh entered the first form at Broughton Secondary Modern. Her form teacher, Valerie Ivison, was just twenty and had started her teaching career at the school a year earlier. Valerie, who taught her form history and English, was soon impressed with Shelagh's schoolwork: 'she worked hard, and she was really imaginative'. But Shelagh was no conformist good girl – she was passionate about subjects she liked, but did barely any work for those she didn't enjoy. She was also completely out of step with the 1950s idea of feminine beauty. She had 'very black hair. She didn't have a good complexion. She was a tall girl … And she always seemed a bit more mature than the rest of the class.'[11]

Perhaps to her own surprise, Shelagh quickly settled down at Broughton, better than she had done at her primary schools. Her new headmistress, Miss Leek, shared the Ministry of Education's vision for secondary moderns, aiming to 'provide a good all-round secondary education' that addressed pupils' 'social, emotional, physical and spiritual development' and paid attention to 'the interests of the children'.[12] When school inspectors visited Broughton, they noted approvingly Miss Leek's 'enthusiastic support' for 'many cultural and recreative activities which provide colour to a full and useful life enjoyed by all attending this school'.[13] She recruited a young staff who shared her aims, including Valerie Ivison. 'Miss Leek said to me, "You can start from scratch. I want a syllabus."' Valerie constructed a curriculum that delved into local, national and international history. 'I wanted to show how the world came to be as it is, and something of man's inhumanity to man.' The school had many extracurricular activities, including a United Nations society and a Young Farmers club. Shelagh plunged into school life. She joined Valerie's History Society, the aim of which was described in the school magazine as 'learning by looking ... We try to imagine how people lived at different times in the past as we look at their homes, pictures and models of their clothes and things they used.'[14] Valerie 'used to cart the kids about, on trips' to local museums and monuments. Shelagh also became a star of the netball team – a role she reprised in the opening scene of the film adaptation of *A Taste of Honey*. Being tall had its advantages.

Most importantly, Miss Leek encouraged Shelagh's love of literature and introduced her to drama. She took Shelagh to see her first play. 'I'd been kept in after school … I was in the headmistress's study and had just finished some lines. Miss Leek said to me: "I'm going upstairs to watch a performance of Othello. Do you want to see it?" It was by some school amateur group. I said to myself, Anything for a laugh. But I enjoyed Othello. It made a great impression on me.'[15]

Shelagh included Shakespearean lines in many of her plays; there are lines from *All's Well that Ends Well* in *A Taste of Honey*. Miss Leek told her that in his day Shakespeare had been an immensely popular writer, not just watched by nobility as many people assumed. Asked in the early 1960s if she thought theatre was just too highbrow for her work and the people she wanted to reach, Shelagh bristled. 'The working classes in the gallery have supported the British theatre ever since Elizabethan times. Give them good and well publicized plays and they will go to the theatre.'[16]

When Shelagh began her second year at Broughton, Miss Leek taught her English. She encouraged Shelagh to take her writing seriously. Valerie Ivison knew that in many secondary moderns 'children spent months just copying stuff off the board', but this was not Miss Leek's way. 'What I wrote she understood, and she didn't harp so much as others on rigid English,' Shelagh recalled. She appreciated that 'I write as people talk' and encouraged Shelagh to develop her ear for dialogue.[17] In 1952 her first piece of writing appeared in print when Broughton's school magazine carried 'The Vagabond' – thirteen-year-old Shelagh's short sketch of a 'dirty, ragged, weatherbeaten man'. Shelagh's description was compassionate, suggesting that appearances could be deceptive. 'Now and again he would stroke the heads of the two dogs that lay either side of him ... the friends of a man who had none; a vagabond who preferred to roam and sleep with animals rather than his fellow men.'[18] Already she was interested in those people rejected or ignored by society, and keen to find her way past their stereotyping as delinquents or victims.

Miss Leek was well aware of Broughton's limitations, though, and was keen to get her most promising children a broader education. The school was just nine years old when Shelagh arrived, the city's flagship secondary modern, accommodated in a 'fine new building' of which Salford Education Committee was proud. But expectations of the children were low. Secondary moderns were prohibited from entering children for external qualifications until 1953. Shelagh's school had no library or science laboratories, the council choosing instead to provide 'three excellent rooms' for housecraft and two needlework rooms.[19]

By the early 1950s, however, Salford Education Committee acknowledged that the eleven-plus was not foolproof. Rather than invest more in secondary modern schools, the committee urged head teachers to identify promising thirteen-year-olds for transfer to a grammar school. This invitation was not as open as it appeared. Transfers could only happen if there were places available at Salford's sought-after grammar schools, which was rare (the Education Committee recognised that 'transfers from grammars to secondary moderns would be deeply unpopular' with parents – and voters – and did not encourage them), and if a grammar school head was willing to accept a new entrant. Valerie Ivison thought Shelagh was an ideal candidate. 'I went to Miss Leek and I said, "Her English is superb and she's very good at history, she is certainly fit to go to Pendleton High School."' But after Shelagh sat the exam, Miss Leek told Valerie that "'she can't do the maths". I said, "So?" She said, "I know, but she can't go if she can't do the maths …" I was cut up.'[20] Between September 1950 and July 1953, just three twelve- and thirteen-year-old girls were admitted to Pendleton, and Shelagh was not among them.[21]

But her teachers refused to give up. With extra coaching from Miss Leek, Shelagh eventually scraped a pass in the maths paper, and her headmistress was able to convince the Education Authority to admit Shelagh to a grammar school because of her 'outstanding … capacity for English studies'.[22] In September 1953, exceptionally, Pendleton High admitted fourteen-year-old Shelagh Delaney.[23]

Shelagh herself was surprised when Miss Leek told her that she would 'for some reason' be joining the fourth form at Pendleton High. 'I thought, "Oh crikey, I'll be very much behind the door as far as knowing things is concerned."'[24] At first sight, her new school was imposing: Pendleton High School for Girls was a former stately home, set on a hill and surrounded by tennis courts and well-kept gardens. Inside, girls were taught by an entirely graduate staff (at Broughton Modern, only Miss Leek had a degree), in spacious classrooms, dedicated science laboratories and the school's 'light, well-furnished library'.[25]

But Shelagh soon became disenchanted. 'I found I knew a damned sight more than a lot of the girls there,' she recalled.[26] 'The work, though sound, is undistinguished,' the school inspectors bluntly concluded. '[T]here is a lack of distinction in the teaching.' They found that English lessons 'lack purpose' and 'make insufficient demands on the pupils'.[27] 'It was,' recalled Jean Whur, 'incredibly boring.'[28] And the school inspectors noted that large sections of the school library, and the entire library card index catalogue, were 'kept locked up, preventing pupils from using their initiative to undertake research'.[29]

The point was, girls weren't meant to use their initiative. As Mary Evans explained, grammar schools were concerned with teaching their pupils to be 'a "good" girl ... a well-behaved, sensible person who could be trusted not to wish to attract attention to herself'.[30] While girls were told to work hard, they were also expected to accept the status quo of the society in which they lived – one in which middle-class girls, however hard they worked, ultimately got married and had children.

Like many girls' grammar schools, Pendleton High aimed at a pale imitation of the older male equivalent. Girls were divided into four houses to encourage competition, united as a school by a song and a smart blazer. Each house celebrated a male benefactor of the school (there was no thought of naming them after women, despite Manchester's importance in the fight for women's suffrage) – Shelagh was in Armitage, named after a Salford industrialist. The house names were a reminder that while the girls were expected to work hard, in the real world only men were achievers. Their house competitions gently stressed the point, since they had nothing to do with academic success: in Shelagh's second term, competitions included 'wild-flowers' and 'hobbies', in which entries – reported Ethel Rogers, captain of Armitage House – 'ranged from a beautifully worked cushion cover to a delicious-looking chocolate cake'.[31] In summer the school uniform was 'striped dresses with a very full skirt' of regulated length – a New Look costume with an emphasis on modesty.[32]

But Pendleton High did reflect broader ideas about how women of Shelagh's generation should live. Before the war, very few women had received a secondary education and those who did were expected to choose between a career and marriage; it was assumed they could not cope with both. After the war, many more women were given an education, and there were more jobs for them to go to: demand for teachers, nurses and clerks grew rapidly. Yet at the same time, psychologists and social scientists suggested that women had a biological need to be wives and mothers, and those who did not fulfil this were thwarting their nature. In 1948, the educationalist John Newsom argued that 'involuntary virgins' were ineffective teachers since they could not teach girls 'to adjust themselves to the standards and demands of a woman's normal life'.[33]

Such ideas weren't new, but they gained fresh support in the Cold War climate. 'Natopolitan' was how the socialist historian E. P. Thompson described British culture in the 1950s. He traced the reassertion of 'Monarchy, the Church, the State, the Family ... [as] indices of the supreme good – stability'. Thompson argued that this culture embodied a huge contradiction on which the media and politicians remained silent. On the one hand, Western governments declared their belief in individual freedom against the collectivism of the Communist bloc; psychology gained a new authority and collectivities like social class were said to be dead in the new 'affluent society'. In 1951, the Conservatives had won the general election, declaring themselves 'not biased by privilege or interest or cramped by doctrinal prejudices or inflamed by class warfare'; the party of 'national unity', committed to 'individual freedom'.[34]

But on the other hand, individuals who did not fulfil the role to which they were expected to conform were labelled mad, bad or dangerous. Thompson cited the treatment of women as an example of this new dogma. 'Sociologists, psychologists and husbands discovered that women are "different", and, under cover of talk about "equality of difference", the claim of women to full human equality was denied.'[35]

In Salford, the new psychology justified older suspicions of educated women. When, in the early 1950s, school inspectors asked Salford's Director of Education why so many of the city's girls left grammar school at the earliest opportunity, he replied bluntly that 'Salford was over-supplied with grammar school places for girls' – though in fact the two girls' grammar schools accommodated less than 15 per cent of the city's young women, while boys had almost twice the number of places.[36]

Girls of Shelagh's generation were told that their chances surpassed those of any previous generation, but also that wanting to do anything other than get married and have children was unconventional and deeply worrying. Many of her teachers embodied this contradiction. Pendleton High's older teachers were the 'spinsters' who so concerned John Newsom. To girls like Jean Whur they appeared remote and 'unable to teach'; many had ended up back in the classroom because so few other jobs were open to them. Their pupils certainly didn't emulate them. But some of the younger teachers were more puzzling. Jean admired a French teacher, with a degree from Cambridge, who stood out as 'really enthusiastic, and she got wonderful results'. Jean was disappointed to learn that 'she was a real girly girl. When she got engaged she took us in little groups to her home and showed us her wedding dress.'[37] All those years of hard work eclipsed by a walk down the aisle! Jean thought this 'was really, really strange'. Teachers who did think differently – who had watched mothers leading independent lives during the war, and had relished their own independence at training college or university – knew better than to express this to their pupils. Valerie Ivison, born in 1930, felt 'quite revolutionary, insofar as very early on I was advocating that people live together before they get married'; but her ideas caused shock among 'my own contemporaries' and would, she knew, have been unacceptable to Salford Local Education Authority.

Pendleton's pupils were expected to be middle class, or to aspire to be so. Like many grammar schools, Pendleton had charged fees before the 1944 Education Act and prided itself on its social exclusivity. In October 1953, when Shelagh had been a pupil for about a month, the headmistress, Miss Pearson, admitted to the governors and school inspectors that 'the older members of staff had experienced difficulty in adapting themselves to … the new type of pupil' – by which she meant those working-class girls who made it through the eleven-plus.[38] In Salford, a largely working-class city, these girls composed a large proportion of Pendleton's pupils, but the school never considered trying to fit into the community it served; rather the girls were meant to submit to Pendleton's standards. 'We were often subjected to snobbery,' remembered Norma Rowles, who attended Pendleton High in the mid-1950s.[39] And Shelagh was there on sufferance; as a former secondary modern pupil she'd already failed the academic and social test that was meant to handpick the middle class of the future.

She wasted no anxiety on trying to fit in, though. She found the social pretensions of Pendleton High very funny. 'There was never any malice in Shelagh, but she did take the piss,' recalled Jean Whur. She couldn't resist drawing out the petty snobberies of some of her classmates and teachers. 'I remember her grilling one girl [who] was very competitive and a snob, a working-class snob … She wanted to be middle class … And by the time Shelagh had finished, [her victim] had gone bright pink.' Some girls at Pendleton High thought Shelagh 'opinion-ated' when she declared that Broughton was just as good a school as theirs, dismissing her as 'miffed' for not passing the eleven-plus in the first place.[40] But she was at first disappointed and then angry on behalf of her old friends; she knew, she said, 'that back at the secondary school where I'd been half the girls and boys were capable of doing what I was doing'.[41] 'She didn't have a chip on her shoulder,' Jean said, 'and she wasn't cowed by the school … I think she genuinely found us quite tedious, really.'

Shelagh was, thought Jean, 'something of an outsider' at Pendleton High. She didn't fit in with the 'earnest' girls who wanted to pass exams, become a prefect and then a secretary and marry the boss. But she wasn't an outright rebel either, like the 'tough girls' from Ordsall, who came to school in brothel creepers and showed off lipsticks they'd got from sailors in exchange for a kiss or sometimes more; girls who 'got pregnant and couldn't play netball any more'.[42]

Shelagh had witnessed in Ordsall the results of pregnancy for working-class girls: punishing hard work and often gruelling poverty. But neither did she want to be a middle-class matron. Instead, she spent these teenage years envisaging an independent life that did not rely on having a man to look after her. She formed a double act with Christine Hargreaves, a confident young girl who also found Pendleton's pretensions ridiculous.

With Christine, Shelagh flouted the middle-class notions of ladylike behaviour and feminine innocence that their school promoted. They roamed around Salford's markets and streets of dilapidated houses and past the magistrates' court whose cases of drunkenness, wife-battering and burglary filled a full weekly page in the *Salford City Reporter*. In 1960, a reader supportive of 'Shelagh Delaney's Salford' – broadcast on BBC television – wrote to the *Reporter* to express his delight that Shelagh seemed to know the 'two different Salfords. One is the Ordsall and Trafford Road areas with its back to back terraced houses in a state of near collapse ... reminding one of a brick jungle' but peopled by 'the warmest, friendliest people ... [who] could show the rest of the country how to live as one. The other Salford lives in the Height and parts of Broughton ... for all their nice gardens these people seem to enclose themselves in a veil of ... isolation.'[43] Shelagh's home was on the border of the Height. She didn't aspire to the social superiority exhibited by its well-heeled residents held dear (some had opposed the building of her council estate); her parents and her own Ordsall childhood linked her back to that 'other Salford'.

Shelagh and Christine were thought 'sophisticated' at school – not a good thing, because for girls this meant sex. Tight-lipped teachers told their pupils to be 'careful' and wait for the right man and marriage, but otherwise maintained a disapproving silence about the facts of life. Girls were meant to seek a chaste outlet for their passions in crushes on older pupils; loving other women was a wholesome sign of immaturity, as long as it only involved adoration from afar. Shelagh was impatient with such prudery. 'I remember her coming over to me once ... and saying "You've got such beautiful ears,"' recalled Jean. 'I wasn't very streetwise, and I think now she was actually pretending a come-on. She didn't get the right reaction from me, because despite being taught all these dreadful things about sex, the other stuff was never mentioned.'

What gave Shelagh and Christine the temerity to laugh at Pendleton High and to challenge its ideals of chaste femininity? Despite her ambivalence about the move to Duchy Road, Shelagh was aware from a young age that the state considered her worth investing in – the new welfare state declared that families like hers deserved comfortable houses, free health care and a better education than preceding generations. 'I think I would be a very different person now if orange juice and milk and dinners at school hadn't told me, in a covert way, that I had a right to exist, was worth something,' wrote Carolyn Steedman.[44]

Imbued with this sense of entitlement, some girls – Shelagh Delaney and Christine Hargreaves among them – became angry that the world wasn't changing fast enough as far as women were concerned. The moral virtues their schoolteachers upheld were under threat, but were still powerful enough to ruin women's lives – neither of them wanted to end up in an unmarried mothers' home. Crucially, their own mothers encouraged their anger and their aspirations. Christine's mother, a former teacher and a socialist, supported her daughter's ambition to study at London's Royal Academy of Dramatic Arts (RADA). The prudery of Pendleton High was not evident in either girl's home. Elsie Delaney shared Jessie Hargreaves's view that ignorance was not bliss but dangerous. Later, when *A Taste of Honey* was condemned by a Salford newspaper as 'immoral', both mothers wrote letters of protest. 'When will the people of Salford admit that our city is not all that could be desired?' asked Jessie Hargreaves. 'Shelagh is telling the truth.' 'Has he never seen slums or a white girl with a coloured baby?' Elsie Delaney wrote of the journalist who'd lambasted her daughter. 'Are there any girls or boys in the world today who, at the age of twenty, do not know about sex life or pregnant women? I do not think so.'[45] Shelagh and Christine articulated an impatience with sexual taboo, ladylike behaviour and the rituals of marriage that marked the beginnings of a feminist challenge to post-war society. This would find its most conspicuous expression in the 1970s Women's Liberation Movement; many of the activists were members of Shelagh's generation. Their frustration at the way women's lives were circumscribed was already present in working-class Salford in the mid-1950s.

At fifteen, Shelagh's friendships were more eclectic than those of many of her schoolmates. She and Christine were part of a group of Pendleton High and Salford Grammar pupils who met at the Buile Hill Park cafe on Saturday afternoons.[46] But Shelagh was also friends with working-class girls who lived closer to Duchy Road, some of whom had already left school. Yvonne Carter, a classmate at Pendleton High, became a close friend. The daughter of a single mother, Yvonne lived in a poorer neighbourhood than Shelagh's. She introduced her to Shirley Gray (later Evans) and her large family, who lived in an overcrowded, privately rented house in a district earmarked for demolition. Shirley's ambition was to settle down with her boyfriend and get a good job in a bank. But she was also keen to escape the streets where she grew up, and in the 1960s would emigrate to Australia with her husband. 'My parents thought we were crazy. They said, "You're both giving up good jobs, you're giving up a house." But we thought it would be an adventure and it was.'[47]

While her different groups of friends rarely overlapped, their memories of Shelagh are consistent; she didn't adapt her behaviour to suit her audience. 'She was confident, calm ... comfortable ... with who she was,' said Jean Whur, although others noted that she still stooped in order to hide her height if she was with new people or felt uneasy.[48] Boys noticed that she did not defer to them. 'She had charisma,' recalled Harold Riley, a contemporary of Shelagh's and a pupil at Salford Grammar School. Most of her friends thought her attractive but, Jean said, 'unconventionally so, for Salford: she had all this thick, glossy black hair, and olive skin'. The pink-and-white petite prettiness favoured by 1950s films and advertisements was not Shelagh. 'She was not soft and feminine,' said Harold.

She was also openly contemptuous of the conservative ideals held out to young women. 'She would say things to get a reaction,' Shirley Evans recalled. 'This was in the fifties and things were different then ... "straight-laced" is putting it very mildly.' It wasn't only the residents of the Height who thought sex before marriage was a sin; Shirley's family took it very seriously. 'She used to come to our house, there was one time when a neighbour in our street had just had a baby. Shelagh said, "Oh, I would like to have a baby, but I wouldn't like a husband, I don't want to be married." And my mum, the look on her face. When Shelagh had gone, Mum said, "That was a very wicked thing for Shelagh to say." But it was what Shelagh thought and meant and she said it.' A growing tolerance towards lone motherhood is often associated with the so-called 'permissive' years of the late 1960s, when the contraceptive pill became available via the National Health Service, abortion was legalised and no-fault divorce became easier to obtain. More than a decade earlier, Shelagh Delaney and some of her friends were questioning the shame and stigma that attached to women who had sex outside marriage.

But she tempered her provocations with humour, aimed against herself as well as against the social conventions she found ridiculous. 'Shelagh was good-looking, highly intelligent, but mainly she impressed me as a very witty person,' said Harold Riley. 'She had a great sense of humour ... that kind of Salford humour, you talk about death and then you tell jokes ... it's a way of coping with what life throws at you.' But although she was ready to find life ridiculous, she was also kind. She was observant, noticing when people were in trouble, and became, said Jean Whur, 'a very good listener ... she was very, very interested in people ... and she was sympathetic'.

Listening and observing were helping her writing, which she took increasingly seriously. Shirley remembered her 'always carrying a pen and pad with her and she used to take notes all the time'. She had a good ear for dialogue, but in the mid-fifties dialect was frowned upon at girls' grammar schools, so when, in 1954, she submitted a piece to the school magazine she concentrated on description. In contrast to the prosaically factual accounts of games fixtures or whimsical poems that graced its pages, Shelagh contributed 'Learning to Ride a Bicycle'. 'There are few things as terrifying, and at the same time amusing, as learning to ride a bicycle,' she begins. Her prose matches the subject, picking up pace as the cyclist gains confidence: 'A feeling of exhilaration takes possession of you. Round go the wheels, furiously, swiftly over the road. Faster, faster, it's so easy, so simple. Why didn't you learn sooner?' Unlike much adolescent writing, she included more than one point of view: the cyclist but also the 'unfortunate' friend who is helping her and whose exasperation adds humour. And, in the last line, comes a twist, as the friend releases her hold on the bike and the pace is suddenly interrupted: 'Good heavens! She's let go of that carrier. Pick yourself up. Try again.'[49]

'Learning to Ride a Bicycle' introduced some subjects to which Shelagh would repeatedly return: the importance of the everyday, of female friendship, of risk-taking. This piece also suggests why, in 1956, she was so excited and inspired when she saw Samuel Beckett's play *Waiting for Godot* in Manchester. Beckett tried to explore the mundanity of everyday life while keeping his audience gripped – creating, in the words of one rapturous critic, 'an uneventful event'.[50] Later, Shelagh would read and enjoy most of Beckett's work, including *Worstward Ho*, which contained his famous reflection: 'Ever tried. Ever failed. No matter. Try again. Fail again. Fail better' – a sentiment embodied in the final line of her early piece.[51]

Like Beckett she was fascinated by movement as a bid for freedom; though unlike Beckett she would eschew bicycles in her later work for fast cars. But for Shelagh, bicycles represented a different sort of mobility as well: they were the traditional gift for children who passed the eleven-plus.[52] Throughout her work she'd explore the power of objects to symbolise aspirations, if not realise them. In *Dance with a Stranger*, set in the 1950s, Shelagh puts Ruth Ellis – a working-class woman with social ambitions – into 'an excellent copy of a Chanel suit' and gives her huge quantities of possessions 'including an elegant brolly and the very latest portable radio'.[53] In the 1950s, male politicians and writers frequently castigated working-class women for their frivolous consumption: they had to get jobs, argued an editorial in *The Times*, only because of their 'feckless' spending on luxuries they couldn't afford.[54] But Shelagh knew that such objects were important, reminders of how far a woman had come – but also where she wanted to get to.

Where Shelagh herself was going was, by the summer of 1955, a pressing question. She was sixteen. After obtaining good passes in all five subjects she took for her School Certificate, she decided to enter the sixth form with Christine. But she didn't take her studies particularly seriously, enjoying English but later claiming to be unable to remember her other A-level subjects. 'I forged a lot of notes from my parents and didn't go to school for a year,' she told a friend, and though this is an exaggeration, other friends recall that Shelagh seemed to spend a lot of her time 'roaming around' Salford on her own, perhaps while skipping school.[55]

She wanted to do something creative, probably to write. She knew that a few working-class boys like Albert Finney and Harold Riley were making a name for themselves as budding actors and artists at Salford Grammar School. They were helped by some particularly inspiring and energetic former servicemen who'd become teachers after the war and 'were culturally starved', said Harold. 'They were full of what they wanted to do culturally. And the theatre was, in schools, the principal cultural activity.' It was, recalled Albert Finney, 'extraordinary'; and not entirely to the liking of most of the staff of this conventional grammar school – some of them 'were very, very sarcastic about the school's dramatic activities'.[56] Nevertheless, Salford Grammar became known for its stellar performances, and by 1955 both Albert and Harold had gone to London to pursue their ambitions – Albert at RADA and Harold at the Slade School of Art.

But life was different for girls. When Shelagh asked her teachers' advice about becoming a writer they disapproved. They implied that she should be grateful for the opportunities she already had, and advised she set her dreams aside in favour of applying to a teacher training college.[57] 'God knows that the indifference shown in many cases to anybody contemplating a career such as acting, writing, or painting is often appalling,' she wrote two years later in the *Manchester Guardian*. 'The general reaction to my announcement that I intended to try and write for a living was one amounting to hysteria.'[58]

Girls were meant to look after others, either as paid teachers or secretaries, or as unpaid housewives and mothers. Shelagh and Christine Hargreaves found there was no clear route to a different future. At Easter 1956, seventeen-year-old Shelagh left school after completing two terms of her sixth-form studies.[59] Christine had been offered a place at RADA, and would be leaving school at the end of the summer term. 'Nobody ever thought we would get what we wanted,' recalled Christine when she was interviewed in 1962. '[B]ut we had confidence in ourselves.'[60] Inspired by Christine's success, Shelagh, believing that 'a writer needs to see life', decided that school had nothing more to offer her.[61] Annette Kuhn, a working-class girl at a London girls' grammar school, felt the same way. 'If at this point I was uncertain what I wanted to do with my life, the prospect of being a pillar of the community did not exactly stir the imagination,' she wrote. '[S]urely there ought to be more to life than a choice between bourgeois matronhood and a roomful of schoolchildren?'[62]

Pendleton High liked to keep up to date with former pupils: each girl's entry in the school register had a space for the secretary to ink in their destination after they left school. The register for Shelagh's year shows that most of her contemporaries had left at sixteen for office work in Salford or Manchester. Of those who entered the sixth form, a handful went to university; Christine to RADA; a larger number to teacher training college, and yet more into offices. But by Shelagh's name there is a blank. She'd had enough of being recorded, assessed and classified; at seventeen she decided to map her own escape route from the life she was meant to aspire to.

# 4

# 'I Write as People Talk'[1]

Shelagh walked out of school into a city that boasted greater opportunities for its school-leavers than ever before. Salford's Youth Employment Service observed that 'demands from employers for boys and girls of 15 to 18 years of age remained heavy'; school-leavers were lucky to have a 'wide variety of jobs open to them'.[2] The *Salford City Reporter* regularly praised the council's slum clearance programme, which promised new homes for these school-leavers once they married and started families of their own. The *Daily Mirror* coined the phrase 'Beanstalk Generation' to capture the health and prosperity of Shelagh and her fellow teenagers, their lives, thanks to post-war affluence, a heady mix of 'jeans, jive and juke boxes'.[3] The implication was that Shelagh's generation was lucky to be entering the world at such a time.

But the reality, as Shelagh knew, was far more mundane. The majority of school-leavers ended up in factory, shop or office work. Elsie and Joe Delaney assumed that their grammar-school-educated daughter would become a clerk in the council offices, the Co-op, or perhaps a bank. Clerical work was widely viewed as the best job a working-class girl could get – it was clean, safe and paid more than factory or shop jobs. But when her parents offered to pay for Shelagh to have typing lessons, she turned them down. In the year before she left school, a former pupil, Shirley Hynd, had written in Pendleton High's magazine about her job as clerk at the *Manchester Evening News*. 'Life in an office such as ours can never be dull,' she enthused; but in fact the only excitement came from the vicarious thrill of observing those men who dashed around town collecting stories, or edited them 'at paper-littered desks, in shirt sleeves and with pint mugs of tea and cigarettes always to hand' – while Shirley and her colleagues typed up their stories and poured their tea.[4] This did not appeal to Shelagh.

Exasperated, Elsie managed to get her a job in the smart clothes shop in Manchester where Shelagh's older, glamorous cousin Beryl worked. 'It was a gown shop – what you'd call a boutique,' recalled Beryl. 'Small, very fashionable – we had some famous people pass through.' Another attraction was that the assistants were expected to model the shop's pastel-coloured dresses, demure twinsets and full skirts; Beryl 'loved it'. But Shelagh was less enamoured. She 'drifted in late and when she did get there she wouldn't do much', said her cousin. 'She was untidy. Or maybe she was just lazy. The manager would say to me, "Where's Shelagh?" and she'd be under a clothes rail, "resting".'[5] Beryl was relieved when Shelagh, by mutual consent with the manageress, left after just a few weeks.

Next, Shelagh became an office girl at a milk depot. Though clerical work was meant to be the pinnacle of a working-class girl's ambitions, she offered a different view when, in 1960, she appeared on the BBC's *Monitor* programme. The episode, entitled 'Shelagh Delaney's Salford', was partly scripted by Shelagh, whose many drafts show that she thought carefully about what she wanted to say about school-leavers. 'They have to ... do jobs they didn't really want to do,' she said. 'You know, go into offices and type. Which is alright if you want to type (huh!) but I know too many who didn't want to be typists and all the rest of it.'[6] She left the milk depot as quickly as she'd left the boutique.[7]

Girls were meant to find a good job and stick with it. 'I shouldn't like you to think you can always just throw up a job when it doesn't seem too good,' a teacher warns the heroine of *Joan Goes Farming*, one of many girls' career novels that were published in the 1950s. 'You're seventeen and a half; time to face growing up, with all its hard facts.'[8] One of those 'hard facts' was that women's job choices were still very limited by the assumption they should leave work when they got married or at the latest when they had children. Most of the heroines of career-girl novels or the bestselling Mills & Boon romances of the fifties spend their working lives looking after men – as secretaries, nurses or air hostesses – who they end up marrying and caring for at home instead of at work (Joan's lucky – she can marry a farmer and carry on working as well). But Shelagh had no intention of facing up to a future spent serving other people, or staffing a production line, nor did she cherish any dreams of finding a husband to wait on.

Her third job, as an usherette at Manchester Opera House, was the kind of dead-end job, with no prospect of promotion, that careers advisers warned grammar school girls against. But

Shelagh found it more bearable than her previous forays into the labour market. As she later told Murray Melvin, one of the actors in *A Taste of Honey*, this job allowed her to watch the plays, as long as she remembered to leave just before the interval to serve ice creams, and just before the end of the show to see the punters out. 'By all accounts, she didn't necessarily remember to do so.'[9]

Working at the Opera House in the evenings left plenty of time for walking around Salford in the day. It was a city that epitomised the chasm between the rhetoric of politicians, academics and journalists, and the everyday life of ordinary people. In 1953 Queen Elizabeth II's Coronation had prompted two left-leaning sociologists, Edward Shils and Michael Young, to declare a new age of 'national unity' and 'the assimilation of the working class into the moral consensus of British society' as affluence replaced poverty.[10] At the 1955 general election the Conservatives, led by Old Etonian Anthony Eden, had emerged victorious with an increased majority. 'Conservative freedom works,' declared their manifesto, 'by maintaining full employment, by restoring housewives' choice and by smashing housing records.'[11] Magazines carried advertisements for new bathrooms, newspapers acclaimed the 'end of poverty'.[12] Yet thousands of Salford's residents remained without an inside toilet; it was, said Valerie Ivison, 'an industrial revolution, war-damaged slum'.[13] The city remained resolutely Labour, but Shelagh thought all politicians were out of touch with life. The council had begun pulling down the slums, but they took the life out of the city with them, closing cinemas, theatres and markets – 'the very essence of life so far as I'm concerned', said Shelagh – and removing people to estates on the edge of town 'where nobody knows anybody'.[14]

At home, she was faced with stark reminders of what marriage and motherhood could mean. Her wage was essential because her father was very ill. He'd never regained his strength after the war, and by the time Shelagh left school he seemed permanently exhausted, complaining of recurring back pain. He remained a loving, gentle husband and father, but Elsie told Shelagh that the witty, gregarious young man she had married had disappeared during the war, along with their romantic dreams.[15] It was a salutary reminder to Shelagh of why she did not want to marry.

But the alternatives to married life didn't look very attractive either. Boys were able to get better-paid skilled work than girls, but Shelagh felt no envy for her brother. '[M]y brother wants to be an instrument maker,' she said in 'Shelagh Delaney's Salford'. 'They're apprentices until they're 21, and they've got to go to night school, and doing a man's job in the meantime. And getting paid a pittance for doing it.' Going into the Civil Service or a profession like accountancy meant having to 'slog your heart out until you're about 25, going to night school', which Shelagh had no interest in.[16] Writing in the *New York Times Magazine* in 1961, Shelagh observed that 'Some ... found it hard to believe that a 19-year-old girl should be aware of the fact that some people are lonely, unhappy, miserable, capable of great tenderness and cruelty and possessed of courage'.[17] It was a passage that offered a glimpse into those years between 1955 and 1958, shaped by her father's suffering, her mother's exhaustion, and her own uncertain future.

She instinctively sympathised with anyone who didn't fit into the white middle-class family image so assiduously promoted as 'normality' by politicians and the media. By the time she left school thousands of migrants from Commonwealth countries in Asia and the Caribbean were trying to make a home in Britain's big cities, persuaded by government recruitment drives for bus drivers and factory hands. Newspapers took little interest in their efforts, but in Salford Shelagh could see windows prominently displaying signs stating 'No Blacks, No Irish', and the dilapidated properties, rented out by unscrupulous land-lords, that such discrimination forced the new arrivals to accept.

In 1957, after three years of consultation, the government's Departmental Committee on Homosexual Offences and Prostitution recommended that 'homosexual behaviour between adults in private should no longer be a criminal offence'. But the government dismissed the proposal. More popular was the committee's conclusion that street prostitution resulted from a 'weakening of the family' and 'community instability'. A police crackdown targeted prostitutes, but the men soliciting sex were left alone.[18]

Shelagh, as she would later tell her daughter, Charlotte, 'knew where the brothels were in Salford' from her teenage wanderings. Elsie would always give her straight answers to her questions, but other girls weren't so fortunate, and were very innocent. Kath Wilkie, who became friends with Shelagh in the 1990s, discovered they were the same age and had lived in the north-west at the same time. In 1956 Kath worked in Manchester city centre. 'There was a large chemist's on Market Street. And I went in there one morning before work, very early. And these women had gone in ... I did not know about the sex trade ... They'd got these chains round their ankles. I thought, "How strange. Why are they wearing chains round their ankles?" Then I noticed they were dressed in leather. I told Shelagh and she roared with laughter; she'd have known all about this of course.'[19] When one of Shirley Evans's workmates got pregnant, she was sent by her parents to an unmarried mothers' home. At first Shirley's mother refused to let her visit her friend. 'I'd never known a single woman get pregnant before ... Mum had kept such a tight rein on us, we never saw this sort of thing.' When Mrs Gray 'finally relented', Shirley's visit was 'an eye-opener ... for a start it was very far from home ... this enormous house where there was lots of pregnant girls and they just had their babies and they were put up for adoption. Later she came back to work, and it was never spoken of.'

The disapproving silence around such women, and the sexual double standard that underpinned it, enraged Shelagh. 'Liars made her angry,' said Kath Wilkie, and so did attempts to fudge or evade the truth. 'She liked facts ... if she didn't want someone to know something, she wouldn't tell them. If she wanted someone to know something, she'd tell them straight ... but didn't fabricate.' Harold Riley, who had now graduated from the Slade and was back in Salford trying to make a living from his art, had become a close friend of Shelagh's. He agreed that she could be 'very direct' and was 'a very strong character'.

Some emerging writers and critics shared her views. 'The country was dead from the neck up,' wrote Alan Sillitoe, a former factory worker, by now embarking on a writing career. He condemned the 'miasma of falsity' created by politicians, journalists and broadcasters. 'These purveyors of conformism did not know about the great majority of people, and did not care to consider them worthy of notice. When they did not fear or hate them, they wanted them to be in perpetual thrall to values which the complacent upper few per cent had decided, because they were their own, were the only ones worth living by.'[20] At a time when the Lord Chamberlain could censor literature, theatre and television, the arts provided no riposte. '[A]nyone whose knowledge of England was restricted to its popular theatre would have come to the conclusion that its standard of living was the highest on earth,' concluded the *Observer*'s young theatre critic, Kenneth Tynan, of 1954. 'The poor were seldom with us, except when making antic contributions or venturing, tongue-tied with embarrassment and clutching cloth caps, into the gracious salons of middle-class comedy, where they were expected to preface every remark with "Beggin' yer pardon, Mum".'[21]

By 1956 cracks in the conservative edifice were beginning to appear. In July, the Suez Crisis erupted when the Egyptian leader Colonel Nasser nationalised the Suez Canal, an important trading route for Britain and France. Prime Minister Eden continually claimed he was 'a man of peace' committed to a diplomatic solution, but the American press exposed his secret plan for a huge military invasion of Suez designed to re-establish British control over the region. At the same time, hundreds of thousands of Hungarians rioted against Soviet domination – the first major threat to totalitarianism in Europe since the Second World War. The Hungarian uprising was crushed, but the Egyptians forced Eden into an ignominious retreat; at home he was discredited as a liar by his own ministers and by thousands of demonstrators, while the BBC finally defied the prohibition on reporting matters due for debate in Parliament. Eden resigned in 1957. By then it was clear that politics, far from being a game best left to the experts, was of real and pressing consequence to everyone on the planet – and that ordinary people could make history.

In the theatre, too, 1956 was the year, Tynan declared, when 'there issued the distinct sound of barricades being erected'.[22] John Osborne's *Look Back in Anger* premiered at London's Royal Court Theatre in May that year – it wasn't performed in Manchester, but an enthusiastic theatregoer like Shelagh could not help knowing about it. Osborne's story of Jimmy Porter, an 'angry young man' sick of the social hierarchy, was a hit. '*Look Back in Anger* presents post-war youth as it really is,' wrote Tynan; 'the drift towards anarchy, the instinctive leftishness, the automatic rejection of "official" attitudes, the surrealist sense of humour ... the casual promiscuity, the sense of lacking a crusade worth fighting for.'[23] Twenty-four-year-old Arnold Wesker, then working as a pastry chef in London, *agreed with* Tynan that Osborne's debut was 'a call to arms'. He already had aspirations to act and to write when he saw the play. 'The war had been a formative part of our lives, followed by the hope of 1945, and the general decline from then on,' he said. '[W]e were the generation at the end of that decline, desperately wanting to find something, being tired of the pessimism and the mediocrity, and all the energy that was spent on being anti-Soviet and anti-Communist.' *Look Back in Anger* 'triggered something off in me, and I felt the Theatre [*sic*] was somewhere where something could happen'.[24] The result was *Chicken Soup with Barley*, Wesker's play about the Kahn family, anti-fascist East End Jews fighting Oswald Mosley's Blackshirts in 1936. Its premiere in 1958 launched his career as a playwright.

Shelagh shared many of Wesker's opinions, and his ambition to write. 'I didn't know what to do with myself,' she later said of this time. 'I knew I wanted to do something, but what I couldn't find out. I was lucky. I thought I could write.'[25] She had a particularly good ear for dialogue, relishing the sardonic, absurd humour of Salford, the frequent use of non sequiturs, and the forthright manner in which people spoke. It was what drew her to the Gray family. 'She used to laugh a lot in our house,' recalled Shirley. 'Because my father was a natural comic.' He was also, said Bill, Shirley's younger brother, 'a real storyteller – if anything happened at work he'd come home and by the time you heard about it you didn't know whether to believe it or not, his stories were so fantastic', often involving amazing athletic feats, like his claim to have jumped the width of the Salford canal to avoid being hit by a crane.[26] Shelagh listened and learned. 'He'd tease Shelagh,' Shirley remembered; 'he'd warn you "be careful what you say, Shelagh's writing all this down!"'

Her friends sympathised with her desire to become a professional writer, for several of them also wanted to work in the arts. Albert Finney and Christine Hargreaves were at RADA, Harold Riley had only recently graduated from the Slade. In the holidays they met up at Buile Hill Park. 'We'd saunter round the park to the cafe, singing the latest songs, eyeing the boys eyeing us,' recalled Lilian Barker, one of Shelagh's contemporaries.[27] When it rained, said Harold Riley, 'it was jukebox time' – they crammed into the small cafe and pooled their money on coffee while they talked about what they were reading, the plays and films they'd seen and where they planned to go next. And across the country similar conversations were happening. 'We all wanted to be involved in something creative,' said 'Polly', in a group biography of women who'd attended the same grammar school in Stratford-upon-Avon in the late 1950s.[28] Jean Whur, who wanted to be an actress, thought that 'it was something about the times'; acting, writing and painting promised self-fulfilment and self-expression that a respectable niche in the suburban middle class didn't offer.[29]

They were influenced by a post-war spirit of optimism in the arts. In 1945 the incoming Labour government had established the Arts Council to fulfil its commitment to 'the provision of concert halls, modern libraries, theatres and suitable civic centres'.[30] John Maynard Keynes, the Council's chairman, argued that culture was not a luxury in those cash-strapped times, but essential to the creation of a fair and civilised society. 'There can be no better memorial of a war,' he said, 'than to save the freedom of the spirit of the individual.' Keynes believed that every town and city that had been made 'half a ruin' by war should be transformed into 'a great artistic metropolis'.[31]

Among the Labour councils to respond enthusiastically to Keynes's rallying cry were Manchester and Salford. These cities boasted a radical artistic tradition on which to build. In 1936, the Salfordian Communist activist, actor and writer Ewan MacColl, had joined forces with avant-garde director Joan

Littlewood to form Theatre Union. They aimed to 'present to the widest possible public, and particularly to that section of the public which has been starved theatrically, plays of social significance'.[32] In the late 1940s Manchester Council proposed a cultural quarter, accommodating 'artists, writers, dons, students, Continentals, journalists, architects, actors, musicians, engineers and others whose jobs or leisure interests link them with the cultural centre'. Theatres and 'studios' would be built alongside blocks of flats with communal dining rooms to promote 'congenial, appreciative and stimulating company'.[33]

That ambitious vision came to nothing, but both councils put some scaled-down plans into practice. Manchester Council launched a youth drama festival (as did Salford soon after) and in 1946 granted the city's Libraries' Committee power to establish a theatre for 'the performance of stage plays for or in connection with the advancement of art, education, drama, science or literature'.[34] Situated in the basement of Manchester Central Library, it opened its doors in 1952. And, much as Shelagh disliked Pendleton High School, she benefited from the regular theatre trips offered to Salford students, particularly sixth-formers. 'I didn't know anything about modern plays until I was sixteen,' she later said. 'My teacher gave me tickets to see Arthur Miller's *Death of a Salesman*. It left a deep impression on me. I read a lot after that – Chekhov, who really means a lot to me, and O'Neill ... and Brecht and Beckett.'[35] By 1955 Shelagh and Christine Hargreaves had joined the Salford Players, an excellent amateur company. 'Shelagh had experience before *A Taste of Honey* – she'd acted, and she wrote sketches,' said Murray Melvin.[36]

Her time at the Salford Players also introduced Shelagh to David Scase, artistic director of the Library Theatre. David was to be an invaluable ally for Shelagh. The son of a bricklayer, his first job had been in a bicycle factory. In 1945 Scase had joined Theatre Workshop as a technician, but, as Ewan MacColl wrote, he was quickly 'able to do any job in the theatre from rigging and de-rigging a stage to acting a major role'.[37] When Scase left in 1954 to take up his new appointment in Manchester, he remained on good terms with Joan Littlewood – not easy given her irascible temper. That was to prove fortuitous for Shelagh's future. In the meantime, he appears to have been responsible for getting her the job as usherette at Manchester Opera House.

Being an usherette allowed Shelagh to see the Manchester debut of Samuel Beckett's *Waiting for Godot* in 1956. The play's London premiere the year before had provoked condemnatory notices in the popular press, and mass walkouts from theatregoers disgusted by Beckett's apparently formless play about two tramps waiting for a third man who never arrives. But the theatre critic Irving Wardle was stunned by its originality. 'Conflict, we learnt from Beckett, was not an indispensable component [of drama]; neither was the torture chamber of moralistic plotting; nor characters who finally emerge as winners or losers.'[38] Shelagh said that *Waiting for Godot* provided 'her chief inspiration to write'. It reinforced her growing belief 'that there were other voices that absolutely needed to be written and to be heard'.[39]

But Shelagh did not think of writing a play herself. Instead she embarked on a novel. She was motivated by the new job she took in January 1957, as an assistant in the research photography department of Metropolitan-Vickers, a large engineering firm on the Trafford Park industrial estate. Metro-Vicks, as it was known, employed 23,000 people so 'there were a great variety of people to get to know' – a golden opportunity for an aspiring writer, as Shelagh later told interviewers.[40] Working on the Trafford Park estate, and travelling through Salford every day, gave her plenty of material for her notebooks – and fed her own strong sense of the absurd. She regaled her friends with stories of Metro-Vicks, including the tale of a young man who 'raced for the bus she was on, made it, sat down next to her out of breath – and put his head on her shoulder. She looked over, and he'd died.'[41] The element of absurdity in tragedy, and of the ridiculous within the everyday, greatly appealed to her. 'She had the one thing from Salford that she felt was the essence of what she was, and that was that humour,' said Harold Riley. 'That sense of talking about dying on the one hand and laughing on the other – it's a Salford thing. In the face of everything, you can make a joke.' 'Usually North Country people are shown as gormless,' she later complained about the theatre, 'whereas in actual fact they are very alive and cynical.'[42]

By 1957, writers and film-makers were becoming more interested in the life that Shelagh knew best. This was the year when documentary film-maker Lindsay Anderson directed *Every Day Except Christmas*, a short film about workers at London's Covent Garden market. Michael Young and Peter Wilmott published a study of life in the modern East End, *Family and Kinship in East London*. Their book became a surprise bestseller. So did John Braine's novel *Room at the Top*, about a young working-class man on the make in a northern town. Young and Wilmott wrote out of concern that working-class communities were about to disappear forever as slums were demolished and people departed for new, suburban council estates. Others, like Anderson, a left-wing former public schoolboy, disenchanted with the snobbery of his upbringing, thought the working class offered a more honest, authentic way of life than Britain's discredited establishment. Many of their viewers and readers were interested in the changes that the welfare state, and particularly the 1944 Education Act, had wrought on working-class life. It was in 1957 that Phyllis Bentley, who had enjoyed interwar success as a novelist writing about middle-class life in Yorkshire, observed that there was no longer any market for books like hers. Suddenly, a 'younger generation portrayed and expressed a kind of life hitherto inarticulate'; predominantly that of a 'good-looking upstanding young fellow, with waved hair, a well-tailored suit, a colourful pullover and a sophisticated taste in discs; well paid, enjoying the benefits of the Welfare State [*sic*] ... but thoroughly dissatisfied, struggling towards a code of ethics as yet unformulated'.[43]

A few of these writers, and many of their readers, hailed from the places and backgrounds they wrote about. For many of Richard Hoggart's middle-class readers, *The Uses of Literacy*, published the same year, was a revelation, an insight into a life of which they were ignorant.[44] But it was even more shattering for his working-class readership, who saw their lives treated seriously, as the stuff of art and culture, for the very first time. 'My own life was being described as if it merited serious scholarly attention,' recalled Annette Kuhn.[45] Tom Courtenay, the son of a Hull dockworker, had his sights set on RADA when he read *The Uses of Literacy*. It 'made a great impression on me

... I loved seeing the people I had grown up among taken seriously.'[46] For Stan Barstow, a Yorkshire draughtsman and aspiring novelist, Hoggart's work was an inspiration. '[T]he bright young men from the provinces were no longer content to sit back and accept what was given to them,' he wrote. 'They were reaching out and taking for themselves. The air crackled with a new energy. Anything seemed possible.'[47]

But Shelagh's novel took a different perspective. There was no place for prostitutes or single mothers in Hoggart's community; no recognition of the resentments or exhaustion of women like Elsie Delaney.[48] Shelagh wanted to explore their lives and passions. She focused on a pregnant woman and her mother, aiming to capture the 'restlessness' of youth, but also what she called the 'chaos of middle age where ... it's too late to start again – and it's too early to give up'.[49] No trace of the novel survives, but her later notebooks suggest that she would have begun by writing down fragments of conversation overheard in the street, on the bus home from work, and in the offices and canteen at Metro-Vicks. Ideas for characters would follow, but she always began with the phrases she heard and enjoyed writing dialogue most of all. 'I write as people talk,' she declared in an interview with *The Times* in 1959.[50]

Perhaps for this reason, her book did not progress very far. She found it hard to sustain the pace and narrative pull that a novel required. Description struck her as tedious – she would never give very full stage directions – and plot was a bore: she was interested in exploring episodes from life, and from several points of view, not telling a linear story of a single hero or heroine. Other working-class writers were grappling with the same dilemma. Alan Sillitoe spent 1956 'stitching the narrative [of *Saturday Night and Sunday Morning*] together by ploughing in a dozen Nottingham stories [which had been rejected by magazines] which seemed to concern the main character … Perhaps it was this technique which gave the work a somewhat episodic effect.'[51] Stan Barstow wrote short stories before finally finishing his debut novel *A Kind of Loving*; Keith Waterhouse, author of *Billy Liar*, was a journalist by trade and vocation. Like Shelagh, they had to earn a living and it was easier to write a short story in the evenings than to think one's way back into a novel. If they sought to make writing pay then columns or stories produced quicker returns than a book. But the novel also posed a structural challenge for writers intent on recreating a whole community rather than charting the progress and triumph of a single, self-made protagonist. That form of writing had gained popularity among middle-class authors and readers in the nineteenth century as the ability of men (chiefly) to make their fortune through industry or finance became popularised and celebrated. Of course women and working-class writers had managed to adapt the novelistic form to accommodate different stories, but it was still a challenge to write about a character who didn't want to escape his or her past – like Arthur Seaton of *Saturday Night and Sunday Morning*, described by Sillitoe as 'a working man who, though not necessarily typical of the zone of life he lived in, belonged to it with so much flesh and blood that nothing could cause him to leave it – not even his mother'.[52]

Meanwhile, Shelagh was developing an interest in the visual arts. Partly this was because of her friendship with Harold Riley, who was trying to launch his artistic career while teaching part-time at a school in Ordsall. 'She came down because of the school play,' Harold recalled. 'She was involved with the Salford Players. I showed her the kids' drawings. And I got them drawing their back doors ... Shelagh said, "Oh, that's interesting. Back doors ... What did they make of that?" So I said, "Well, at first they don't know why they're doing it. But then they explain what the back door is in their life: somewhere that keeps them in, or somewhere that keeps them out ... It's also, in fact, the gateway into their home." We talked about that for quite a while. She said, "They won't get any of that, Harold. But what they will make of it will be very interesting" ... She was interested in tangents. Like you'd say, "I like the shape of that salt pot," and she'd look at it and say, "Oh, have you seen ..." which was very stimulating.'

Conversations with Harold, and her job as a photographer's assistant at Metro-Vicks, sparked her interest in perspective – how your choice of viewpoint could alter what you saw, and the importance of the frame in communicating a particular message about the place or people being represented. Possibly Harold helped her to get the Metro-Vicks job, as Geof does Jo in *A Taste of Honey*: 'That's a nice little job you got me, retouching those bloody photographs. What was it supposed to do, prove I was the artistic type? Of course we can't all be art students, going to our expensive art schools, nursing our little creative genius.'[53] Her interest in the visual arts was to have an important impact on her career. 'I thought she'd gone to art school because she always had an eye for the best shot, the right location, the perspective,' said Stephen Frears, who worked with her on the film *Charlie Bubbles* in 1968; many other collaborators made the same assumption.[54] Place was always integral to what Shelagh wrote, though she was often better at visualising this than describing it on the page.

But in the summer of 1957, the chances of Shelagh becoming a writer seemed more remote than ever. Metro-Vicks gave her money to spend and a new circle of friends. 'I was too busy enjoying myself, going out having a good time' to write and her novel languished in a drawer. Years later she and Kath Wilkie compared notes and found they'd both spent Saturday afternoons at Manchester's Kardomah coffee bar on bustling Market Street. 'It was the atmosphere, and the coffee and the smoke – they would smoke inside in those days.'[55] In the evenings she and her friends went to the cinema – she loved Hollywood musicals like *Oklahoma!* and *Funny Face*, which brought glorious technicolour vistas of sunlit prairies or glamorous Paris into Salford's smoke-filled auditoria – or to the theatre. 'There was a very active theatre-going public in Salford amongst young people,' recalled Harold Riley. Shirley Evans, by now in a different coterie, went to 'musicals, stage show and variety shows. We used to go to the Opera House in Manchester. And we went to the Hallé Orchestra.' Shelagh preferred jazz clubs to classical concerts, but she was a regular at the Opera House and the Library Theatre. Most of all, though, she loved jiving at one of Salford and Manchester's many dance halls. 'It turned out we both used to go to the Ritz, in Manchester, of a Saturday night,' said Kath Wilkie. 'That was the place to be seen … you'd get BBC types upstairs on the balcony, the hoi polloi dancing below.'

Richard Hoggart disapproved of young women like Shelagh, who he deemed 'flighty, careless and inane' factory girls, pursuing mindless fun 'at the "Palais", the "Mecca", the "Locarno"' rather than leading respectable lives helping their mothers.[56] But for Shelagh, dancing and music were the stuff from which dreams of a different future were woven. In her 2004 play *Baloney Said Salome* – named after a fifties children's skipping rhyme that celebrates an impudent dancer – sixty-year-old Nina, who is dying, regrets having eschewed fun for respectability. 'I should've been dancing all my life. I should have been jitterbugging and jiving every night at the Ritz instead of sitting at home … to please my parents.'[57] Dance would crop up repeatedly in her work, most conspicuously in her 1985 screenplay *Dance with a Stranger*. It was vital for Shelagh that 'Ruth dances superbly'. She captured the importance of dancing as an escape from the everyday hardships, social snobbery and contempt that a working-class single mother had to endure in the 1950s. She also showed that dancing was a form of self-expression as well as courtship. Ruth is a glamorous but generous partner on the dance floor, while David Blakely, the arrogant Etonian racing-car driver with whom Ruth falls hopelessly in love and who she eventually murders, lumbers around 'like an ape', thinking only of himself, never of his partner.[58]

Dancing was also about having fun while you could. That had a special pertinence for Shelagh's generation, who knew they were living under a mushroom cloud. 'Today's adolescents live within a world sharply divided into two immense blocks of power; and a world under a constant threat of nuclear catastrophe,' observed the government's Committee on the Youth Service in England and Wales, commissioned in 1958 to 'examine ways of assisting young people to play their part in the life of the community, in the light of changing social and industrial conditions' (Richard Hoggart was one of its members). 'These issues may only be made articulate by a few ... [but] they ... lie immediately behind the small stage of many an adolescent's activities, like a massive and belittling backcloth.'[59] Shelagh grew up watching cinema newsreels of atomic tests; they were a frame through which she understood the world. In a pivotal scene in *Dance with a Stranger*, Ruth and her young son sit together in a cinema auditorium watching a newsreel. Shelagh's directions described Ruth being disturbed by a man who 'decides to sit next to her in spite of the fact that ninety per cent of the seats are empty. As he sits beside her she, knowing full well what his intentions are, gets up and leaves.' The next item on the news is 'about the H-Bomb test at Eniwetok, the huge explosion that changed the world'.[60] Ruth Ellis, like Shelagh, lived in a world where life was cheap, particularly if you were a working-class woman.

Despite having a good time with her friends, Shelagh was still yearning to become a writer and leave Salford. She found her home town 'alive' and 'restless', but 'at the same time, somehow or other, it seems to be dying'; it had never really recovered from the industrial recession of the 1930s.[61] She also had an inkling that to write properly about the town might mean moving away. She told Harold Riley that Salford was 'the creative force' in her life, but that 'it obstructs me'.[62] At home she was subject to the expectations and obligations that came from living under her parents' roof. London was her goal. Despite all the high-flown rhetoric of the 1940s, the Arts Council hadn't delivered much money to the provinces; the new plays and exhibitions were in the capital. At times, escape was more important than the writing itself. 'Christine had used drama to get away, and Shelagh saw writing as a passport to getting away,' her daughter recalled; 'that was her chance at a new life.'[63] 'I could not know it then,' reflected Alan Sillitoe on his failure to gain a scholarship to secondary school in the 1930s, 'but I wanted to go in[to that new life] by the ceiling, not enter by the cellar.'[64] At eighteen, Shelagh felt the same.

Shortly after her nineteenth birthday in November 1957 Shelagh's father was diagnosed with terminal cancer. After several weeks in hospital, he came back home to see in the new year of 1958 in a sickbed in the Delaneys' sitting room. Shelagh was very close to her father; 'she really loved him', recalled her cousin Beryl. 'She had this leaning towards her dad more than her mum,' said Kath Wilkie. 'It was not what she said, it was the tone of voice she said it with ... always quite gentle.' Her father's illness could have prompted Shelagh to give up any hope of leaving Salford and a career; several of her later plays would explore the lives of women whose ambitions were over-ridden by a need to look after an ailing or widowed parent.[65] But in fact she was galvanised to write, in the hope of producing something of note before he died. In the first weeks of 1958 she tried to complete her novel, but was soon mired in the same problems she'd had before. She toyed with the idea of writing for the stage, recalling *Waiting for Godot*, and turned to David Scase for help. He agreed that a play might be a better form for her ideas.[66]

She needed one final provocation to pick up her pen. In February 1958 she accompanied some workmates to a performance of Terence Rattigan's latest drawing-room drama, *Variation on a Theme*, at Manchester Opera House. She and her friends found themselves laughing at Rattigan's portrayal of 'safe, sheltered, cultured lives in charming surroundings', as Shelagh put it, 'not life as the majority of ordinary people know it'. She was never, she'd later say, 'an angry young woman – what have I got to be angry about?' But she did have a strong sense of the ridiculous. At school this had prevented her being intimidated by Pendleton High's social pretensions; now she was 'convinced I could do better' than Rattigan. She 'just went home and started work'.[67]

The plays she enjoyed the most – *Death of a Salesman* and *Waiting for Godot* – offered some insight into life, grief, and the desires of men and women like her parents, scarred by circumstances beyond their control. They were concerned with ordinary people's imagination as well as with their everyday lives. They were also controversial – something, Shelagh later told her daughter, she wanted for her own play. She didn't mind courting disapproval; her friends could attest that playing by the rules wasn't always rewarded. Jean Whur had wanted to go to drama school but 'I was bullied out of it' by her headmistress and her parents, who argued it offered neither security nor respectability. Jean 'ended up' being a nurse 'out of sheer desperation.' Shelagh was determined to escape that fate, but she had no role model to follow. Instead, she sought to learn from her own experience. She'd come to believe that she'd got to Pendleton High because 'I was more cheeky than the rest or a bit more conspicuous'.[68] Now she set out to challenge convention once more. Two weeks later, she had written a play she called *A Taste of Honey*.

# 5

# A Taste of Honey

When Shelagh sent her play to Joan Littlewood in April 1958, her covering letter presented a shrewdly selective version of the truth. She omitted to mention that she had been writing for the Salford Players and that David Scase had advised her to send the play to Theatre Workshop. Instead, she wrote to Joan that she had 'nothing – except a willingness to learn – and intelligence'.[1]

Shelagh's letter betrayed her apprehension and nervousness, but it was also a cleverly crafted self-portrait, one that offered Joan a pliable provincial protégée. Being working class and young were, in selected quarters, just beginning to be points in an artist's favour. And Shelagh learned from Scase that Littlewood was an imaginative, visionary director, who'd never lost the left-wing principles that caused her in the 1940s to turn down the BBC's offer of Head of Features in favour of joining a group of left-wing writers and actors determined to create, in the words of Ewan MacColl – Littlewood's husband and partner in the venture – 'a popular theatre with a broad working-class base'.[2]

This made Theatre Workshop appear the obvious choice for *A Taste of Honey*. But Shelagh knew that, as a female playwright, she was a very different prospect from Arnold Wesker or John Osborne. She thought hard about how to present herself to Joan. She'd learned from her upbringing that working-class girls, even educated ones, were expected to be docile, not ambitious, and grateful for every opportunity bestowed upon them. Shelagh trod a careful line between her claim to have something Joan might want – a teenage girl's native insight into northern working-class life – and gratitude laced with humility. '[I]f you can gather a little sense from what I have written – or a little nonsense – I should be extremely grateful for your criticisms,' she wrote, presenting herself as 1958's answer to Eliza Doolittle.

Shelagh contacted Joan at an opportune moment. For the first eight years of its existence, Theatre Workshop had been a touring company, but in 1953 Joan had decided to make a permanent home at the Theatre Royal in Stratford, in east London. This new base made heavy demands on the company. Joan had hoped that they might attract funding from the Arts Council, but the Council proved far more elitist than many of its advocates had hoped. 'In the climate of the Cold War, the left-wing perspective of [Theatre Workshop] was incompatible with the establishment ethos and prevailing cultural conservatism embodied by the Arts Council,' the theatre scholar Nadine Holdsworth has written.[3]

To attract and keep a regular audience the company had to find endless new productions to perform – rather than staging the same play night after night, as they had on tour – and the Theatre Royal needed constant upkeep, so the productions had to be popular. In 1955 MacColl departed; he and Joan had split up and he often found himself on the losing side of arguments with Gerry Raffles, Joan's new partner and Theatre Workshop's manager. Raffles insisted plays had to have wide appeal but MacColl was suspicious of what he saw as an overly commercial outlook.

Theatre Workshop was struggling when, in 1956, Raffles recruited the young Irish writer Brendan Behan. His play *The Quare Fellow* was an immediate hit, not only with the critics but with Stratford's office and factory workers who Littlewood was determined to bring into the theatre. A series of minor successes followed, most of them introducing new writers. In 1957 their production of *You Won't Always Be On Top*, a play about a day on a building site written by construction worker Henry Chapman – and praised by Kenneth Tynan for making 'ordinariness fascinating'[4] – incurred the theatre censor's wrath. The Lord Chamberlain decreed that the Workshop must cut 'an imitation of Sir Winston Churchill ... called upon to open a public lavatory'. Littlewood refused; she and Raffles were prosecuted and fined.[5] Shelagh read newspaper reports of this case with interest.[6]

A week after she had sent the script to 'Miss Littlewood', Shelagh learned that Theatre Workshop was going to perform her play in just six weeks' time. She immediately accepted Littlewood's invitation to attend rehearsals, and handed in her notice at work. Shelagh was sure that she was on her way. 'Joan Littlewood is the most valuable person I've ever met as far as work's concerned,' she told *ITN News* in 1959, a conviction she stuck to, even when, in later years, she and Joan fell out.[7]

Arriving in London in April 1958, Shelagh was introduced to the frenetic life of a professional theatre. At Theatre Workshop, everyone had to muck in with every task, partly because money was so short, and partly because Joan wanted to break down the hierarchies that existed in conventional theatrical companies. Actors turned their hand to set construction or lighting. The wardrobe mistress, Una Collins – soon to become one of Shelagh's closest friends – served drinks in the interval.[8]

Shelagh relished it; but she was also daunted by trying to work out how she could fit into this company. She arrived, recalled Murray Melvin, 'wearing a huge white man's mac – she was tall – and she said, "I could murder a cup of tea," in this wonderful voice – deep, northern'. She was welcomed, but as the northern ingénue she'd presented herself as being in her letter to Littlewood. 'Joan and Gerry were very, very strong personalities,'[9] and Gerry, in charge of publicity, was keen to make the most of Shelagh as the new working-class voice. His press release for *A Taste of Honey* described her as 'a nineteen year old factory worker from Salford, Lancashire'; a slight twist of the truth, since Shelagh had not worked on an assembly line at Metro-Vicks, as Raffles implied, but as a technician, assisting in the processing of photographs – a new sort of job on the borderline between manual and clerical work.[10] She wanted to be a full-time writer, and the requirement to play the part of the northern factory hand would quickly begin to grate on her. Later, Brendan Behan would say that 'Shelagh Delaney and I are creations of Joan Littlewood's imagination'.[11] To Joan they were stock characters, the Irish rebel and the northern, working-class heroine.

For now, though, Shelagh was content to sit in on rehearsals, learning her trade. She lodged with Avis Bunnage – cast as

Helen – some of the time, but she also stayed at Joan's house in Blackheath. Joan, always generous to new talent, was willing to subsidise Shelagh from her own pocket, confident that her protégée's play would provide ample compensation.

Almost as soon as *A Taste of Honey* opened, critics were saying that Joan Littlewood had written it, implying that a young working-class woman from Salford wasn't capable of this. In fact Joan's Workshop was grounded in the radical assumption that creativity was collaborative: an individual's contribution would inspire and be reshaped by others. Oscar Lewenstein, the left-wing theatrical manager partly responsible for staging *Look Back in Anger* at the Royal Court, agreed that *Honey* was the result of collaboration. 'It has been said that a certain amount of the play was created in production. I do not know how much of the original was in the final script and I do not think it matters. Author, director and cast had worked together to create a joyful evening from a story that in other hands might have been tragic.'[12]

But in fact Shelagh's original manuscript, now held in the British Library, refutes the suggestion that Joan Littlewood was responsible for *A Taste of Honey*. The plot and the vivid dialogue are already present in her script, as Murray Melvin, who Joan had cast as Geof, recalls. 'Technically there was a lot wrong, of course. She was nineteen! But the actual words were very assured ... and her humour came out in the writing.'[13] 'I like this romantic half-light,' says Jo, lying on a dilapidated couch in her cramped flat as dusk draws in, 'it just goes with this Manchester maisonette!'[14] Shelagh's characters all have an imagination – they often dream of a different world – yet they also have a sense of the ridiculous, ever-conscious of the chasm that exists between the romances played out by Hollywood idols on the big screen and the reality of their own lives. 'I dreamt about you last night,' Jo's boyfriend, Jimmie, tells her. 'Fell out of bed twice.'[15] Frances Cuka, who played Jo, agreed that 'most of the best bits were Shelagh's'.[16]

Shelagh had come to Theatre Workshop at a transitional moment in the company's history. Joan wanted to find authentic working-class voices, and in Shelagh she had one. As Cuka recalled, Joan was adamant that 'it was a young girl's play and we mustn't wreck the flavour of it'.[17] Joan was increasingly using improvisation, but in the rehearsals of *Honey*, her desire to keep the authenticity of the working-class, northern voices Shelagh had created triumphed. She used improvisation to get the actors into character for their roles, rather than to change the plot. Joan had Cuka and Bunnage running around the theatre carrying heavy suitcases to imitate the journey around Manchester that Jo and Helen are meant to have taken before the play begins.[18] Once rehearsals were properly under way, 'if you improvised, the question you had to ask was, "what was Shelagh's intention?"'[19]

The cast recognised that they'd been handed an outstandingly original play. Shelagh's Salford dialogue was something completely new to post-war London theatre. So too were the settings she'd created, in the cramped, squalid bedsit in which Helen and Jo live, and the meetings between Jo and Jimmie by the canal. But most original of all was that *A Taste of Honey* took a woman's perspective. 'When I started this play, I had only two people in it – the mother and daughter,' Shelagh later said. 'Then I realized there had to be other characters so that these two could reveal themselves more fully. It built up on its own.'[20] But Jo and Helen remained her focus. From the moment they barged onto the stage, carrying suitcases as they 'flitted' from one rented room to another, they railed against the roles women were meant to fulfil in fifties Britain – and ripped apart the romanticism that shrouded so many depictions of working-class life. '[W]hat's wrong with this place?' asks Helen ironically as she and Jo survey their new home, a bare flat in a Manchester lodging house. 'Everything in it's falling apart, it's true, and we've no heating – but there's a lovely view of the gasworks, we share a bathroom with the community and this wallpaper's contemporary. What more do you want?'[21] It was what Shelagh knew women back home were meant to settle for: a bit of modern decor and the comfort of 'community' – a word used repeatedly by writers like Richard Hoggart and Michael Young. In Shelagh's hands, 'community' is a metaphor for overcrowded homes and poverty.

Shelagh's women told the world that they wanted more than marriage, motherhood and fashionable furnishings. Yet unlike the 'angry young men' of the 1950s – John Braine's Joe Lampton, for example – they did not aspire to join the middle class. Helen's repartee includes music-hall gags and songs, Jo is a lover of contemporary jazz tunes from black America; theirs is a culture borne out of oppression but which offers richer dreams and speaks to deeper emotions than the 'respectable' life of suburban domesticity. There's a suggestion that Jo could have been an artist, given the training, but she thinks 'it's too late' – a recognition of just how limited young women's educational chances were – and in any case, she's 'had enough of school'.[22] She wants to be independent and make her own decisions – but quickly learns that for women adulthood is defined by responsibility for others rather than by one's rights.

Shelagh offers no explanation of how Jo might achieve a different life, but plenty of evidence of her scant opportunities to do so. Jo's baby is both a burden and a blessing; it is her chance to create and love something, yet also a heavy responsibility. As a child of the post-war years, Jo is the repository of all those promises of a brighter future that the welfare state and affluence were meant to bring. She is angrier at her situation than Helen, who never expected much. But at the end of the play the similarities between them are more evident than their differences. Radically, Shelagh suggested that Jo's desire for 'a taste of honey' was a perfectly understandable reaction to a largely loveless world – and is all she is likely to get from it. Even more radically, she proposed that single motherhood was a better option for Helen, Jo and their children than marriage; for at least this way they could retain their independence without having to care for a man as well as a baby.

Although Shelagh said that her addition of male characters was almost an afterthought, they had a great impact on the play. Colin MacInnes declared *A Taste of Honey* to be 'the first English play I've seen in which a coloured man, and a queer boy, are presented as natural characters, factually without a nudge or shudder'.[23] Jimmie, the black sailor with whom Jo has a brief affair, and Geof, the young man who moves in with her, are drawn sympathetically. Jimmie, like Jo, is out to have fun, but clearly feels great affection for her – it is him, not her, who proposes marriage and tells her off for not taking this seriously enough – 'No more food, no more make-up, no more fancy clothes; we're saving up to get married.'[24] MacInnes highlights Geof's difference from most dramatic portrayals of gay men in the 1950s. In the drawing-room dramas of Terence Rattigan and his peers they were tragic or comedic characters whose needs and desires were presented as entirely alien. Geof is 'an art student' with all that this implies, but Shelagh has him propose marriage to Jo, and he clearly hankers after domesticity. She wanted to make the point that there was no one way to be a man – just as there was no right way to be a woman. When Geof, aghast at Helen having left Jo on her own, asks 'What kind of a woman is she?', Jo replies defensively, 'She's all sorts of woman.' Shelagh's treatment of Geof indicates her distaste for the sly innuendo employed by dramatists and journalists when discussing homosexuality. Jo is made to apologise for teasing Geof about 'what you do'.[25] Shelagh saw sexuality as an intensely private matter that should not be subject to political censure or a topic for public discussion – a view she would hold for the rest of her life.

Shelagh's treatment of sexuality and race caused conflict with Joan. In Shelagh's version, the play ends with Helen visiting Geof while Jo is in hospital having her baby. Helen's reaction to her grandchild's parentage is philosophical. 'Has Jo told you anything about the father of the baby?' Geof asks her. 'Nothing too significant – so far we've established his sex,' Helen responds. It is Geof who tells her 'He's a coloured boy'. Jo has not mentioned this, possibly out of shame but more probably because she's more preoccupied with becoming a mother. 'Huh!

Black!' Helen responds. 'I often think it signifies something that the majority of men should care so anxiously and fret for the pure strain of their animal stock and yet attach such little importance to the breed of their children. Still! A black man ... It can't make much difference now.' She tells Geof that 'I want her – and her chocolate coloured coon', to which Geof, already established as a sympathetic character, takes great exception. 'I hate to hear people use that expression ... That's the sort of talk that makes me cringe.'[26]

Joan, however, makes Helen far more vehement in her reaction to Geof's sexuality and to Jimmie's race. In Joan's amendments to Shelagh's script, there are more explicit references to Geof's sexuality (although Joan toned these down before the play was sent to the censor). Helen throws Geof out: 'Go on take your simpering face out of it you pansified little apology for a man.' It is Jo who nervously tells Helen that 'my baby may be black'. Helen is initially disbelieving and then descends into insults. 'You filthy little bitch ... Oh my God, a chocolate drop, I need a drink.' She threatens to 'drown it'.

Joan's treatment of Jimmie and Geof offered far less nuanced, and more stereotypical, characterisations than Shelagh's original script. Shelagh seems to have objected, because Joan agreed to modify her preferred ending. When the play was staged at Theatre Workshop, Helen simply responded 'Then the father was Jimmie, wasn't it?' When Stuart Hall, a black academic and one of the founders of *New Left Review* in 1957, saw *A Taste of Honey* in 1958, he thought the ending was 'true to the way the relationships have been treated elsewhere in the play. The colour of the baby and Jo's lover is immaterial. Helen absorbs this, together with Jo's pregnancy, with an immediate, direct human acceptance of the facts ... For the first time in a recent play, the question of "colour" is contained within the framework of the human values established for us on other, more authentic grounds.'[27] This achievement was Shelagh's.

Nevertheless, Theatre Workshop's original staging depicted Jimmie, Peter and Geof as far less developed characters than either Jo or Helen. Jimmie and Peter conform to stereotypes of working-class men as feckless or violent, or both. Jimmie deserts Jo and Peter is a spiv who throws Helen out. Yet Shelagh had created male characters who were more romantic than the women. Like Richard Hoggart, they idealised motherhood and marriage, since neither cost them any personal pain or sacrifice. When Jo is distressed to learn her father was, in her mother's words, 'a half-wit', Peter remonstrates with Helen. 'You could have made up some fairy-tale about him.' 'I told her the truth,' Helen retorts, 'if she didn't like it it's a pity but she got it.' She, unlike Peter, knows what a hard world Jo must enter; but both of them return to Jo at the end of the play to ask her to live with them, at Peter's behest. Jimmie, meanwhile, wants Jo to marry him immediately in Shelagh's script; it is Jo who equivocates, realising that, as Helen advises her, 'Marriage at your age is a death – it kills something – but it never does the favour of killing you.' At the end of Shelagh's version of the play, Geof is left in despair; the curtain falls on him clutching, as he says, 'a carving knife and a rubber doll! ... that's the nearest I'll ever get to a son and heir'. Women were stronger than men, because they bore new life. When Geof melodramatically worries that Jo 'might die!' as she goes into labour, Helen drily observes,

'I think not. There'll be no tragic death scene in our play – we'll all live to see another day.'

Jo and Helen are simultaneously exasperated by and protective of the men. Helen, who in Joan Littlewood's edits is made to despise Geof because he is gay, exhibits far more ambivalent feelings towards him in Shelagh's script. 'You're a nice enough person but oh! There are some things I can't take – and your unwholesome tendencies are among them,' she tells him when Jo goes into labour. But she also decides that 'I'd better stay with you a while. You're upset', and later offers him her address, 'if you ever need anything. I'm very free with my husband's money.' She does so with Peter's blessing; younger than her, he affectionately refers to their 'mother and son relationship'. She calls him 'my little love'. The shadow of war helps to explain why the men crave domestic stability. 'In the army I realized how much a man's family means,' Peter says. Shelagh shows that the post-war years placed a huge responsibility on women to remedy the mental and physical wounds of war. They do so partly from affection, but ultimately the lure of domesticity for women is largely explained by financial security – it is often easier to make ends meet with a man than without one.

As well as changing Shelagh's male characters, Joan altered the relationship between Helen and Jo. In Shelagh's version, the women's affection for each other is far more evident. 'I'm not sorry to see you go,' says Jo as Helen leaves for her new life with Peter, 'but I'm not glad either.' It is to Jo that Helen confides that she dislikes the new house Peter has bought. While Peter, Jimmie and Geof are all keen to settle down in lives that will help them to erase the past, Helen values experience. 'I'll

Eight-year-old Shelagh (standing) with neighbour Jackie Shaw on Hartington Street, Ordsall, the Delaneys' home between 1939 and 1947

Shelagh slouching sulkily at Pendleton High School, the girls' grammar school she attended between the ages of fourteen and seventeen

Dedicated to educating young ladies, Pendleton High School placed more emphasis on maintaining the flower gardens than the library

Shelagh aged about thirteen with Micky, the Delaneys' dog, outside 77 Duchy Road, Salford, the council house they moved to in 1947

A TASTE OF HONEY

A play by

Shelagh Delaney.

74 Duchy Rd.
Salford 6
Lancs.

April 1958

Dear Miss Littlewood,

along with this letter to you comes a play – the first – I have written and I wondered if you would read it through and send it back to me – because no matter what sort of theatrical atrocity it might be it isn't valueless so far as I'm concerned.

A fortnight ago I didn't know the theatre existed but a young man, anxious to improve my mind, took me along to the Opera House in Manchester & I came away after the performance having suddenly realised that at last, after nineteen years of life, I had discovered something that means more to me than myself. I sat down on reaching home & thought – the following day I bought a packet of paper & borrowed an unbelievable typewriter which I still have great difficulty in using & I set to and produced this little epic – don't ask me why – I'm quite unqualified for anything like this. But at least I finished the play and if, from among the markings out, the typing errors and the spelling mistakes you can gather a little sense from what I have written – or a little nonsense I should be extremely grateful for your criticism – though I hate criticism of any kind.

I want to write for the theatre – but I know so very little about the theatre. I know nothing. I have nothing – only a willingness to learn – and intelligence. At the moment I seem to be caught between a sort of dissatisfaction with myself & everything I'm doing and an enraptured frustration at the thought of what I am going to do – please can you help me? I don't really know who you are or what you do – I just caught sight of your name in the West Ham magistrates court proceedings – but please help me – if you think I'm worth helping – I'm willing enough to help myself.

Yours sincerely

Shelagh Delaney

'I seem to be caught between a sort of dissatisfaction with myself and everything I'm doing and an enraptured frustration at the thought of what I am going to do – please can you help me?' The letter that nineteen-year-old Shelagh sent to Joan Littlewood, director of Theatre Workshop, about *A Taste of Honey* in April 1958

ACT ONE.

Scene I

PAGE 1 (ADAPTED TO STAGE.)

Time - the present.

Scene. a section of a street and a flat. On the left of the
stage ~~and~~ there stands a street lamp. The main entrance
to the flat is also on the left. Inside the flat -
of which only the main living room is visible -
there is a bdroom door - standing far back on the right -
and further forward another door which lads into the
kitchen. The room is badly furnished - giving a generally
down-at-heel impression. A divan stands against one wall.
On the back wall there is a window which overlooks
a river. As the curtain rises the stage is in darkness.
The flat door opens and a woman, follo ed by a young girl,
enters. The woman - Helen - switches on the light - a
light which dangles from the ceiling on the end of a long
flex - (an unshaded electric light bulb) - they walk
round the room - taking in the general features. Between
them they carry a lot of luggage - including a smallish
wooden crate.

Hel. This is the place. (She speaks with an Irish accent)

Jos. I don't like it.

Hel. I don't give a damn what you like. When I find a place
for us to live I have to consider something far more
important than yours, or anybody's, feelings - the rent!
It's all I can afford.

Jos. You can afford something better than this old ruin.

Hel. Listen! I'm the sole financial support of our little
combination and until that happy day when you contribute
to the family income you'll, the disposal of the said income
to me -

Jos. I hate living off your immoral earnings.

Hel. Allright - but you would enjoy starving. And what is so
wrong with this flat? We've seen worse. The furnishings
are ~~lousy~~ enough - (opens window) - and the outlook isn't
too inspiring -there's no heating and we share a bathroom
with the community but otherwise it's pleasent - it'll do
for two weary, seasoned old travellers like ourselves. Have
you seen my glasses?

Jos. Have you lost them?

Hel. I never loose things - it's just that I can never find
anything. Pass me that bottle, Jo -it's in the brown bag.

Jos. If you want it you can get it yourself. Why should I run
around after you?

Hel. Children owe their parents these little attentions.

Jos. I don't owe you a thing.

Hel. Except respect - and I won't be getting any of that from you.
(gets a bottle of cheap whiskey from one of the bags and taking

Shelagh composed *A Taste of Honey* in a fortnight on 'an unbelievable typewriter'. Graham Greene, who loved the play, gifted her a new one

Shelagh backstage with the cast of
*A Taste of Honey* at the Theatre Royal,
Stratford, London, 1958. Left to right:
Nigel Davenport, Clifton Jones and
Murray Melvin

Shelagh with her now-mentor Joan
Littlewood in Paris, April 1959, to see
Brendan Behan's play, *The Hostage*

Shelagh and her mother, Elsie, on
the opening night of *A Taste of Honey*
at Wyndham's Theatre in London's
West End, 10 February 1959

Shelagh outside her family home at 77 Duchy Road. At six feet tall,
she cut a striking figure around Salford wearing her white mac

Shelagh delighted in the glamour of London's West End, but she felt most at home in the smoky East End pubs and cafes that Theatre Workshop friends introduced her to

After years working in low-paid jobs, Shelagh could now enjoy shopping sprees in London. She adored handsome American idols like Elvis Presley and Humphrey Bogart

Shelagh was interested in the latest fashions, but always determined to be original. By 1959 she'd devised her own version of the beatnik look

like it in a couple of years – when it isn't so new and clean,' she tells Jo; 'at the moment there in't a line on its face – quite unblemished and unutterably dull.' And while in the staged version, Jo admits to Geof that 'I don't know much about love', suggesting that Helen is to blame for this, in Shelagh's original script it is Helen who tells Jo to avoid marriage: 'You think you're in love? What do you know about love? How much love has there been in your life?' Within the manuscript that Shelagh wrote, Helen's statement is meant as an indictment of a society that consigns millions of people to slum dwellings, a substandard education and boring work, and offers no compassion or understanding to single mothers or homosexual men.

The ambivalence and affection between Jo and Helen is the central relationship in *A Taste of Honey* – far more vital than any courtship. This was radical at a time when educators, politicians, social investigators, novels and films treated marriage as the bedrock of society and the pinnacle of women's dreams. Once again, Shelagh anticipated the concerns of the Women's Liberation Movement of the 1970s. Many of the writers and activists central to second-wave feminism celebrated the relationship between mothers and daughters as a sign that a woman didn't need a man to complete her. But Shelagh was not afraid to explore the tension and hostility within this relationship, too. Helen's guilt at her inability to be a selfless mother provokes an antagonism that is resolved at the end of the play when it becomes clear that neither she nor Jo want the kind of self-sacrificial 'mother love', idealised in 1950s advertisements and films, which they recognise would 'smother' both giver and receiver. Another cause of tension between them is Jo's father

– 'how could she inflict a man like that on me?' Jo asks. Ultimately this, too, is resolved as Jo comes to learn that women's chances to enjoy 'a taste of honey' are often fleeting and rarely planned; in a world that can be callous and lonely, both she and Helen grab the chance of affection and fun where they can.

Shelagh's was a story about the power of sex and class to shape people's lives, but also about their resilience – her women never gave up their hope of that elusive 'taste of honey'. Joan, by contrast, made *Honey* into a generational clash. Like James Dean's *Rebel Without a Cause*, Jo's antipathy to Helen is presented as an existential teenage sulk requiring no explanation. While many of Shelagh's snappy one-liners remained in place in the staged version – as when Geof remonstrates with Jo and Helen for squabbling and Helen silences him by retorting: 'We enjoy it' – the women's relationship is far less comprehensible.[28] At the end of Shelagh's original manuscript, Helen and Peter ask Jo to live with them, partly because of Peter's yearning for a child. Love binds this unconventional family together as they seek comfort in the face of memories of war, the atomic threat and an unforgiving post-war morality. But Joan's insistence on having Peter throw Helen out weakened Shelagh's portrayal of a mother and daughter who are bonded by love as well as by obligation and circumstance. 'What Joan understood was what London audiences wanted,' observes the director Sean O'Connor. 'And that's important, but that's also the problem, that you end up making things that will titillate or entertain those people who dominate the theatre.'[29]

Shelagh accepted most of Joan's changes. She was aware of her inexperience, and delighted that her play was going to be performed. She was particularly appreciative of Joan's technical suggestions, knowing that here she was a total novice. In many ways, Joan's ideas developed her own intentions. Shelagh had had Helen speak in monologues almost to herself, particularly when she related dreams or recalled her past. Joan adapted these so that Helen directly addressed the audience at critical moments. This was a highly innovative venture in 1958, and received enthusiastic endorsement from Shelagh, who'd long aspired to recapture that sense of connection between the audience and the action that she remembered from the cinema matinees of her childhood. Joan taught her that they were breaking down the 'fourth wall' between actors and spectators. 'I think she is a genius, the greatest woman in the theatre today,' Shelagh said of Joan. 'She has taught me so much.'[30] By May 1958, Theatre Workshop had crafted Shelagh's manuscript into a pacy, lively, technically novel production. But this could not have happened without the startlingly original script that she had written herself on an old typewriter at home in Salford.

Shelagh faced a serious attempt to suppress *A Taste of Honey* before it was even staged. In May, Gerry submitted the script to the Lord Chamberlain for inspection. The anonymous reader was undecided; he recommended that the so-called Assistant Comptroller – the arcane job title of the flunkey within the Lord Chamberlain's office who dealt with censorship – read it himself. Assistant Comptroller Brigadier Norman Gwatkin proposed banning *Honey* from British theatres. 'I think it's revolting, quite apart from the homosexual bits,' he scrawled in red pencil on the bottom of the reader's report. 'To me it has no saving grace whatsoever. If we pass muck like this it *does* give our critics something to go on.'[31] 'After some misgivings' his office grudgingly passed *Honey*, judging that 'because it depicts such a sad collection of undesirables it will not do the public any harm',[32] but it was 'a borderline case'[33] – just as Shelagh herself had been classified aged eleven.

On 27 May 1958 *A Taste of Honey* opened at the Theatre Royal. Within a week it had attracted a wave of enthusiastic admirers. Ken Tynan, the *Observer*'s theatre critic, was one of the most influential. In 1956, he had championed John Osborne's *Look Back in Anger*; in 1957 he had strongly recommended John Braine's novel *Room at the Top*. Now he emphatically endorsed *A Taste of Honey*. 'Miss Delaney brings real people on to her stage, joking and flaring and scuffling and eventually, out of the zest for life she gives them, surviving,' he wrote a few days after the first night.[34] Doris Lessing thought the play a rare 'glimmer of light ... [a]t a time when the word Art has become the alibi for every sleek gentleman's timidity'.[35]

The *Listener* praised Shelagh for 'what is called "an ear for dialogue". This is much more than being able to reproduce what people say in real life ... Miss Delaney project[s] speech, just as an actor projects his voice ... giving what seem to be conversation, but heightened, shaped, selected – the right words to illuminate the characters who utter them and the circumstances under which they are uttered.' And she did this with 'people who up to now have usually been shown to us only in terms of cliché'.[36] Shelagh professed herself even more delighted by 'the locals ... bricklayers, cleaners ... when *they* said it was good, that they enjoyed it, I knew they meant it, and it was much more rewarding for me'.[37]

But she also faced a deluge of vitriolic criticism. The right-wing press immediately dismissed the play as a flop, its content vulgar and its author untutored. 'Once, authors wrote good plays set in drawing-rooms. Now, under the Welfare State [*sic*], they write bad plays set in garrets,' grumbled the *Daily Mail*.[38] To many critics, the recipients of the 1944 Education Act were overindulged, educated beyond their talents or station in life and, in Somerset Maugham's phrase, 'scum'.[39] The *Spectator* thought *Honey* 'an awful, amateurish mess'.[40] The *Mail* advised Shelagh to stop writing until she 'has seen a few more plays'.[41]

Shelagh, however, was hardly going to defer to established ideas about what constituted art, taste or culture. She retaliated that her work drew on 'the background of my experience', asserting the worth of where she came from against the sneers of her critics.[42] In 1963 E. P. Thompson would give her stance scholarly justification, arguing in *The Making of the English Working Class* that the lived experience of ordinary people was worthy of study precisely because out of this came political and cultural change; 'taste' was not absolute.[43] But that was several years off. Shelagh was brave to cite 'experience' because for a woman that meant sex. 'Culture' was the preserve of men with degrees and posh accents.

Back home in Salford, some thought Shelagh had brought their city the wrong sort of attention. Her local newspaper, the *Salford City Reporter*, was openly contemptuous of *Honey*. Its initial reports were favourable – 'Shelagh has the right idea,' the newspaper declared shortly after the play's premiere, and gave good wishes to 'her father, Mr Joseph Delaney, a Salford busman, for when the *Reporter* called to interview Shelagh

Mr Delaney was still in bed in the back room of his council house home, recovering from a recent serious illness'.[44] Cancer was another taboo in 1958. But then Saul Reece, the editor, got involved and the tone changed. In June 1958 he described Delaney as 'a very, very lucky young woman' whose 'literary fling' had succeeded because her 'rough sketch ... was "meaty" enough for the versatile players of an experimental group to get hold of'.[45] Once it became clear the play was a hit, Reece, who had close connections to Salford City Council, oscillated between denying the existence of single mothers and slums, and asserting that if they did exist this 'sordid tale of a prostitute's daughter' certainly wasn't suitable theatrical fare.[46]

Shelagh saw much of the local newspaper coverage because she was at home for most of May and July 1958, as her father's health deteriorated. In July she postponed an interview on BBC Radio's *Woman's Hour*, citing her father's ill health. She was desperate not to cancel her appearance, as Mollie Lee, the producer of *Woman's Hour*, very much wanted to meet her. No stranger to controversy herself – she ensured the programme pioneered lively discussions on subjects generally avoided by the BBC, including the menopause – Lee had expressed a warm interest in Shelagh's success. But shortly after postponing her interview, Joseph Delaney died at home.

His loss was a huge blow to Shelagh. While her work focused on women's relationships with one another, most of her male characters were compassionate, even supportive figures. Feminists from middle-class backgrounds like Ann Oakley would write of physically or emotionally absent fathers, whose neglect illuminated the unimportance of homes, wives and children, all distant from the men's world of power.[47] But Shelagh, like Carolyn Steedman, grew up with 'a relatively unimportant and powerless man', whose hard work and hard war showed how little men, as well as women, had to gain from the confining gender roles that psychologists and politicians presented as 'normal'.[48]

Friends and cousins were aware how close Shelagh was to her father, and even friends who got to know her in the 1980s knew 'her father was something special; she was particularly close to him'.[49] A stranger when he'd returned home at the end of the war, he'd become her greatest ally after she'd returned from Lytham, offering the sympathy of a fellow invalid, and his stories of Ireland and North Africa connected her to a world beyond Salford. He'd been her biggest supporter, determined the council must have made a mistake when she'd failed the eleven-plus, and always quietly encouraging her to enjoy her freedom and follow her dreams. He had lived to see her first taste of success, but now he was dead.

Richard Hoggart had talked of the uneasy position of the scholarship boy, caught between the world of home and the vista his education offered him. But far crueller was the position in which Shelagh found herself, balanced between a family that needed comfort and a career just beginning. Writing to offer Shelagh her sympathy the following week, Mollie Lee suggested that 'Perhaps later on, we can revive our project'. Shelagh replied quickly, 'I do hope it will be possible, as you say, to revive our project later on.' But her main object was to 'express the thanks of my mother and brother, and of course myself, for your condolences'.[50] As the older child and only daughter, she'd taken on the role of family correspondent. Nevertheless, she was desperate not to lose her big chance.

# 6

# The Lucretia
# Borgia of Salford

By September 1958, Shelagh knew that *A Taste of Honey* was
a success. The theatre manager and producer Oscar Lewenstein
had arranged for it to transfer to the West End in 1959. Shelagh
grew confident that her new status as a professional playwright
was assured. Now she faced a new challenge – defying convention to become the independent woman she wanted to be.

After her father's death, she began to spend more time in
London, where she lived out a teenager's dream of the bohemian
life. Joan Littlewood and Gerry Raffles became trustees of her
earnings – essential because nineteen-year-old Shelagh was two
years short of the age of majority – but paid her a generous
allowance. Shelagh accepted Joan's invitation to lodge permanently in the attic of her large house in Blackheath, where the
American film-maker Gerry Feil first met her. He was enter-
tained by Shelagh's sardonic humour and her desire to spend
as much time as possible sleeping in or lounging in front of
the television.[1] She was enjoying the sort of life that the press
represented as that of the typical late-fifties teenager – one of
leisure and spending money. In reality, this was beyond the

means of most young wage-earners in Salford, as Shelagh knew only too well.

Shelagh gave little sign of being the pliant protégée who had written to Joan. Feil was amused by her ability to cope with Joan's forcefulness by apparently acquiescing to her suggestions (usually about how much Shelagh should be writing – Joan wanted another play) before quietly doing exactly what she wanted. One thing she loved doing was eating, especially if journalists were paying. 'In spite of an enormous appetite she is slim and supple,' noted the *Observer*.[2] She liked being dined at London's upmarket restaurants, but she also savoured the East End haunts frequented by her Theatre Workshop friends, relishing 'sausage, cabbage, beetroot, and weak tea at the local caff'.[3]

She was negotiating two very different worlds: that of Salford, where she still spent much of her time, and of the artsy London scene she was getting to know. 'She's got a taste for foreign foods, like spaghetti,' her mother told the press, 'but she still likes my meat and potato pies.'[4] Joan took her to theatrical and literary parties; Shelagh became friends with Alan Sillitoe, whose first novel *Saturday Night and Sunday Morning* appeared in the autumn of 1958.[5] She also met some influential supporters, among them John Osborne and Tony Richardson – a director at the Royal Court who, with Osborne, had established Woodfall Films to produce realist dramas about contemporary Britain. But while she enjoyed this glamorous life, she was lukewarm about the theatre world's elitism. 'I am shy of coming into a crowded room and of meeting people,' she told one journalist. 'I still don't like the sort of party where you stand around balancing little glasses and murmuring sweet nothings. I don't feel part of the theatre. I don't like all the idle gossip in it.'[6]

But she wasn't interested in playing the working-class heroine, a role foisted upon her as her fame grew. In autumn 1958 she was awarded an Arts Council bursary of £100 and the prestigious Charles Henry Foyle £100 prize for the best new play of the year, which took her another step towards establishing her writing career. Emlyn Williams, the fifty-three-year-old playwright presenting the award, made no direct mention of Shelagh's background, but praised her 'individuality, imagination' and 'wayward talent', against the 'smooth construction' of 'college-taught dramatists'.[7] Williams, himself from a working-class background, implied that Shelagh's experiences had made her a better playwright. By contrast, the *Manchester Guardian* – the only national newspaper to report her award – dwelled on the 'obstacles' she had 'had to overcome', and described her as 'working in an engineering factory in Lancashire'.[8]

On 10 February 1959, *Honey* transferred to Wyndham's Theatre. This brought Shelagh into the limelight of the West End, where she was treated as a curiosity from 'up north', not a writer embarking on an exciting career. She was quite happy to admit writing from experience – 'To write plays you have to observe life,' she told one journalist. 'You have to be part of this mad business of living to know what it's all about.'[9] But she wanted credit for using her imagination. 'My play is not a bit autobiographical,' she stressed. 'The play is 25 per cent observation and 75 per cent imagination.'[10] Tom Courtenay, whose big break came when he landed the lead role in the stage and film adaptations of *Billy Liar* in 1961, knew that 'my early fame as an actor was due in some measure to my background, but I never beat my chest about being either North Country or working class ... I wasn't proud of it and I wasn't ashamed of it ... It's just the way it was.'[11] Shelagh felt likewise. She didn't want where she came from, and people's assumptions about what that meant, to define her career. She wanted recognition for her achievements; writing wasn't as easy as simply holding up a mirror to one's surroundings – it took effort and skill.

Her new London social life, and the success of *Honey*, might have been expected to imbue her with confidence for the West End premiere. 'Art must be disciplined,' observed Emlyn Williams when presenting her award in 1958, 'but discipline can come only with self-confidence and that is what we can foster with this prize.'[12] But the glare of publicity took its toll on Shelagh. Nervous of the West End's scrutiny, she acquiesced to some of the revisions that Joan had wanted to make to her original manuscript, including Helen's response to Jo's revelation that her baby might be black. The critics disapproved; Ken Tynan disliked the 'unattractive jokes about piccaninnies and "bloody chocolate drops"', while Stuart Hall thought the changes 'deny the spirit of the rest of the play ... They are gratuitous and arbitrary.'[13] As a result, Helen was transformed into an unsympathetic character at the end of the play. Later, Shelagh regretted this change, and revised it once more for *Honey*'s Broadway debut in 1960, but Helen's reaction to Jo's baby remained harsher than in the original manuscript. While Shelagh's relationship with Joan was often tempestuous, she nevertheless felt huge admiration for Joan's work and, faced with the chance to change her published play back to her original, she chose not to do so. Years later, Polly Thomas, a BBC producer who adapted *Honey* for radio, asked Shelagh whether she would prefer them to use the first version. 'She said, "No. I'm really proud of what we did. I'm really proud of ... the published play."'[14]

Shelagh wanted to show working-class women in all their complexity and contradictions. But many critics chastised her for writing about deviants. News of the West End production galvanised her critics. In January 1959 'E. L. Norton Esq' of Woodford Green wrote to the Lord Chamberlain to protest about *Honey*'s transfer. Norton had seen it at Stratford East and condemned it as 'sordid'. He was particularly incensed that 'blasphemous dialogue' was 'added to the general filth ... We are rightly appalled when we read of militant atheism in Communist countries.' Whether Shelagh's characters were realistic was not, he said, something that should influence the censor; they simply should not appear in the theatre.[15]

When *Honey* transferred to the West End, Saul Reece, the editor of the *Salford City Reporter*, relaunched his vendetta against Shelagh. Rather than send a journalist to review it, he employed his own son, a research chemist. Reece junior pronounced the play 'disgusting', in a piece that denied such conditions existed in Salford, and suggested Shelagh's drama was reminiscent of 'the magistrates' court, when slummy neighbours were summonsing each other'.[16] The irony that the *Reporter* carried a lengthy weekly account of proceedings at the magistrates' court, dwelling on particularly salacious or scandalous cases, was lost on Reece.

Local newspapers were widely read in 1959. Shelagh and her family could not escape the debate that the *Reporter* ignited. Shirley Evans recalled 'neighbours saying, "Oh, fancy doing that, you know, writing about Salford like that." I don't think they'd even seen the play.'[17] Others wrote to the *Reporter* to express outrage at Shelagh's depiction of their city, fearing it would prejudice their own children's chances. A Mrs Crewe complained that Shelagh was dragging Salford's name into the mud. 'One of my sons is a qualified teacher, having taken his examinations at Salford Grammar School ... how do boys like this, who have struggled to reach the top, feel about such as Shelagh Delaney's play? I don't wonder respectable people can't settle in Salford ... Surely the council have the influence not to let this young woman ... have our decent citizens be looked down on.'[18] This was a world where the entitlement to a free education was still very new, and the chance of a grammar school education or a professional job was available to only a few working-class children. Many feared that the post-war gains, limited though they were, might be snatched away if their recipients were not sufficiently grateful.

But others came to Shelagh's defence. Praising Shelagh's depiction of teenage motherhood and a mixed-race relationship, her friend Yvonne Carter – herself the daughter of a single mother – asked, 'Don't these things happen in our garden city of Salford? Perhaps Dr Reece would like a tour of Salford day nurseries.'[19] The newspaper's first review of *A Taste of Honey* had run alongside an account of a brothel in Broughton. The life Shelagh depicted was not so unknown to the *Reporter*'s staff after all.

Richard Hoggart, meanwhile, questioned whether Shelagh's characters had any basis in real life. He'd argued in *The Uses of Literacy* that conceiving a child outside marriage was anathema to the 'respectable' working class.[20] Shelagh offered a different view, and he disapproved, taking to BBC Radio to criticise her and pronounce that authors 'should write about what they know'.[21]

Alan Sillitoe was bemused and scornful in the face of similar criticisms of his own debut novel. He argued that the writer's job was not to produce 'typical' figures but to explore those crises or dilemmas that revealed people's struggles to assert their individuality in circumstances they didn't choose. '[T]ypical is not what I wanted Arthur Seaton to appear,' he pointed out, 'as much as an individual in some way recognizable by those who worked and lived in similar conditions.'[22] *Marxism Today*, the magazine of the Communist Party of Great Britain (but attracting a readership that stretched well beyond the CP's membership), greeted Shelagh's work with greater enthusiasm. While agreeing with Hoggart that '*A Taste of Honey* ... deals with figures ... who are not typical of the working class', the magazine argued that the play 'is a serious work, a tragi-comedy', whose appeal was heightened by the skilful drawing of characters whose frustrations and hopes would resonate with many of the audience. 'This picture of youthful confusion and defeat of youthful aspirations is surely typical of Britain today.'[23] The *Daily Herald* concurred that it was 'a Honey of a play' made sweeter by the fact that its author was a 'former usherette'.[24]

But labels like 'ex-usherette' were unwelcome to Shelagh, who recognised the danger of becoming typecast as a 'working-class' writer. By March 1959 *Honey* was a West End hit, and there was talk of a Broadway run. And yet many theatre critics, journalists and directors were loudly suggesting that they'd now heard quite enough about the working class, and that the new playwrights were already passé. 'There's nothing very shocking to experience,' commented T. C. Worsley, the *New Statesman*'s theatre critic – and a close friend of Terence Rattigan – in his review of *A Taste of Honey* at Wyndham's. 'The English play can now break through the class barrier at will ... Plays will be accepted ... purely on their subject.' He claimed that the fashion for working-class voices, rather than talent, determined 'Miss Delaney's' success: 'She has no distinctive voice, is not original or out of the common.'[25]

Critics like Worsley assumed there was only one tale about working-class life to tell and that it had been told. Arnold Wesker, a great admirer of *A Taste of Honey*, retorted that 'Delaney, Behan, myself and others ... [have] just started, most of us with only one play performed, we are just getting into our stride and beginning to learn about it all, and now some "fashion-conscious" young smoothy comes along and declares with a bored yawn that "we've really had enough darling!"' Wesker pointed out that no similar objection had ever been made to drawing-room dramas.[26]

They also assumed this was the only story that writers like Shelagh were capable of telling. 'I could go on writing plays if I never saw Salford, Manchester, or any northern working-class district again,' Shelagh declared.[27] She would have been cheered by a letter from Gerald Hodcroft, a Salfordian who wrote to the *Reporter* to protest at the paper's criticisms of *A Taste of Honey*. Hodcroft pointed out that 'a dramatist uses a certain amount of personal observation and much more imagination in the writing of a play … To suggest that … she considers the characters and situations to be typical of Salford is arrant nonsense.'[28] When the *Reporter* belatedly gave Shelagh the right to reply in October 1959, she stressed that 'it's wrong to say I intended reflecting life in Salford. It could be anywhere.'[29] She wrote about subjects of wide contemporary concern – sexuality, morality and poverty – and rejected the accusation that these were parochial.

While male authors like Wesker and Sillitoe faced similar criticisms, Shelagh had a particularly hard struggle to be taken seriously because she was a young woman writing about women. The *Salford City Reporter* lamented that outsiders would think Salford 'a place where girls of around nineteen are sufficiently informed on the subjects of half-wits, half-castes, half-tarts, half-pimps and half-homosexuals to write about them with ease and confidence'. 'She seems to understand emotions which most women acquire only through long and harsh experience,' wrote Reece. Like 'maturity', 'experience' was not considered a valuable asset in young women; defined by their bodies, they were either virgins or defiled.[30] The local press was not alone in suggesting that Salford's newest playwright was immoral at best, or depraved. 'The honey cake is obviously baked out of personal experience,' concluded a critic in a Scottish newspaper, condemning the play as 'sin'.[31] The London media were only slightly more restrained. 'Miss Delaney, what are you prepared to give in exchange for our society's present manners and morals?'

asked one BBC Radio interviewer sent to Stratford East to report on the performance. 'I don't know,' replied Shelagh dismissively, knowing full well that 'society' meant 'genteel', at a time when the majority of middle-class people thought women should have no sexual experience before they married.[32] Any flippant remark was picked up and used against her – not that she cared. She told the *Daily Mirror* that she wanted a car – 'I can't drive yet, but I shall probably pick up someone who will teach me.'[33] That a working-class girl from up north might have the audacity to send them up, let alone have written a play based on her imagination, never seemed to occur to her interviewers.

Her face didn't fit the accepted notion of a writer, even the new wave of northern authors. 'By every train from King's Cross and Euston and Paddington, it seemed, actors, writers, artists, musicians, were pouring into London,' recalled Keith Waterhouse, who was among them. 'The artists brought images the south-east had only read about, the writers wrote about the working class and the lower middle classes as if D. H. Lawrence hadn't been a one-off after all … and the actors no longer spoke in anyone-for-tennis accents.'[34] But this crowd did not include women. 'If you wanted to identify with a rebel when you were growing up in the late fifties and early sixties,' said Sally Alexander, at the time a student at RADA, 'the rebels were young men like Albert Finney.'[35]

Shelagh's writing had challenged the fifties feminine ideal. Now her refusal to conform to that role caused at least as much consternation. Even sympathetic reporters fixated on her wedding plans. 'I understand you're getting married soon?' asked an earnest young reporter from *ITN News* when he interviewed her in 1959. His question prompted the smile that had lurked at the corners of Shelagh's mouth throughout their two-minute exchange to finally break into an incredulous grin. 'No! I'm not getting married soon!' she said. Her interviewer pointed out that news of her wedding was being 'reported' in the media. 'Yes, but that sort of thing isn't very reliable, is it?' she responded archly.[36]

She was used to fending off such enquiries – getting married was what turned a girl into an adult, not finding success on the London stage. This was, if anything, even truer of the middle-class milieu she was now mixing in than in her Salford neighbourhood. Middle-class girls were taught to seek fulfilment as helpmeet to a man. 'We fondly imagined we would find ultimate happiness as the wife of some bohemian genius,' said 'Polly' of the middle-class teenage clique she belonged to.[37] Elizabeth Wilson, born into a middle-class home in London, was twenty-two when *A Taste of Honey* appeared. Oxford-educated, she wanted to write, spending her first earnings on a typewriter, and yet she could not reject her childhood training. In her daydreams about entering 'sophisticated bohemia … I … played the part not so much of Writer, or Artist in my own right, but rather of Great Artist's Mistress'.[38]

Shelagh, whose mother had to work for a living, and to whom wifely support meant making the tea and dressing wounds, didn't cultivate such dreams. Asked if she was 'the Sagan of Salford' – a reference to Françoise Sagan, the young French novelist with whom she was constantly compared – she retorted that 'I'd like to be Lucretia Borgia' – the beautiful, powerful and ambitious

Italian Renaissance aristocrat who was rumoured to have committed incest, adultery and murder to achieve her goals.[39]

By 1959 Shelagh was becoming the object of some teenage girls' admiration. Carol Dix and her friends were thirteen-year-old middle-class grammar schoolgirls in the Midlands when *A Taste of Honey* was staged. They'd never have been allowed to see the play, but they knew all about its author. 'The women's life-style we noticed, and wanted to copy, were bohemians like Sheelagh [*sic*] Delaney,' Carol recalled.[40] By now, Shelagh had adopted the 'beat' style – an androgynous look of short hair, black jerseys and jeans. It was a rejection of the overtly feminine New Look and its connotations of domesticity, but also of smart office wear and the 'prophylactic make-up' Lorna Sage remembered from a one-off cosmetics lesson offered at her grammar school.[41] Women who wore sweaters and flat heels were labelled as immature – 'the perennial schoolgirl' according to a feature in the *Manchester Evening News* – while those who 'make up too much' were 'unlikely to be trusted'.[42] Women's main concern was meant to be how men saw them. Shelagh had no time for this stifling conservatism, apparently made modish by drip-dry fabrics in assorted pastel shades. 'Smart clothes stifle me,' she declared.[43] She liked to dress comfortably, attending interviews wearing fisherman's sweaters and 'paint spattered jeans'.[44] It was this which made her an icon for those girls who wanted more from the world than a wedding dress, but weren't sure what, or how to get it.

Shelagh did not aspire to be a role model, though. Like the beat writers of the late 1950s – she read Jack Kerouac – she sought authenticity by asserting her individuality, and believed others should do the same. In a world that defined women by their sex and the working class by their stupidity, she had no interest in identifying as part of an undifferentiated mass. 'My usual self is a very unusual self, Geoffrey Ingram, and don't you forget it,' Jo says in *Honey*. 'I'm an extraordinary person. There's only one of me like there's only one of you.'[45] 'Fashion,' Shelagh said, 'is usually followed slavishly by women who have too much time on their hands, too much money and too little imagination.'[46]

But she was discovering that women had little control over how they were represented. At the end of 1958, Osborne and Richardson's company had bought the film rights to *A Taste of Honey* and she'd earned £20,000. Now the media became interested in how she'd spend it. Far from typical of young wage-earners, Shelagh nevertheless became an emblem of the new, modern teenager, her lifestyle a hook on which critics of assertive, financially independent young working-class people could hang their disdain. Her spending plans were seized upon to suggest that working-class women in particular were too feckless to make sensible use of their new affluence. 'Spend, spend, spend. Quickly, rashly' was how the *Daily Mail* judged her plans, though aside from the 'fast sports car with an open top' she wanted, her ambitions hardly sounded racy: 'New clothes for brother Joe. Lots of holidays for Mum', and travel 'to France, Italy, China'.[47]

Shelagh disliked being described as a 'teenager' even more than she loathed the epithet 'working-class writer'. It was factually inaccurate – she turned twenty in November 1958, as she announced to every journalist who would listen, but most of them conveniently knocked a year or two off her age (a myth that persisted; several of her obituaries erroneously reported that she'd been eighteen at *Honey*'s premiere). But she also railed against 'the image of Youth as a race apart'. She thought that the portrayal of the affluent teenager, whose only interests were buying new records and rebelling against parental discipline, 'is becoming more and more distorted and exaggerated'.[48] For all the press hype about young people's new freedoms, she found the label infantilising, a convenient means of ignoring or condemning any activity or aspiration that couldn't be confined to a youth club or dance hall.

Given the chance, she described herself as 'an apprentice playwright'.[49] Graham Greene, a fan of *A Taste of Honey*, presented her with a new typewriter to replace the 'ancient' one on which she'd typed her first manuscript. By 1959 she was, reported *The Times*, 'employed at the Theatre Royal, Stratford, where she is engaged on writing a new play in a dressing-room there. "I can work better at the Theatre Royal," she says. "I feel it's friendly to me"' – a dig at the *Salford City Reporter* which sent journalists to her mother's home whenever they thought Shelagh was in residence.[50] She loved Stratford and enjoyed learning more about the theatre; she took a walk-on part in Frank Norman's *Fings Ain't Wot They Used T'Be* when Theatre Workshop staged it in February 1959.[51] She became more confident at challenging people's assumptions about her. She began to tell different stories about herself to those she'd initially fed Joan Littlewood. 'I've always known I could write,' she told one journalist; 'I read a lot too. The Goncourt Brothers. Zola.'[52]

Yet the press intrusion didn't infuriate her as much as Joan and Gerry did. When *Honey* transferred to the West End Shelagh was still almost a year away from being twenty-one, and so Joan and Gerry continued to act *in loco parentis*, taking charge of her money and trying to organise her life. Gerry also persuaded Shelagh to let him, rather than a theatrical agent, manage her affairs. At first she was grateful for their help, but by 1959 she resented being treated as the gauche, northern girl she'd presented herself as being when she'd first contacted Joan. Whatever grain of truth that letter had possessed, Shelagh had changed. She had watched her father die; seen her first play become a West End hit; and as a wage-earner she had the right, she thought, to be treated as an adult. But despite their much-vaunted opportunities for self-expression, young people lacked the right to be taken seriously, remaining children in the eyes of the law. Gerry was furious when she independently negotiated the sale of the film rights for *Honey*, but eventually acquiesced.[53] Then, when the money from Woodfall Films arrived, Gerry refused to let her buy the sports car she wanted. 'Who's going to drive it?' said Gerry. 'In any case, your money is in the bank and will remain there till you're twenty-one.' 'You have no right whatsoever to order me about like some Industrial Revolution employer,' Shelagh wrote to Gerry from Salford in autumn 1959. Joan was exasperated – 'as if we hadn't enough on our plate without trying to control Shelagh'.[54] But the northern novice had found her voice, just as her twenty-first birthday approached – and with it, a new decade.

# 7

# Coming of Age

In November 1959 Shelagh celebrated her twenty-first birthday by buying herself a sports car she couldn't drive. Within weeks she had decided 'she wasn't much interested in it and gave it to her brother, Joe',[1] but she didn't regret the purchase. Murray Melvin, by now a firm friend, was sympathetic. 'She couldn't drive, but that had nothing to do with it. When you've got nothing, and you've had nothing, and suddenly there's the wherewithal, then you want something that is ridiculous and outrageous.'[2] Adulthood was meant to be about settling down, which for women meant getting married and having babies – but Shelagh had just found her freedom and wanted to have fun and take risks.

The risk-taking began with writing her second play, *The Lion in Love*. Joan had encouraged her to think about a sequel or companion to *A Taste of Honey*, but Shelagh was intent on doing something different. 'I would rather write a terrible play than a mediocre one,' she declared, meaning she'd prefer to try something new than stick to a tried and tested formula, whether her own or someone else's.[3]

*The Lion in Love* took its name from one of Aesop's fables, the moral of which is that 'Nothing can be more fatal to peace than the ill-assorted marriages into which rash love can lead'.[4] In this case the 'ill-assorted marriage' is between Kit and Frank Fresko. They live in Salford with Kit's father, Jesse, and their children: Banner, who is in his early twenties, and teenager Peg.

The Freskos are what 1950s political rhetoric and psychology would have termed a 'problem family'. The Conservative government declared that, in an age of near-full employment and a welfare state, those who lived in poverty – about a quarter of all British households[5] – had no one to blame but themselves. While some Labour MPs on the left of the party argued that welfare benefits were inadequate, others agreed with the Conservative line. '[F]amilies living on ... low incomes usually have parents of inadequate personalities and low intelligence,' said Leo Abse, a former solicitor and MP for Pontypool. '[Their] children are brought up in an atmosphere not only of emotional deprivation but of material deprivation.'[6] Local councils were ordered to seek out that 'hard core of families which consistently fail to observe normal standards of cleanliness and care in the home' and who could become 'a drain' on public money.[7] 'Problem families' filled the sheets of the broadsheet and popular press. Working-class women were held chiefly responsible for their existence. The social investigator Benjamin Seebohm Rowntree declared that a significant and worrying consequence of women's employment outside the home was 'to counteract the lack of skill of some housewives in spending their resources'.[8] In 1958, *The Times* stated that working-class women who took jobs spent their earnings on 'frivolities' such as televisions, and neglected their children.[9]

*The Lion in Love* challenged this picture of problem families by looking at the world through the Freskos' eyes –

particularly Kit's. The Second World War is the backdrop to the story. As the director Sean O'Connor, who first read *The Lion in Love* in the 1980s, says, '*Lion* is about the fact that the war still permeates everyday life and relationships well into the 1950s, 1960s.'[10] *Lion* focuses on the experiences of those left behind on the Home Front. Kit is an alcoholic who has little patience with her children, but we learn from her conversations with Jesse that during the war she visited Banner, an evacuee, every Sunday: 'after the blitz we wondered how we could possibly get to the school ... we went on bikes ... I'll never forget the faces of all them boys ... Banner's face was a picture when he saw me roll up, but them boys whose mothers didn't arrive – I'll never forget their faces.'[11] With this short anecdote, Shelagh Delaney captured the immense pressure that 'keeping the home fires burning' placed on women during the war.

Kit, Frank and Banner find post-war life difficult. Frank seems incapable of looking after anyone, and just wants a quiet life. Banner seeks the heroism that older men supposedly found on the battlefields – he has a brief career as a boxer – but he also wants love and security, and at the end of the play emigrates in the hope of starting a new life in Australia. Meanwhile, Kit is exhausted by the strain the war placed on her, and by her husband's and children's expectation that she is responsible for creating a happy, secure home life. It is she who points out that they are all still struggling to come to terms with the war and its physical and emotional devastation. 'The garden's looking very lovely this year, isn't it?' she asks drily, indicating the bombsite outside.[12]

Like *Honey*, Shelagh's second play presents men as romantics and women as hard-headed realists. Frank is dissatisfied with his ordinary life but his dreams centre on a domestic setting in which women care for him. Nora, Frank's mistress, scorns his assumption that they can simply run off together, and makes clear that looking after him isn't a fate she relishes. Kit tells him that 'We've just got to make the best of a bad job, haven't we?'[13] She recognises that men are fantasists: 'don't tell me we're going to see a bit of action at long last,' she remarks when Frank finally storms out – only to quickly return.[14] But, just as in *Honey*, the women turn out to have much more radical dreams than the men. Kit and Nora long to escape the obligations that domesticity imposes on women. At the same time, they recognise that they are not masters of their own destiny. Motherhood roots them, making it hard for them to reinvent their lives, but also bringing them love and a sense of significance in the world that Frank cannot share.

Shelagh was 'more ambitious' in *Lion* than she had been in *Honey*. Her second play explored three generations of the same family and the relationships between them. Generational conflict was a temptingly easy plot device and one that was providing much of the tension in contemporary films and plays like *Billy Liar*. But Shelagh was keen to highlight the dependence of the generations on each other, and the insights that dependency could bring. Jesse Fresko finds himself sympathising with his daughter's plight, as old age makes him more reliant on her and more able to observe the pressures that domestic responsibilities cause.

She also made clear that men's and women's lives were very different, even among the younger generation. Banner and Peg

Fresko believe that the only way to find happiness is to leave Salford. Banner leaves the country hankering after a pioneer lifestyle reminiscent of Wild West cowboys, in which he can combine adventure and marriage. But Peg pins her hopes on the new tools of post-war life – education, the arts and fashion – to make an independent life. At the end of the play she goes to London with a male art student, Loll. Their relationship is ambiguous but it's clear that Peg, like Jo in her relationship with Geof, enjoys the no-strings companionship that Loll offers. 'It's your life,' her mother tells her. 'You ruin it your own way.'[15] This, Shelagh suggests, is the only kind of freedom a working-class woman can give her daughter in 1960. The real point is that although there is no happy ending, the play is no tragedy either; the Freskos have survived.

Joan Littlewood disliked *The Lion in Love*. 'I read it with growing disappointment,' she later wrote in her autobiography. 'It had more characters, less appeal and even less shape than *Honey*. She had learned nothing from the company's adaptation of her first work.' She told Shelagh to 'go and read some Ibsen or some Chekhov'.[16] Joan claimed that Shelagh's response to her criticism was to write her a letter, declaring: 'If you aren't interested enough in my play to sort out the good from the bad, and generally put me right where I've gone wrong, then I may as well be working on it with the people who think that there is enough stuff there to be doing something with.'[17]

But this is a misleading account, written when Joan was keen to cement her reputation as one of Britain's foremost theatre directors. In 1960, Shelagh was impatient with what she saw as Joan's interference in her writing and her life. Ossia Trilling, who was on the board of Theatre Workshop, recalled that Littlewood, far from refusing to help Shelagh rewrite the play, saw merit in it and undertook 'fruitless attempts at doctoring the text'[18] – fruitless because Shelagh did not want to accept her edits. She was concerned that Joan was seeking to turn *The Lion in Love* into a sequel to *A Taste of Honey*.

Dismissing Joan's criticisms, Shelagh secured the support of Wolf Mankowitz and Oscar Lewenstein, who had staged *A Taste of Honey* in the West End. They recognised the originality of *The Lion in Love*. The 'kitchen sink' novels and plays of the angry young men tended to portray women, especially middle-aged women like Kit Fresko, as long-suffering, self-sacrificial, stoical 'mams'. These women were deeply conservative, content to remain in their communities, or to recreate them on new housing estates. Young men were the adventurers and rebels. In more conventional post-war theatre, marriage tended to be the backdrop to a storyline rather than the focus of it. On the rare occasion that a marriage was dissected – as in John Osborne's *Look Back in Anger* – it was the man's discontent that was probed, not the woman's. Shelagh's women were not guardians of tradition or upholders of domestic stability. They wanted more from life.

Mankowitz and Lewenstein were, however, too cautious to offer Shelagh the Royal Court run she'd hoped for. They arranged a fortnight's provincial tour beginning at Coventry's new Belgrade Theatre, to see how her play got on. Although they agreed with Joan Littlewood that *The Lion in Love* lacked pace and form, they chose a novice director – twenty-eight-year-old Clive Barker. Barker was known to Shelagh from Theatre

Workshop where he'd acted in Brendan Behan's play *The Hostage* in 1958.[19] His background was in improvisation, not in giving structure to scripts. He was a very risky appointment for a play that had a large cast and was expensive to produce.

*The Lion in Love* was not the roaring success that *A Taste of Honey* had been. Its premiere at Coventry on 7 September 1960 was watched by a packed house, including Hugh Stewart, a BBC drama producer sent by his bosses 'so that we can register copyright interest quickly if it is worth following up'. Stewart's report echoed the mixed feelings of many who saw the play that night. 'She showed us a lively, colourful handful of characters,' he wrote, 'loving, hating, wrangling, in their seedy home in a slum backstreet in the North of England.' But, he went on, 'having created these undeniably interesting and real people, in scenes often tenderly brilliant and amusing, she does nothing with them at all. She explains nothing and resolves nothing ... at the end one is left frankly puzzled and frustrated. Last night's audience could scarcely believe that it was the end and after being a wonderfully responsive and captivated house for barely two hours their applause at the last curtain was less than half-hearted.'[20]

The critics agreed. Most concurred that *The Lion in Love* offered – in the words of the *New Statesman*'s Jeremy Brooks – 'vivid, salty back-streets dialogue'; Shelagh had proved that *Honey* was neither a fluke nor the product of Joan Littlewood's pen.[21] But they united in viewing *The Lion in Love* as formless and slow. 'The play is a series of sketches more than an entity,' said John Mapplebeck of the *Guardian*.[22]

Nevertheless, Shelagh's second play accrued considerable admiration. John Osborne condemned its 'vicious reception' as 'the classic example of a second play being demolished on the grounds of feigned admiration for a first play's privately resented success'.[23] George Devine, director of the English Stage Company, saw *The Lion in Love* in Bristol and thought it good enough for a Royal Court run. When it appeared at the Court in December 1960, most of the critics who had seen its provincial premiere did not bother to attend. That, thought Ken Tynan, was a mistake. He'd seen the play at the Belgrade, and was able to observe the changes when the play appeared in London. 'Partly rewritten and recast since I saw its premiere in Coventry last September, Shelagh Delaney's *The Lion in Love* has arrived at the Royal Court much improved, with several loose ends neatly knotted and many rough edges smoothed off the playing.'[24] Philip Hope-Wallace for the *Guardian* was another who saw it at the Royal Court; he praised Shelagh's 'wonderful ear', and – ironically, given Littlewood's criticisms – called her play 'Chekhovian'.[25] It had twenty-eight performances at the Royal Court and took a respectable £3,049 at the box office – about average for the twelve Royal Court productions that year.[26]

But *Lion* was not a hit. One reason was that Shelagh found it hard to develop her female characters. The play does lack pace and resolves nothing. The fates of Kit and Peg are particularly uncertain, and this is frustrating because Kit is such a central character. For Shelagh, this was the point: Kit and Peg are discontented but can't envisage a way out of their situation. As a younger woman, Peg discerns that she has some advantages (education, no children, the possibility of earning enough money to live independently) that her mother lacks. But Peg cannot imagine what her future might look like, outside the frame of domesticity. Very possibly, Shelagh couldn't either – the media attention she received testifies to her exceptional circumstances as a young, working-class woman forging an independent life in London.

Writing a play in which little happens – and indeed about the fact that little happens – takes huge skill. In *Honey*, Jo's pregnancy provides a sense of time passing and some dramatic tension: the audience knows that at some point she'll give birth. *Lion* lacks this tension, and Shelagh lacked the experience to resolve this, but refused to take up Joan's offers of help. Joan's curt dismissal of *Lion* riled her. 'She was probably a bit arrogant and wouldn't take Joan's advice,' says Sean O'Connor, who discussed *Lion* with Shelagh in the 1990s. As she had written to Joan back in 1958, she hated criticism. And she was reluctant to learn about those elements of her craft that she had no interest in or was apprehensive about – including form, structure and different ways of writing. Theatre Workshop provided the perfect training ground for a playwright to learn about all aspects of writing and production, but it was a training Shelagh couldn't be bothered with. 'A lot of the time she left us to it,' recalled Murray Melvin of the later rehearsals of *Honey*, when form and pace were being discussed. Her early success emboldened her to follow her instincts rather than take advice. 'She never, ever wanted to take on something she didn't feel passionate about,' says her daughter, Charlotte. 'She'd been a big star, very young, and she'd got used to being able to say, "I'm not interested, I won't do it – I've written a masterpiece, why should I?" She was a real bolshie teenager, and she was also very hurt by a lot of the press, especially around her family, and so she could get defensive very, very easily.'

Shelagh's inexperience meant she undervalued what Theatre Workshop offered her. She quickly discovered that there was little support available to young, working-class writers as they sought to turn a successful debut into a career. Shelagh was exasperated with Joan Littlewood's blunt and ruthless methods, but her first director was unusual in understanding that fresh talent required a long apprenticeship with seasoned mentors. Although the Royal Court shared Theatre Workshop's gift for spotting new writers, Shelagh found little consideration of how to nurture and develop them. 'It was produced too early, and by people who just weren't experienced enough,' says Sean O'Connor of *Lion*. 'They were doing this radical stuff at the Royal Court, and so [after she rowed with Joan] she thought, well, I'll leave; but then they didn't give her the support. Decided to open it at the Belgrade – well, it was a great theatre, yes; but it wasn't right for her. *Lion* needed an experienced director, someone who was totally focused on it, within the Court.'

Arnold Wesker, who had enjoyed success at the Royal Court with his *Roots* trilogy, suggested that Shelagh didn't get the backing she needed because she was a working-class woman. 'I admired *Lion in Love* which though not wholly successful seemed to me a more ambitious work [than *Honey*], which is what the critics should have praised her for. But no, they wanted more of the same. I thought she was doing what we should expect of the true artist – not to repeat herself.'[27] Most of the theatrical establishment did not see Shelagh as a 'true artist', but as a working-class girl from Salford who was in the arts world on sufferance. Even those sympathetic to her were not prepared to give her the financial and practical assistance she needed. This, as Sean O'Connor says, was 'because she was a woman, and because of her class. They let women in, give them one chance, and that's it. They aren't given the support to develop in new directions. Then when the second play is a flop, or it's derivative, based on the first, they're condemned. But what choice do they have?' He is right to conclude that *Lion* was 'a remarkable achievement in those circumstances'.

Despite these issues, by the end of 1960 Shelagh was a noted playwright with a sizeable income and a promising future. The film rights for *Honey* had brought her considerable wealth. She was in demand: the BBC was keen for her to work for its drama department, but she told them she was more interested in writing plays for the theatre.[28] Mankowitz and Lewenstein were firm allies, and a Broadway run of *A Taste of Honey* was due to begin in October, directed by Tony Richardson.

But the critical response to her first two plays from the media and the artistic establishment had convinced her that writing alone wasn't going to get her the kind of life she wanted. Being treated as an adult was not as simple as turning twenty-one, or even becoming financially independent. And while she had been keen to share her good fortune with her family, she hadn't been able to make a difference where it mattered most. Her brother Joe had failed the eleven-plus exam and followed Shelagh to Broughton Modern. In 1960 he was an engineering apprentice in Salford and spending long hours at night school after work, trying to fill in the gaps of his education. Joe loved writing and drawing, and he was often bored by work; Shelagh was incensed at what she saw as the waste of his talents.[29]

She was adamant that her writing 'advocates no political philosophy other than "common sense and kindness"', but she took an interest in how these qualities could be infused into public life.[30] In *A Taste of Honey*, she'd hinted that if only Jo had been able to find an outlet for her artistic talent her life might have been easier, or at least more fulfilling. But having achieved artistic success, Shelagh discovered that being a woman from a working-class background continued to count against her. Changing yourself was apparently not enough; she began to consider how she might help to change the world.

Already, she had publicly opposed the eleven-plus exam. When she picked up the Charles Henry Foyle prize in 1958 she declared she was an eleven-plus failure, immediately provoking the wrath of Salford Education Committee and their allies at the *Salford City Reporter*. 'The implied sneer at the eleven-plus and the city's educational system is unfair and unworthy,' said Salford's Director of Education, Mr F. A. J. Rivett. 'Ingratitude to her Teachers,' screamed the *Reporter*'s headline.[31] Shelagh was undeterred. She took no public notice of the *Reporter*'s attack, but when Rivett wrote to the *Guardian* to suggest she should be grateful for her opportunities, she replied that grammar schools were deficient in their treatment of the arts, and that the eleven-plus was unjust. 'I am not ... anxious to promote myself as a native genius,' she wrote. 'I have many friends who would have benefited from a more advanced education but were denied it ... which all goes to show the mistake of educational segregation at 11.'[32]

Shelagh's intervention came as public debate about the eleven-plus was growing. The baby boomers of the late 1940s were reaching secondary school age, but while the number of children had increased, the number of grammar school places had not. Most parents wanted their children to have a grammar school education and the greater opportunities it offered. The system's inability to cope with demographic change made its iniquities clear, and their anger grew. Meanwhile, the originality of those few working-class writers like Shelagh made some wonder whether extending educational opportunities to *all* children might not be beneficial. Shelagh's protest was a portent of the not-too-distant future. By 1964 an increasing number of local authorities would have introduced non-selective comprehensive schools, although Salford did not follow suit until Harold Wilson's Labour government requested comprehensive schools be introduced in all local authorities in 1966.

In 1960, Shelagh used a television appearance to air her more general concerns about politicians' neglect of and contempt for ordinary people. She was the subject of one of the BBC's *Monitor* programmes, which explored the background and inspirations of selected writers and artists. Those involved were invited to curate an episode alongside the presenter, in Shelagh's case Ken Russell. The script for 'Shelagh Delaney's Salford' went through several incarnations as she sought to express all that she wanted to say about Salford Council's destruction of the city's heart, their removal of people to new housing estates, and the lack of interest in, or opportunity for, most Salford people to realise their ambitions. She lambasted selective education. 'I was dead lucky,' she told Russell, 'but so many aren't lucky – and this is the tragedy.' Her old friends and her brother, she said, were just as ambitious as she was; 'so many of them wanted to do a job that a grammar school education prepares you for, right from the age of eleven ... if they'd started off with a proper chance they wouldn't have this terrible fight to try and discover what it is they want'.[33]

Shelagh had once again managed to stir up controversy. Maurice Richardson in the *Observer* thought she seemed 'in some inexplicably significant way to be able to spark across the gap in working-class life between the thirties and the sixties'.[34] In contrast to male writers like Hoggart, she wasn't interested simply in documenting working-class life, but in evaluating the political significance of her experience; a preoccupation that connected her back to writers and artists who'd cut their teeth in the thirties, like Salford's own Ewan MacColl. But Mary Crozier of the *Guardian* thought that Shelagh was not clever enough to offer a political analysis and should simply have described Salford: 'she is not highly articulate and it might have been better value to hear her simply talk about the place, which the film showed indeed to be full of a fierce, indigenous life needing no theories to explain it'.[35] This was a condescending hint that the educated working class were ruining the unspoilt, 'indigenous', inarticulate provinces by becoming too cocky by half.

In Salford, the council and the *City Reporter* launched their fiercest attack yet on Shelagh. The mayoress pronounced herself 'disgusted'.[36] Rivett weighed in once more to claim that Shelagh 'was speaking on behalf of a very tiny segment of the population'.[37] But Elsie Delaney staunchly defended her daughter.

'I thought it was a lovely film",' she told reporters;[38] and at least one reader wrote to the newspaper in praise of her 'truthful picture of the Salford she loves'.[39]

Shelagh joined the Campaign for Nuclear Disarmament (CND), which had been established just months before *A Taste of Honey* premiered. Most of the press dismissed CND as a collection of eccentrics led by – in the words of journalist Alistair Cooke – the 'midget … frail figure' of the philosopher Bertrand Russell.[40] But for E. P. Thompson, the movement was the first post-war attempt to 'place the postwar generation's desire for love into politics and power relations'.[41] Shelagh attended CND's annual Aldermaston march along with Thompson, John Osborne – she marched with him behind the Royal Court banner – and thousands of others. Leila Berg, a children's writer and editor twenty years older than Shelagh found a 'creative joy' among the marchers. '[P]eople were ungagging themselves, and their boldness was creative and imaginative; and the columns with tugging banners on the way to Aldermaston were happy to find themselves in such stimu-latingly diverse company, and were jubilant with song.'[42]

CND was a radical riposte to the mantra that nuclear weapons were essential, and that opposition to NATO was tantamount to Stalinism. Campaigners, many of them young, adopted non-violent tactics and democratic decision-making, consciously distinguishing their movement from the aggression, secrecy and high-handedness of both Western and Eastern European governments. 'They marched fifty miles in cold rain and bitter wind – in protest and hope,' Shelagh later wrote. 'Hope that with the end of the whole evil business the world's hunger for food and knowledge might be addressed.'[43] But like Bertrand Russell and many other members of CND, Shelagh quickly decided that peaceful marching was insufficient. In September 1961, she took part in a huge sit-down protest against nuclear weapons in Trafalgar Square; her arrest, along with those of John Osborne and Vanessa Redgrave, was reported in all the national newspapers.[44]

But writing remained her passion, and Theatre Workshop the place she felt most comfortable. Although she did not return to work there, she remained very supportive of the company's aims and close friends with several of its members. *The Lion in Love* helped her to establish the adult relationship with Joan Littlewood she wanted. Joan may have felt some gratification that many critics agreed with her low opinion of the play, but she also respected Shelagh for having stood up for her work. 'Joan felt she stayed friends with Shelagh,' recalled Philip Hedley, Joan's assistant. 'They fell out at times, but ... falling out with Joan [was a common occurrence].' When Gerry Raffles died in 1975, Joan asked Shelagh to join Philip Hedley in running Stratford East as a playwright-cum-director – testifying to her faith in Shelagh's abilities. Shelagh, however, replied that this was 'a ridiculous idea, don't be stupid'.[45]

But it wasn't such a ridiculous idea; Joan knew that back in 1960, Shelagh had toyed with the idea of setting up a kind of Theatre Workshop herself. That year's prosecution of Penguin Books for their publication of D. H. Lawrence's novel *Lady Chatterley's Lover*, under the 1955 Obscene Publications Act, suggested that the political elite were out of touch with the public. The prosecuting counsel, Mervyn Griffiths-Jones, opened his case by asking the jury whether this was 'a book that you would even wish your wife or your servants to read' – he was taken aback when some of the jurors laughed.[46] But the trial also hinted that art and culture were realms where political and moral conservatism could be challenged, for the jury unanimously found Penguin not guilty.

In the same year, Shelagh joined a small group of writers she'd come to know through CND, including Doris Lessing, to discuss how to create some alternative artistic spaces more fitting for the new decade than London's gilt-encrusted theatres. They discovered they were not alone in wanting to challenge the artistic establishment: the Trades Union Congress of 1960 unanimously passed Resolution 42, which urged unions to initiate cultural activities that encouraged popular participation in the arts. Arnold Wesker set out their vision in the *New Statesman*. Resolution 42 aimed, he said, to encourage:

> orchestras tucked away in valleys, people stopping Auden in the street to thank him for their favourite poem, teenagers around the jukebox arguing about my latest play ... a picture of a nation thirsting for all the riches their artists can excite them with ... arguing about Joan Littlewood's latest.[47]

Wesker was worried that 'the in-people ... said they were beginning to get *tired*' of working-class plays and their writers. 'And immediately there loomed up an image of all of us being simply fashionable, you know, rather quaint specimens ... I knew that it was all going to come to an end, if something else didn't happen, if somehow it wasn't consolidated.'[48] Wesker's attempt at consolidation resulted in Centre 42, established in London in 1961 to promote the arts nationwide.

Shelagh did not get involved with Centre 42 – she was preoccupied with plans for a community arts centre in Salford. A few beacons of provincial theatre were beginning to appear by 1960. Coventry's Belgrade Theatre, opened in 1958, had showcased several exciting new productions (including *The Lion in Love*), with support from the city's Labour administration and the Arts Council. Shelagh had a personal motivation for starting a similar venture in Salford: life there looked more appealing now she had established herself as a playwright. 'I've learned something in this year. It's the value of having a home,' she told one magazine in 1960. 'That sounds sentimental or clichéd, but it's true all the same. I've found out if you've got no home, you've got nothing.'[49] 'Everyone thinks it's funny – the neighbours and all – that she hasn't altered,' her mother told an American journalist. 'She's met all those people in the West End, but she's not impressed. Her head hasn't been turned. She's not gone all lah-di-da – like some of those you see on the telly. She still goes around with the friends she went to school with in Salford.'[50]

It was possible to have a private life in Salford, away from the prying eyes of London journalists. Her old school friend Christine Hargreaves was back home too, working in repertory theatre (she would soon become a television star on *Coronation Street*). She remained one of Shelagh's staunchest supporters, telling an interviewer that 'Everyone was surprised when Shelagh had such a hit with [*Honey*]. I wasn't. The only thing that surprised me was that she succeeded so soon.'[51] Shelagh had also grown closer to Harold Riley. As he recalls, she had no intention of marrying him 'but we lived together on and off during those years at my studio, and we had a lot of fun'. London had originally attracted Shelagh as a bohemian place where she could live more freely; but she had reckoned without the media's unquenchable desire for salaciousness. Her relationship with Harold was far easier to conduct away from the glare of publicity.

Salford and Manchester were at the centre of exciting changes in the arts. Almost half of Britain's households had a television set by the end of the 1950s, and Manchester was the heart of the television revolution. The BBC's studios on Oxford Road had been joined by Granada Television, the small but ambitious company that had won the ITV north-west franchise after the third television channel was established in 1955. Mike Newell arrived in Manchester to work at Granada at the age of twenty-one, just weeks after graduating from Cambridge:

Manchester was the centre of the world. No one behaved in any expected or accepted way … I'd got the overnight bus. And I was in a cafe in the centre of town. Packed. Roaring. And the condensation running down the windows. And I wanted the brown sauce. And I said to the person on the next table, 'Could you pass me the … ?' And immediately, Manchester said, 'What do you want, love?!' 'Pass the … it's the brown …' 'He wants the sauce! Could you pass up the sauce? Pass …' And the whole cafe cooperated in getting me my brown sauce. And of course, I realised afterwards that that was one of the great lessons of the place – that it was freer than the south; it was liberated in a way that the south wasn't. Which of course must have been part of Shelagh.[52]

Granada could have its pick of ambitious young graduates like Newell, but the company was also keen to recruit local talent. Their new writers included Jack Rosenthal from Manchester and Tony Warren from Swinton, on the outskirts of Salford. In 1960 Warren created *Coronation Street*, Granada's first soap opera, set in 'Weatherfield' (working-class Ordsall).

Shelagh was an important inspiration for this new wave of northern achievement. Tony Warren, only two years older than she was, had regularly skipped school to haunt Manchester Central Library, including the 'real theatre in the basement where talents the like of Joan Littlewood and Harry Latham [who would go on to produce the first episode of *Coronation Street*] were doing experimental seasons'.[53] Then in 1958 'I saw the original production of *A Taste of Honey* at Stratford East before I wrote *Coronation Street*'. By 1960 he knew Shelagh 'a little' and tried to persuade her to come and work at Granada.[54] Shelagh declined, considering the soap opera too cosy and nostalgic. '"Caps and muffler," she said. "That's all it is: caps and muffler. No, *Coronation Street* doesn't interest me."'[55] But the soap's success – it was the most popular programme on television by 1961 – made clear that there was a large appetite for drama about working-class people, including women.

Shelagh's political activities brought her new friends from a swathe of Salford society far removed from the *City Reporter*'s editor and his fans. In 1960, Manchester audiences finally got to see *A Taste of Honey* when the play had its first British performance outside London. The *Reporter*, meanwhile, kept up its campaign against the play and its writer. In one diatribe Saul Reece paraphrased Shelagh's story of how she had come to write *Honey*: 'she saw a production of one of Rattigan's plays and said to herself that if she couldn't do better than that she wanted kicking – or words to that effect'.[56] Further attacks brought 'a delegation of Salford Direct Works Department employees to the *City Reporter* office' to protest at the newspaper's treatment of Shelagh. Faced with eleven angry men, Reece agreed to publish their letter, under the headline '"We Should be Proud of Shelagh" Say Building Workers'. These trade unionists described how they had met Shelagh 'to discuss our campaign for peace and disarmament in which she was most interested'. Shelagh, they said, had not besmirched Salford's reputation. 'Indeed, we recall that in the edition [of the *Reporter*] that first reviewed *A Taste of Honey*, there was alongside the review an article concerning a case of brothel keeping in Broughton, and on another page the proceedings at a trial at which people were charged with incest.' If readers perused the *Reporter*'s lengthy weekly accounts of the magistrates' court, '[t]he impression gathered thereby (wrongly we are sure) would surely be that our city is populated by drunks, reckless drivers and petty thieves'. With a swipe at Saul Reece they went on: 'We wish that some of those who lecture most on morals would give us the same support that Miss Delaney is giving and show us that they have faith and conviction in the ability of people usually described as ordinary.'[57]

Shelagh's 'support' was directed at establishing a community theatre in Salford. Inspired by Resolution 42, local trade unionists thought the time was ripe not just to defend the city's cinemas and theatres from demolition, but to insist that cultural activities of a much wider variety be embedded in the council's plans for Salford's redevelopment. Shelagh was keen to be involved and she recruited Clive Barker to the cause.

Over the next few months the group expanded to include local clergy, youth club workers and supportive Labour councillors. They regularly met at Elsie Delaney's house and evolved a plan for 'a theatre in Salford that would reflect life as lived today and [that] could comment on it', and 'for a community centre where people could meet and mix'.[58]

They were concerned at the lack of cultural activities available to Salford's residents, particularly young people. Talk of modern teenagers in the national press contrasted sharply with the reality of life in many towns and cities. Salford's Chief Constable waged a one-man war against jukeboxes in cafes. The city's cinemas and theatres were closed on Sundays, and were not particularly welcoming when they were open. The Manchester Branch of the Musicians' Union complained that 'many existing theatres [should] be condemned as unfit places for persons to be employed in ... they are, in fact, in the state of slum properties.'[59] By 1960 the city council was demolishing most of them to make room for shopping centres, car parks and offices. Meanwhile, thousands of Manchester and Salford residents were being rehoused on large council estates with few amenities. Women living on two of the largest estates, Wythenshawe and Langley, told interviewers that they still felt isolated after three years there. 'Many families had gone regularly to the cinema once or twice a week before moving', but '[t]here is no cinema on either estate', and nowhere for the children to play.[60]

Shelagh's dream was to acquire Salford Hippodrome, also known as the Windsor Theatre. A decrepit building in the centre of Salford, it had closed its doors just weeks before *A Taste of Honey* had premiered in 1958. Two years later the theatre was scheduled for demolition but it wasn't due to be pulled down until 1965. Shelagh's group told the local press that they thought 'the Windsor would make a good temporary home ... to test if public reaction was favourable'.[61]

Unfortunately, their plans did not impress senior members of Salford Council. Shelagh and her supporters were shocked when the Council's planning committee suddenly announced that they were buying the Windsor – and intended to knock it down immediately. Hostility to Shelagh's plan emerged when the full Council debated the matter. Alderman Cowin, a member of the planning committee, sought to reassure his stunned colleagues that they 'would in time get a theatre which could be used by the people of Salford' rather than hosting 'professional producers, actors ... with the Corporation paying for them'. Alderman Hamburger, the leader of the council, managed to persuade a majority of councillors to vote in favour of the purchase by insisting that 'it had nothing to do with any plan for a Civic Theatre'. The council, he said, 'need it for redevelopment'.[62] But when Clive Barker pursued the matter he was told by Jack Goldberg, a sympathetic Labour councillor, that antipathy towards Shelagh was the real reason. 'I have been surprised ... to find out how much prejudice there is amongst members of the Council against Shelagh on the grounds that her plays have brought Salford into disrepute,' Goldberg wrote to Barker. '[A] ny project with which she is known to be connected starts off at an enormous disadvantage when we ask for Council support.'[63] Their hopes for a community theatre were over.[64]

Shelagh retreated from active participation in politics after this. Both Salford and London possessed plenty of people in authority willing to congratulate themselves on allowing the 'younger generation' a voice, but they weren't prepared to hear what was said. London's press and arts establishment, whether or not they liked Shelagh's work, wanted her to fulfil their image of a working-class female writer – the cruder the better. Meanwhile, Salford's journalists and dignitaries exhorted her to act as an educated, civic-minded young woman, which really meant putting her writing behind her as if it were a childish hobby. It was reminiscent of Keith Waterhouse's Billy Fisher, the eponymous hero of *Billy Liar*, who wants to escape clerking to write for TV, to the disapproval of his employer, family and local councillor, Alderman Duxbury. 'Grateful! Grateful! Grateful! ... That's all I've heard, ever!' he declares. 'I even had to be grateful for winning my own scholarship!'[65] Shelagh, too, was expected to be forever beholden to those who took credit for giving her a start in life, not to ask why everyone couldn't have her chances.

In September 1960, Tony Richardson directed the first production of *A Taste of Honey* outside Britain, in Los Angeles. In October, *Honey* transferred to Broadway and Richardson with it. When he invited Shelagh to join the company in New York early in 1961 she jumped at the chance. America beckoned: a young, vibrant country, an ocean away from London's snobberies and the disapproving eyes of Salford's dignitaries.

# 8

# New Horizons

Shelagh arrived in New York in March 1961. America was the dream her generation had grown up with, a young country untouched by war and defined by rock and roll, fast cars and film stars. Shelagh was heading to one of the most glamorous and atmospheric spots in the city – Broadway. Her friend Brendan Behan, arriving with his play *The Hostage* just a few months after *A Taste of Honey*'s New York debut, marvelled at the contrast with London. 'Piccadilly at midnight is dark and deserted … Broadway is not lonely at any hour … it is a complete blaze of colour and you can get anything you want there twenty-four hours a day.'[1]

Shelagh received a warm welcome from Tony Richardson and the cast. Some were old friends – Murray Melvin remained as Geof – but others were new faces: Joan Plowright played Jo and Angela Lansbury was cast as Helen. Shelagh was more surprised to receive a rapturous reception from the American press. *A Taste of Honey* was a hit. Richardson's production was more romantic than Theatre Workshop's. He told friends in New York that 'Joan Littlewood ruined Shelagh Delaney's beautiful play. It's not a play. It's a poem set to jazz.'[2] Richardson played up the love story between Jo and Jimmie, made Geof more pliant, and

Jo less angry. The overall effect was to render Helen a less sympathetic character than in Littlewood's production, and to emphasise a divide between the older generation, jaded by war and poverty, which Helen represented, and the hopeful, loving younger generation represented by Jo and her friends. Oscar Lewenstein 'did not think the New York production was anything like as original and unsentimental as Joan Littlewood's production. However, that would almost certainly not have worked on Broadway.'[3] Shelagh apparently took a similar view.[4] In a country where the arts depended heavily on private patrons, theatre managers were less willing to risk failure. But Shelagh was accepted as a serious writer; she arrived in time to receive the New York Drama Critics' Circle Award for best foreign play.

Shelagh loved New York's exhibitionism. She had no interest in museums or galleries; instead she treated Manhattan as her neighbourhood, hanging out at Gerry Feil's small apartment on the Upper West Side, attending after-show parties at Sardi's restaurant close to Broadway, and whiling away hours in Washington Square in Greenwich Village, where Allen Ginsberg gave readings, guitarists strummed folk songs and old men played chess. In New York people weren't afraid to make a statement. In Washington Square Shelagh passed girls wearing pearls and long velvet dresses, women with cropped hair and pink plastic sunglasses, young men with trilby hats pulled low over long manes of hair. Back home she'd told journalists that 'I don't like diamonds ... I'd much rather buy big things that aren't real ... bangles and earrings that look like toned-down stage effects – chunky bracelets'.[5] In New York, though, nobody appeared to 'tone down' anything. She dragged friends to see the transvestite prostitutes parading around Eleventh Avenue in colourful dresses and wigs; so different from home, where the controversy over *Lady Chatterley's Lover* simmered on.

Shelagh loved America because, she said, 'it is a passionate place'.[6] Passions were running high in 1961. Many of the friends she made there had fallen victim to the government-endorsed anti-Communist witch-hunts led by Senator Joe McCarthy in the 1950s. Some had had their careers ruined; others had only recently been released from jail. In Washington Square, she was caught up in huge rallies called by the National Association for the Advancement of Colored People (NAACP). Unlike southern states New York had no official racial segregation, but in 1961 campaigners were contending with white flight from inner-city neighbourhoods, and political corruption. Carol Greitzer, a resident of Greenwich Village, was a member of the Village Independent Democrats, reformists opposed to the patronage-infused Democratic leadership in the city government. In her words, 'We were having to fight for our public spaces, for our communities, against the vested interests of Tammany Hall.'[7] Police and city politicians blamed black and Hispanic residents for rising levels of crime and violence. Shelagh, already a supporter of the growing anti-apartheid movement (in 1963 she would join forty-eight other play-wrights in prohibiting the performance of her work in South Africa), became deeply interested in the civil rights movement; she bought James Baldwin's novels and essays, books she kept all her life.[8]

Despite these tensions, New York was a magnet for those who felt angry or dispossessed. Will Macadam, an aspiring actor in his late teens, had recently arrived from New Jersey. As a gay adolescent, 'I was one of the people that had to leave high school because of the bullying. I wasn't physically bullied. It was more like mental cruelty.' In his provincial home town anyone dreaming of a future that didn't involve marriage, two children and a home in the suburbs provoked suspicion. 'Our drama coach was forced to leave the school. Because the productions were too polished. Can you imagine? A football team does well, that's the best thing that can ever happen to a school, a town. But good drama productions? That was suspect. Very suspect.'[9]

What made *A Taste of Honey* so welcome to spectators like Carol Greitzer and Will Macadam was Shelagh's treatment of black people and gay men as normal citizens of society – not as deviants, delinquents, or as a cause célèbre. Will saw every play he could, but '*A Taste of Honey*, where there was a gay character who wasn't a raving queen, who was a three-dimensional person, it was a breakthrough. The big issue of this play is not him being gay! That was the honesty.' Carol Greitzer, a regular theatregoer for years, wrote to the *New York Times* to note that Jimmie's 'color ... gets the audience set for a play about race relations'; but in fact 'it is altogether misleading to summarize the action of Miss Delaney's play by saying a girl becomes pregnant by a Negro sailor ... his being a Negro is almost entirely irrelevant'.[10] While some London critics reviled Shelagh's play as depicting lowlife who had no place in the theatre, American reviewers admired her ability to capture the everyday. They welcomed the implication that race and sexuality were artificial divisions. '*A Taste of Honey* is as real as your neighborhood,' commented the *New York Times*.[11]

American audiences weren't as interested as British ones in *Honey*'s portrayal of working-class life, but they were attracted by Shelagh's own rags-to-riches tale. In a country defined by the American dream that anyone could achieve greatness by their own efforts, reviews often wildly exaggerated the poverty of her childhood – *Time* claimed that she came from 'one of the most ferocious slums in Britain'.[12] Far from sneering at her audacity like their British counterparts, American newspapers invited her to explain her success. 'There is a lot of amazed comment and discussion on the so-called exceptional maturity of some young novelists, playwrights, poets, painters and musicians,' Shelagh wrote in a four-page feature for the *New York Times Magazine*. She suggested that her generation was capable of making an artistic contribution thanks to the post-war welfare state – far stronger in Britain than in America – and the growth of mass media. 'Education is no longer the privilege of a particular class,' she wrote. 'Reading provokes thought. Thought provokes questioning.' She defined education in its broadest sense, suggesting Shakespeare, rock and roll and *Coronation Street* were all valuable: 'young people today, with a stack of newspapers, magazines, a radio, free public libraries, television, films and theatre to draw on, and all geared up to keeping them informed, are probably more aware of the beauty, ugliness, cruelty and injustice of the world than ever before'.[13]

Shelagh's piece was entitled 'Never Underestimate Eighteen-Year-Old Girls'. This touched on what, for Carol Greitzer and many other women, was the truly outstanding feature of *Honey*: its exploration of 'the ambivalent aspects of a ... mother-daughter relationship'.[14] 'It made an impression because I was a daughter, and had just become a mother,' recalled Carol. 'I had a somewhat difficult relationship with my mother. And I was wondering how to be a mother myself. So it spoke to certain elements of my life.'[15] In her letter to the *New York Times* she praised the play and gently suggested that male critics missed *Honey*'s 'powerful emotional impact that is probably best understood by women'.[16]

Carol's excitement over Shelagh's portrayal of women wasn't confined to American theatregoers. In Britain women had also observed this – Frances Cuka, who played Jo in the Theatre Workshop and West End productions of *Honey*, considered it the most original aspect of the play. But it didn't occur to most of them to see women as an oppressed group like black Americans or the British northern working class. Shelagh certainly did not, though she had become increasingly annoyed by the sexual hypocrisy and humiliation to which women were subjected. As she pointed out in the *New York Times*, those who claimed to be shocked by *A Taste of Honey* were less bothered by the plethora of strip clubs, brothels and pornography vendors that studded London's Soho, just a few minutes' walk from the West End. 'It is middle-aged men who regard sex either as a mystic ritual, a dark secret or a dirty joke,' she wrote, 'eminent business men, politicians and other respectable members of society – the very society which condemns youth for its transgressions and indulgences.'[17] Youth, not women, were the victims here.

'At the time we weren't thinking about feminism,' said Carol. 'That came later.'[18] Already, though, women in Greenwich Village were leading a fight against the authorities' neglect of their community. In the late 1950s, Carol had become involved in a campaign to remove traffic from Washington Square, initiated by women concerned about the dangers for their children and neighbours. The leaders were women like Shirley Hayes and Edith Lyons 'who organized other mothers and started the loud – and, yes, sometimes strident – protestations'. Their struggle mushroomed into a sustained attack on City Hall's contempt for this socially and racially mixed neighbourhood, large swathes of which the politicians wished to flatten for a highway. Carol and the other women noticed that once 'this campaign began to steamroll and look as if it had a chance to succeed, several other people (mostly men) formed their own group so as to present a more "respectable" approach to city officials, in contrast to Shirley's stridency, which was what aroused their interest in the first place!'[19]

Eventually, the Villagers won their fight for a car-free square and the survival of their neighbourhood, but the role of the women – vital, yet underplayed by the men – prompted Carol to demand that the Democrats take women's representation more seriously. By 1963 she was a New York City Council Member. In the same year, the American journalist Betty Friedan published *The Feminine Mystique*, the seminal feminist text that defined 'the problem that has no name' – the discontent that thousands of women felt with lives centred on domesticity.[20] By 1967, Carol had joined with Betty Friedan to campaign for women's right to legal abortion – together they launched the National Association for Repeal of Abortion Laws. In 1970 she and Friedan marched together in the city's first Women's March. By then, *A Taste of Honey* was being performed and discussed by feminists across the world for exactly the qualities that Carol Greitzer had recognised a decade earlier.

With the Broadway run garnering warm reviews, Shelagh and Tony Richardson planned the film adaptation of *Honey*. The finances were in place – Woodfall had made enough money on their adaptation of *Saturday Night and Sunday Morning* to cover the cost – but Tony had to convince Film Finance to underwrite the film. Film Finance was a bond company set up in 1950 to provide completion guarantees for British film-makers – an insurance policy which avoided the likes of Richardson having to acquire corporate sponsorship. The key figure at the firm was John Croydon, a skilled film producer who assessed each application. His report described *A Taste of Honey* as 'sordid in the extreme and [a story] for which I do not particularly care'. Nevertheless, he recommended funding – *A Taste of Honey* was, he noted, 'enjoying considerable success as a play' and Richardson himself was 'a hard worker with a basic sense of responsibility' who had already established an excellent reputation as a director, and was also hugely committed to the project.[21] Rita Tushingham, who starred in the film, recalled that Tony 'didn't give a fuck if it was popular [with the critics], but he wanted to make something for the ordinary working class, he had that sense of purpose'.[22] Shelagh agreed with his views.

Not everyone at Woodfall shared their vision for the film. Oscar Lewenstein, one of Woodfall's directors, thought they needed a famous face to play Jo and suggested Audrey Hepburn.[23] In 1961 it was still hard to 'sell' a working-class, northern woman as a serious, sympathetic character, despite the new novels and films dealing with the working class. The actress Pat Phoenix had discovered this to her cost when she'd auditioned for the role of Alice Aisgill in the film adaptation of John Braine's *Room at the Top*. To her disappointment, and Braine's chagrin, the film's sponsors demanded the French actress Simone Signoret be cast, arguing that the independent, passionate and articulate woman Braine had created was rendered unconvincing by Alice's northern pedigree.[24] But Richardson, supported by Shelagh, wanted to recruit an unknown actress from northern England. His argument for authenticity won out when they alighted on Rita Tushingham, a nineteen-year-old Liverpudlian working in repertory theatre. 'I was young and naive, fresh ... and grounded too, because of where I came from,' said Rita. Like Shelagh, Rita had to put up with London critics' assumption that her upbringing mirrored that of the character she played, when in fact 'my dad owned a grocer's shop and he was a Conservative councillor'. But she believed that *A Taste of Honey* reflected real life. 'It never seemed scandalous to me. Which was probably my upbringing. My mum and dad ... weren't prejudiced about people' – and running a shop meant they 'knew all sorts of people'.[25]

*A Taste of Honey* was the first British feature film to be shot entirely on location, and the cast and crew's arrival generated huge interest and publicity in Manchester and Salford. The glamour of film caused even the *Salford City Reporter* to change its tone towards Shelagh. '[D]on't be surprised if you feature in the final film,' it told readers; the director was 'determined to use "real" people in everyday settings'.[26] In fact Shelagh was chiefly responsible for identifying locations; it was her knowledge that fired Tony Richardson's desire to make the landscape so central to the film, and to recruit Salfordians as 'extras'. John Croydon of Film Finance had worried that 'the frequent use of groups of children' would 'prove troublesome'; but in the event the only troublesome aspect to this was ensuring that the children looked suitably urchin-like.[27] Tony Richardson and Shelagh recruited local children who they thought looked 'particularly scruffy'. When filming day arrived, however, one of the children turned up 'in her best party frock, her hair all done up, and Tony had to tell her mother "get her back in the clothes she wore yesterday"'. The child was Hazel Blears; thirty-six years later she was to become Salford's 'New' Labour MP.[28]

On 14 September 1961 the film of *A Taste of Honey* premiered in Leicester Square. 'It has the qualities of sincerity and heart … the sweet taste of success,' concluded the *Daily Mirror*.[29] Shelagh won a BAFTA for her screenplay – the first time a woman had ever won this award for a role behind the camera. But she was 'not very happy with the film'. She'd thought Rita Tushingham was too 'sweet' for Jo, but had acquiesced to Tony's judgement.[30] He assured her that she would be heavily involved in writing the script, but he'd then told John Croydon 'that the script should be read with discretion as it was his intention to adapt the content of the scenes to the chosen locations'.[31] As filming got under way, Shelagh departed for New York, where *Honey* was transferring from the Lyceum to the Booth Theatre – 'It's a busy life for Shelagh!' observed the *Salford City Reporter*[32] – leaving Tony free rein. In his adaptation of Shelagh's script, Jo became the star of the film, and Helen was relegated to a more minor role. Tony's insistence that the children in the film look like 'urchins' reflected his desire to present the film as a generational conflict, between adults corrupted by post-war materialism – Helen and Peter spend their time shopping and on trips to Blackpool – and youthful representatives of a supposedly traditional working-class culture of nursery rhymes, untamed moorland and fairs. Shelagh had created in Jo a young woman who was excited by music and dancing, and was very much of her time. Tony Richardson's version brought *A Taste of Honey* closer to the concerns expressed by Richard Hoggart and some of the other northern, working-class male writers of the late 1950s, by lamenting the loss of an older working-class culture.

Tony Richardson was far less concerned with situating *Honey* in the political and economic circumstances of the late 1950s than Shelagh had been. In Shelagh's original script, Jo is personally affected by the time in which she lives – the script refers to the cultural and political preoccupations of the late 1950s, and this contemporaneity was emphasised by Joan Littlewood's use of a jazz band in the Theatre Workshop production. Jo is also affected by the passing of time, most obviously because of her pregnancy. Even in the midst of rage and denial, Jo knows exactly when she is due to give birth. But Richardson set *Honey*, like many of the new northern films, in a vaguely post-war present, and harked back to an equally ambiguous 'authentic' past, while Jo, who conceives just after Christmas, is still pregnant ten and a half months later on Bonfire Night. This allowed him to present 'authentic' working-class life as a timeless cycle of seasonal festivals; Jo lived in Hoggart's 'cosy burrow', removed from the linear passage of time in the harsh outside world.[33]

Shelagh did not express her disquiet to Tony or the cast. She was, recalled Rita Tushingham 'very shy' on set and seemed to 'trust Tony'. Just as she'd been aware of her inexperience at Theatre Workshop in 1958, she was conscious in 1961 of being a novice in the film world. And she recognised and respected the director's role; later in the 1960s Lindsay Anderson would praise Shelagh for 'letting me get on with it' when he worked with her. But there was another reason which prevented her from speaking out when she may have wished to: it was very difficult for a young woman to challenge the authority of an older man, particularly one with Tony Richardson's formidable reputation. 'It wasn't easy being a woman, especially not a woman with opinions,' said Rita. 'You'd say things and people wouldn't like it.'[34] As she grew older, Shelagh would become more confident about expressing her opinions – but she would also choose to work with women, as agents, producers and directors, whenever possible. Rita Tushingham's observations were as relevant to the last years of Shelagh's career as to the early 1960s.

Nevertheless, Tony Richardson's film was also groundbreaking in ways that complemented Shelagh's intentions. Her sense of place shaped the film as it had the play. And Richardson retained a focus on working-class women. Julie Christie, who starred in the film adaptation of Keith Waterhouse's *Billy Liar*, recalled that '[i]n films ... women were there to be disliked by the heroes ... in *Room at the Top* and *Saturday Night and Sunday Morning* and almost all of the rest: they were all about boys who wanted to be free and wanted to screw lots of women, and they always had this person who they were expected to be faithful to, and that person was a nag and a whiner and a restriction on them'.[35] Lizzie, her role in *Billy Liar*, was a rare exception, but the protagonist was still male. And the film adaptation of *Billy Liar* did not appear until 1963, two years after *A Taste of Honey*.

Not only did *Honey* have a female lead, but it helped to establish that such a role did not need to be filled by a conventional beauty. 'Lancashire lass' Rita Tushingham had 'a face and figure that would never win her a beauty queen award', commented the *Daily Mirror*, but was 'the liveliest prospect of the year' due to her 'wonderful, vital eyes; offbeat, warmly wry smile; enthusiasm and … an instinctive flair for being directed'.[36]

The film introduced Shelagh and *Honey* to a far wider audience than the theatre could reach. 'My brothers and their friends knew nothing about it until it came to the cinema,' said Shirley Evans. 'Then everyone knew about her. She was famous.'[37] Among the fans were a new pop group from Liverpool called the Beatles. Their 1963 song 'A Taste of Honey' appeared on their bestselling album *Please Please Me*, introducing Shelagh's story to thousands of their followers. They were awestruck when they finally met Shelagh at a party; she became good friends with Ringo Starr.[38] Suddenly, the world of celebrities seemed to include other people like her, who understood and admired her work – though most of these rising stars were men.

Away from the limelight, many of *Honey*'s new fans were young women, who echoed what Carol Greitzer had found so startling and significant in the Broadway production. For cinema-goers in Eastern Europe, where the film was widely released, *A Taste of Honey* was startlingly original. Zdena Tomin, a young Czech student, attended a showing at a film festival in Prague. 'It was taken as criticising Western capitalism, so we were able to see it.' She found its representation of women and sexuality eye-opening, 'even though they sort of tried to suppress the fact that Geoffrey's gay. I absolutely loved it.'

*Honey*'s admirers were also intrigued by Shelagh's personal story. Zdena 'was immediately aware that the author was a teenage girl, we all knew that somehow'.[39] In Israel, twenty-year-old Ahuva Weisbaum was living on a kibbutz, one of the country's collective farms, when she saw *Honey*. 'I was a young, working-class woman, and here was this film about a young, working-class woman. Israel was a very conservative society … Her environment was different to ours, but where we were was bleak. Desert. It sounds crazy perhaps, but the griminess, the urban feel – that was glamorous to us. Northern England was where it was all happening! We'd seen *Saturday Night and Sunday Morning*, all of that. We were in love with Albert Finney. But [those stories were] all about men. This was about women who were so different, but in other ways the same as us. It made me think I could maybe do something different with my life.' Later in the 1960s Ahuva set off on a round-the-world trip. She hoped to make it to Manchester – but fell in love in Los Angeles and stayed there.[40]

Love also explained why Shelagh returned to America as often as she could. Harvey Orkin was her chief companion there and, by 1963, her lover. Known as 'the Mighty Ork' on Broadway and in Hollywood, Harvey – twenty years Shelagh's senior – was a hugely successful comedy writer and talent agent: he'd written for *The Phil Silvers Show* and represented stars like Peter Sellers. Charismatic and sociable, he could be found at all the best parties, 'his Scotch in one hand and cigarette in the other as he opined wittily on the subjects of the day'.[41] But he was also unpretentious and ready to laugh at himself. 'He had a quick, biting sense of humor,' recalled the American playwright Neil Simon. 'Once when I was riding with him in a crowded elevator, Harvey looked down at his shaking hands and said aloud for everyone to hear, "Christ, I have a hangover the size of India and I've got a twelve o'clock surgery call. Well, I can only do my best."'[42] Shelagh found him a refreshing change after the snobbery and pretensions of the London arts scene.

Shelagh would repeatedly be attracted to, in her daughter Charlotte's words, 'very manly men', reminiscent of Hollywood stars of the 1930s and 40s like James Cagney and Humphrey Bogart, 'in a sharp suit'. They combined charm with sex appeal and had 'the kind of masculinity that doesn't need to make others feel small to feel big'; men who weren't afraid to take risks and have adventures. Harvey introduced Shelagh to Studs Terkel, whom she loved for the alacrity with which he turned his hand to different crafts – acting, broadcasting, writing on jazz and oral history – and the effort and ingenuity he brought to each. Harvey's own eclectic career impressed her – he worked with television and film stars, writers and directors, his interest in people and culture driving him to discern what made each of them tick. And he was fun – 'she liked the playfulness of men, which she felt women just weren't encouraged to pursue', recalls her daughter.

But Harvey was also married, with two young children. The 'manly men' Shelagh was attracted to were rarely fans of monogamy. Her relationship with Harvey reinforced her own ambivalence about marriage. She'd learned from her mother that being a wife could add to women's burdens rather than relieve them. Now she saw that wealth couldn't overcome this – Harvey's own wife, Gisella, decided 'not to see Harvey's numerous "indiscretions" and to forget those she'd been compelled to confront'. Shelagh, who was intensely private about her love life, could not bear the idea of breaking up Harvey's marriage, especially since she knew that she would be 'seen as a home wrecker' while Harvey 'might be portrayed as a hapless oaf who was seduced'.[43] More than that, she could not stomach the wilful ignorance that marriage to such a man must bring.

Harvey became her guide to the America she knew from books and Hollywood films. They mingled with celebrities at the ornate, modernist Russian Tea Rooms – Harvey introduced her to Katharine Hepburn, who shared Shelagh's irreverence for social convention. They ate cheesecake at Lindy's diner off Broadway and visited 'every joint he knew I had read about and some I hadn't – Sloppy Louie's on the docks where I ate a shark steak for the first time'.[44] Shelagh loved the glimpses of glamour in American life; the way that aspirations for a different sort of life became embodied in fast cars or outrageous hairdos. American cars would continually crop up in her work; in *Dance with a Stranger* she would capture the hidden depths of Desmond Cussen, the wealthy banker who holds a candle for Ruth Ellis, by having him drive 'a Zephyr, a car that looks very American and rather flashy'.[45] It made the point that beneath his reticent and respectable appearance he harboured dreams and desires.

In 1962, with Harvey's assistance, Shelagh secured a book contract for a volume of short stories. This appeared in America in 1963 and then in Britain the following year. *Sweetly Sings the Donkey* took its title from the longest piece Shelagh included, a semi-autobiographical account of a ten-year-old girl's stay in a Blackpool convalescent home. All the stories were narrated by children or women and all drew on her own experiences. She used a child's perspective to pinpoint the bullying and elitism in fifties Britain: her protagonists spear totalitarian teachers and superior sociologists. The *New York Times* praised her 'authentic voice of youth, greedy for life ... The impudence and bravery of these English working-class children in their narrow streets and crowded homes are described with the minimum of detail and maximum of effect'.[46] But this was no English *Catcher in the Rye* tale of clashing generations. In Shelagh's stories, parents are benevolent and humane, but powerless in the face of illness or officialdom. This was, she suggested, one of the realisations of a work-ing-class childhood: that your parents have very little control over the world you inhabit.

Shelagh also explored her experience of fame and how being a woman affected this. 'All About and To a Female Artist' strung together excerpts from the mail she'd received since *Honey*'s premiere. Some were violent: 'how are your Teddy-boy boyfriends. Do they carry flick knives? It would be rather fun if they jab their flick knives into you one night.' Women begged for cash: 'I hope you will be kind and read and understand the letter of a humble and honest Catholic mother.' Men assumed that if she'd managed to find an audience for her writing, they could too: 'I come from Lancashire like you ... Should you be interested in acting as my agent for this play then I will give you 20 percent of all profits and later you can help me with another play I have in mind.'[47]

As Shelagh's title for this piece suggested, the common thread linking these letters was that they defined her primarily as a woman, not as a writer. She was either immoral or self-sacrificial, but either way, as Lorna Sage put it, 'a creature of mythology', defined by her body not her mind.[48] When *Sweetly Sings the Donkey* was published in Britain, some critics dismissed 'All About and To a Female Artist' as 'a rag-bag … almost wilfully disorganised'.[49] But Shelagh had no model for talking about women's 'objectification', the word that feminists would begin to use in the 1970s. Her book came out a few months after Betty Friedan's *The Feminine Mystique* (they were published by the same firm: W.W. Norton). By the end of 1964 Friedan's exposé was a bestseller on both sides of the Atlantic.

American reviewers were particularly intrigued by Shelagh's 'new way of writing one's autobiography', as the *New York Times* put it. The newspaper's reviewer found Shelagh's approach refreshing, 'omitting unnecessary facts but in its bare, bold, derisory fashion showing both background and attitude with startling clarity and direct appeal'.[50] Her book had similarities to a genre of American countercultural writings made famous by Jack Kerouac's 1957 travel memoir *On the Road*. But there was a striking difference between the beats and Shelagh. Beat writers were far from convinced that women could be free spirits, as Joyce Johnson, Jack Kerouac's lover, and an aspiring writer herself, had discovered. 'Could he ever include a woman in his journeys … ? Whenever I tried to raise the question, he'd stop me by saying that what I really wanted were babies. That was what all women wanted and what I wanted too.' Johnson was only able to describe this encounter thirty years after it occurred.[51] There simply wasn't the language available in 1963.

Respect for the individual's right to fit their narrative to the shape of their life would become more powerful in both Britain and America over the next twenty years. Shelagh's generation of women would initiate this change, as they began to write about subjects that male writers had consigned to the footnotes: intimate relationships, frustrations and failures as well as worldly success. Shelagh was an early pioneer. *Time* thought *Sweetly Sings the Donkey* 'breaks the rules by offering no one quite credible except the subject'.[52] In other words, Shelagh allowed her narrators – women and children – to present the world as they saw it, asserting that their reality was just as valid as that offered by politicians or journalists. In trying to find a language that expressed what she wanted to say, she fused memory, fiction, letters, anecdote and song.

From the late 1970s, feminists of her generation began to write memoirs that were not concerned with charting an individual's rise to greatness but rather, as the feminist sociologist Ann Oakley – born in 1944 – put it, to capture the 'eccentric authenticity of the individual' while also locating 'oneself in ... a particular culture' and, above all, to 'claim the right to pain and passion'; to life in all its messiness, not reduced to predetermined standards of success.[53] Many of them owed a debt, directly or indirectly, to Shelagh's work. Like her, many of these feminist memoirists eschewed a simple, linear chronology. They focused on particularly significant episodes or life stages, often childhood or youth, to make sense of their formation as women – just as Shelagh had done. In the words of Carol Dix, who in 1978 wrote a collective biography with former school friends, they offered 'no moral, resounding ending ... no concern with dramatic outline ... only ... very honest, intimate revelations' about how they 'responded to certain changes, freedoms, in the world around [us]'.[54] They explored the ambivalent relationship between mothers and daughters, a relationship foregrounded in Carolyn Steedman's 1986 memoir, *Landscape for a Good Woman*. Steedman suggested that 'the stories that people tell themselves in order to explain how they got to the place they currently inhabit are often in deep and ambiguous conflict with the official inter-pretative devices of a culture'. That was certainly true of *Sweetly Sings the Donkey*, whose narrators were, like Steedman's mother, 'not to be found in Richard Hoggart's landscape'.[55] Shelagh's book was a tentative exploration of the feelings and experiences that these feminists recounted years later.

*Sweetly Sings the Donkey* was published in Britain in the spring of 1964. By then, Shelagh was back in London, sharing a flat in Judd Street, near King's Cross, with her friend Una Collins. The two women had become close during the run of *Honey*, for which Una had worked on the costumes, and she had subsequently been the costume designer for *Lion*. Una was just three years older than Shelagh. 'They shared the same sort of dream, of getting away from home, living the life of young, independent women in London,' recalled Una's daughter Sophie. 'And they both had this passion for the arts, and were both a bit surprised to have ended up able to do what they did.'[56] While Shelagh could be shy, sulky and lethargic, Una was gregarious, warm-hearted and full of energy. 'Una was tiny,' remembered Zdena Tomin, who became friends with Shelagh in the 1980s. 'Lots of frizzy black hair. She was all fluffy. And they had this very warm, involved friendship.'[57]

Shelagh had found the American launch of *Sweetly Sings the Donkey* in September 1963 exhausting and felt nauseous when she returned home. When the sickness didn't go away, a friend gently suggested she should consult a doctor. Shelagh's GP confirmed her friend's suspicion: she was three months pregnant.[58]

Her pregnancy was a shock. The future was daunting. Harvey, her lover, was on the other side of the Atlantic, with a wife and children. Abortion was illegal. Single motherhood carried a stigma. But Shelagh, friends recall, 'was thrilled'; 'surprised, but very pleased'.[59] Ten years earlier she had shocked Mrs Gray, Shirley's mother, by declaring she wanted a baby but not a husband. As 1964 arrived, her teenage wish was about to come true.

# 9

# Happy Ever After

On 4 March 1964 Shelagh gave birth to Charlotte Jo Delaney in a private nursing home. Journalists were waiting when she returned to the fourth-floor flat she shared with Una in Judd Street Mansions. 'Yes, it's true, I've just had a baby,' she told them. 'I don't want to discuss it anymore.'[1] The *Daily Mirror* carried the news on its front page, informing readers that '[s]he stayed silent about the identity of Charlotte's father' and refused to say whether she had married.[2] The journalists, said her friend Kevin Palmer, a stage manager and actor at Theatre Workshop, were 'camped outside the door, and outside the flats. She couldn't go out. They wanted to see Charlotte, they wanted to know if Shelagh was married, and who the father was ... and they thought because she wasn't married, that she was public property.' She had no rights; had given them up in deciding to flout convention and present her sin to the world. Harold Riley visited her and found 'she was very distressed by the press'.[3] Kevin and Harold were horrified to hear that some journalists were so desperate to get a photo of Shelagh with her baby that they 'set off a fire alarm in the corridor in her block of flats so that everyone ran out in their pyjamas'.[4]

Unmarried motherhood, Shelagh wrote, 'hung like the Sword of Damocles over women's heads' when she was growing up.[5] This had not changed by 1964, but *A Taste of Honey* had broken the taboo on discussing it in the arts. And in the years since 1958, the number of illegitimate births had risen, from eleven births among every thousand unmarried women in the mid-1950s to nineteen by 1964.[6] By then, a handful of young women were making their name as novelists by writing about the choices and dilemmas that confronted their generation. Lynne Reid Banks's debut novel, *The L-Shaped Room*, appeared in 1960; Maureen Duffy's *That's How It Was* in 1962; Margaret Drabble's *A Summer Bird-Cage* in 1963; Margaret Forster's *Dames' Delight* in 1964. These novels focused on the new opportunities available to young women for sexual, emotional and financial independence – not least university and professional work. The protagonists believed marriage would curtail their freedom, but single women who wanted a sex life feared the stigma of illegitimate pregnancy and the burden of childcare. It is no accident that both Jane in *The L-Shaped Room* and Rosamund in Drabble's 1966 bestseller *The Millstone* have wealthy and helpful relatives to rely on. Nevertheless, each of these novels ends shortly after they give birth – their writers found the single mother's future hard to envisage. How to lead a satisfying adult life was a question they had to leave unanswered. Duffy's *That's How It Was*, which centres on Paddy, a teenage schoolgirl who is desperate to escape the hardships endured by her working-class single mother, is constructed 'towards its very last line, the question "And what the hell do I do now?"'. Duffy believed that 'the ending which leaves the reader to answer is appropriate for our times of rapid change'.[7]

In real life, marriage was often the answer to Paddy's question – particularly for working-class girls who got pregnant. Lorna Sage, who got pregnant aged sixteen in 1959, knew that if your family couldn't afford to keep you or weren't prepared to do so, 'you repented on your knees (scrubbed floors, said prayers), had your baby (which was promptly adopted by proper married people) and returned home humble and hollow-eyed'.[8] Such was the stigma that even contact with the sinner could taint a respectable girl's reputation; this was why Shirley Evans's mother had proved so reluctant to allow her daughter to visit a workmate consigned to an unmarried mothers' home in the late 1950s.[9]

For those who wanted to keep their babies, the best route was up the aisle – Lorna Sage married her boyfriend Vic.[10] But she discovered that while marriage eradicated the stigma of illegitimacy, it brought fresh problems. Married women were considered to be fully absorbed by their family commitments; they required their husband's permission to get a mortgage and, as Sage found, were barred from many universities. She was refused entry to Oxbridge women's colleges, and, more seriously, denied a grant by her Local Education Authority. '[F]or girls sex was entirely preoccupying,' wrote Sage of her treatment; 'your sex was *more of you* than a boy's appendage, you *were* your sex, so you had to do without if you were to have enough energy, self-possession and brains left over to do anything else.'[11] Her refusal to accept this eventually resulted in her being awarded a grant and a place to read English at Durham (the university had to change its rules to let her in). She and her husband were both awarded first-class degrees, while Lorna's mother cared for their daughter. But as the first married couple to enrol at the university, their story made the newspapers when they graduated in the summer of 1964, four months after Charlotte Jo Delaney was born.

Harvey Orkin had no intention of leaving his wife, and Shelagh did not intend to ask him – she only told him about Charlotte once the baby was born. She wanted to go on living with Una in their flat in London. But she decided that the only way to gain control of her life was to lead it as privately as possible. She had always seen sexuality as a personal matter, deflecting prurient press enquiries with talk of her next project. In 1964 she gave up the fight to be taken seriously by the newspapers. Bruised by six years of sneering criticism, and exhausted by new motherhood, she could not summon up the humour she'd rebuffed her critics with in the past. Then, she could rely on the support of Theatre Workshop, and later her friends at the Royal Court, to defend her work. But with Charlotte's birth the media's attention was squarely focused on Shelagh, not on her writing. She also had other people to consider: Charlotte, Harvey – whose family did not know about their relationship – and her mother and brother back home. Elsie and Joe were solidly supportive of Shelagh but disliked media intrusion as much as she did (though they weren't daunted by it; in 1960, Elsie had written to the BBC after *Monitor* was filmed to ask for compensation for the 'time [the crew] were at the house, and the inconvenience').[12] Shelagh and her baby stayed inside the flat until the press finally decamped. She did not give another press interview for twelve years.

She was secure in the knowledge that she did not need publicity or press approval to lead the life she wanted. Her creativity did not need to end with the birth of her child. She still had powerful allies, contacts at the BBC among them. Despite the scandalised tone that the press adopted about her motherhood, many in the real world proved less bothered. Shortly after Charlotte's birth Shelagh began writing for *Z Cars*, a realist police drama on BBC Television. She'd rejected approaches from the BBC's drama department following *A Taste of Honey*, telling them she wanted to focus on the theatre. But by 1964 she'd had enough of the snobbery of London's theatrical world, and the regular work that television offered was attractive – she now had a baby to keep. She liked the grit of *Z Cars*, which had begun in 1962, dealt with topical issues like police violence and corruption, and used northern actors like the Mancunian John Thaw, a recent RADA graduate.[13]

In the summer of 1964, Harry Moore, a BBC drama producer, commissioned Shelagh to adapt one of the short stories in *Sweetly Sings the Donkey* into a *Wednesday Play* for BBC1. This new venture, broadcast at peak viewing time, showcased contemporary social dramas in a realistic setting. Ken Loach was a regular contributor. Shelagh's story, 'The White Bus', followed a young woman on a city tour of Salford. She'd got her inspiration from what the *Salford City Reporter* described as 'the celebrated vehicle which toured Salford during Civic Week' in 1962.[14] This was Salford Council's incredible and costly riposte to *A Taste of Honey*, which they persisted in seeing as a slur on the city. The *Reporter* praised the tour as 'an eye-opener to many people who had no idea of the progress made in recent years'. Highlights included 'the attractiveness of the housing estates' and a demolition site which would eventually house 'a shopping precinct with car park'. No library, theatre, museum or cinema was included in the thirty-one sites visited. Pendleton High School was glimpsed – though its famous playwright alumna did not merit a mention.[15]

Shelagh's white bus was a satirical inversion of the original, populated not by ordinary residents but by pompous civic leaders. Her tour's commentary parodied those politicians, academics and London critics who treated 'the north' as an exotic outpost to be stared at, or as a playground for planners. They saw the 'less fortunate members of our community' as simpletons, who needed to be spoken for rather than listened to, and who could be treated as subordinates. 'You don't mind me talking to you in a paternal way, do you?' the Lord Mayor asks the story's narrator, as she resists his attempt to grope her leg.[16] Shelagh's tour was reminiscent of a colonial safari.

But she found it impossible to adapt her story into the kind of play she wanted. The BBC's *Wednesday Play* favoured a small set; she wanted it to be on location. And as a writer who'd always been as concerned about people's imaginations as their surroundings, she felt constrained by the realism that the drama department demanded (later, writers like Dennis Potter would challenge this).

When, in 1965, Oscar Lewenstein suggested she turn the story into a film, she leapt at the chance. Lewenstein proposed that Woodfall Films make a trilogy of films, one segment each to be directed by Lindsay Anderson, Tony Richardson and Karel Reisz, and each inspired by one of Shelagh's stories. Anderson 'liked the story ['The White Bus'] and I liked Shelagh, and I agreed to do it'.[17] In 1963 Anderson had directed *This Sporting Life*, David Storey's semi-autobiographical account of a Yorkshire Rugby League player. But he was becoming more interested in surrealism as a means to express people's emotions and fantasies, and to convey the huge gulf, as he saw it, between Britain's institutions – whether public schools or town halls – and the people they claimed to represent. When Shelagh met him in March 1965 they hit it off straight away. Anderson, who could be very critical, confided to his diary that 'She is sympathetic, direct, and I feel creative'. He remained enthusiastic even when, at a follow-up meeting, Shelagh characteristically 'hadn't brought her papers!'[18] She was clearly finding it hard to turn 'The White Bus' into a screenplay, and saw in Lindsay a collaborator who could assist with this task.

Typically, she avoided conflict with the BBC by simply failing to tell them she'd changed her mind. Harry Moore sent her increasingly pleading notes culminating in a telegram when he got word of her new project: 'Desperate stop must speak to you urgently stop contact me at BBC tomorrow afternoon.'[19] She probably didn't.

*The White Bus* was shot in Salford in October 1965. Civic dignitaries eagerly accepted Anderson's invitation to take part, believing that Shelagh had seen the error of her ways and that the film was intended to promote Salford. The white bus was filled with councillors and Salford's Lord Mayor; a school assembly was filmed at Pendleton High. None of those involved had any idea that the film would satirise their authority. Anderson and the crew sought permission from the town hall for filming 'feeling like assassins with knives under our cloaks'.[20] Shelagh had no such scruples – she regularly had to walk away from filming so that none of the participants would catch her laughing at their self-importance.[21]

*The White Bus* represented those in authority as out of touch with most people's lives. Speeches by civic leaders and scenes of hymn singing in Pendleton's school hall were juxtaposed with young people dancing on desks in offices, or the main character – played by Patricia Hewison – screaming. *The White Bus* asserted that Salfordians had dreams and ambitions that found no outlet in the city's schools, workplaces and shopping centres.

Although Shelagh focused her attack on Salford's dignitaries, she saw the film as ridiculing the social conventions still widely upheld in much of Britain. In the mid-1960s Shirley Evans, who had not seen Shelagh for years, met her at a mutual friend's wedding in Salford. 'In those days, weddings were always in a church and women always wore a hat, *always*. Well, Shelagh arrived in this enormous sombrero. It was so big that it was ridiculous, it was like a joke sombrero. Shelagh was very tall, and she had this enormous hat on. And it was very brightly coloured. You didn't do that; you didn't go to weddings looking like that – but she did.'[22] Shirley thought it was hilarious, and also admirable; she and other friends got Shelagh to pose for a photo with them.

*The White Bus* provoked similar reactions among some of its audience. It became a cult film, with the mixed consequences that implies. United Artists had undertaken to distribute the trilogy – originally named *Red, White and Blue* – but by 1966 plans for the second and third films were falling apart, and they never materialised. *The White Bus* was only ever screened privately, though these showings generated favourable publicity in London, Venice and, particularly, Prague; Czechoslovakia was the homeland of *The White Bus*'s innovative cameraman, Miroslav Ondricek.[23] Ardent admirers in the United States considered it, in the words of a *New York Times* reviewer, 'a surreal, funny examination of postwar England'.[24] But many viewers found it incomprehensible. As one American critic perceptively commented, 'its strength is in its documentary reality, not in calculated absurdities, which, I suspect, might have been found in reality had Anderson simply looked for them'.[25] Shelagh's original story had certainly been more grounded in the preposterousness of everyday life than Anderson's surreal film was, but she later told a close friend that 'she was happy with *The White Bus*'.[26] Aware that her own strength lay in writing – especially dialogue – and lacking any directing experience, she was generally cooperative, and sometimes overly deferential, to those like Littlewood and Anderson who proved supportive of her work.

*The White Bus* did nothing to enamour Shelagh to Salford's civic leaders but that didn't matter – her life was now firmly rooted in London. In 1966 she moved out of the flat she shared with Una and bought herself a four-storey Georgian house in Gerrard Road, Islington. The area reminded Shelagh of Ordsall – almost a quarter of Islington households lacked hot water or a bath, and there was overcrowding and poverty, but the large numbers of families meant there were always children playing on the street, and many neighbours had known each other for years.[27] And, like Ordsall, households took a variety of shapes, with a high proportion of single-parent families.[28] All the same, Islington was a far grander place to live than Salford; 'it is still possible', found an investigation of housing conducted in 1968, 'to walk for over two miles ... and enjoy an almost unbroken sequence of wide streets and picturesque squares'.[29] According to this report, only a minority of residents in Shelagh's part of Islington were 'middle-class newcomers', and those who were 'had moved to the area not only because property prices were relatively low at the time but also because they liked the liveliness and diversity of the area.'[30]

Shelagh loved her new house. She had grand plans to decorate its large rooms in bright colours, and to sand the wooden floors. New stores like Habitat – founded by Terence Conran in the year of Charlotte's birth – were catering to the tastes of Shelagh's generation, who rejected the thick carpets and ornaments that had spelled comfort to their parents in favour of simple, functional furniture by new designers, which catered for young people juggling careers and childcare. These consumers wanted their homes to be relaxed, informal, easy to maintain and – in contrast to many of their parents' homes – *spacious*. There was room for Shelagh to have a study, for Charlotte and her friends, and for Shelagh's mother, or her brother and his new wife, June, to stay. 'Family was important to her; she adored her brother,' said Stephen Frears.[31] And Elsie's help with Charlotte was invaluable. Shelagh didn't want to do as some of her friends did and employ an au pair; she wanted wealth to give her privacy, not open up her home to strangers. But if she was to work, she needed help. Friends lent a hand, but, like generations of women before her, she relied on family.

Her grand plans for Gerrard Road were never realised. She soon ran out of patience with home decoration, judging it the modern form of domestic drudgery – 'I tend to daub rather than achieve sweeping even strokes,' she wrote to a friend, years later, 'and as for those straight lines between walls and skirting boards ...'[32] 'She never liked housework,' recalled Kath Wilkie. 'She preferred seeing friends, and writing.' Friends regularly called round and stayed for hours or days. 'It wasn't a mess,' said Will Macadam, who visited Gerrard Road in the 1970s. 'It was just this big old house that not much thought went into ... her brother would come down and do things for her. Fix it up.' The garden became an overgrown wilderness. It didn't matter; 'she was happy to have the house and the freedom', said Will.[33] There was no need to consider anyone else's comfort or standards; no rent inspector or landlord to cast a critical eye.

In 1965 Harvey Orkin had moved to London with his wife and two young children to work as an agent at Creative Management Associates. He was part of a new group dedicated to bringing satire to British television and poking fun at politicians, the monarchy and respectability. Harvey became a well-known face after starring on the BBC's new satirical show *Not So Much a Programme, More a Way of Life*, devised by David Frost and Ned Sherrin. He was 'a smart guy, very witty', recalled Stephen Frears who was one of the programme's regular viewers.[34] Harvey's glittering social life involved 'dinners and parties [with] the inner circle of London's theatrical elite, from the brilliant critic Kenneth Tynan to James Mason and Maggie Smith and Peter Sellers ... The conversations were witty and intelligent, sometimes silly, often scandalous ... The talk dealt mostly with British politics, British finance, British sex mores, and the British theater.'[35] Shelagh was often present at these gatherings.[36]

But life as a wife was never on her horizon. In the 1970s, feminist scholars and activists would begin to openly debate whether marriage could ever be a union of equals, or fulfil women's sexual and romantic desires. Shelagh had always been sceptical. She had grown up surrounded by independent women. As a result of the war, they'd had to rely on themselves to make ends meet and on each other for emotional support even more than earlier generations had done. Her father's invalidity had reinforced the lesson that marriage could be hard and thankless work for a wife. She grew up to love men who were worldly-wise, generous and sensual. But she never equated romance with domesticity. One close friend who got to know her later in life thought that 'Harvey was one of the great loves of her life, if not the great love' but was 'not sure whether she would have married him had he been free ... she was very independent'.[37]

Women friends were precious to her. She remained close to Christine Hargreaves and to Una Collins, acting as named guardian to their daughters when they became mothers in the mid-1960s. Like the women of Ordsall, she was quite prepared to care for her friends and their children – relished doing so, in fact. And the value she placed on women's friendships was strengthened by her new life in London, and reinforced by her experience of motherhood. She had become part of a network of friends who were trying to find new ways to live independently of men, usually unmarried and sometimes as lone parents. Her first holiday after Charlotte's birth had been with two other young mothers: Jo Benson, a friend from Theatre Workshop, (Charlotte was given the middle name Jo after her) and her sister, Jane. They went to the Isle of Wight, 'manless', recalled Jane, which felt like an adventure in itself in 1964. The only blight was 'some young man who was in love with Shelagh ... He sent out a message on the ship's tannoy for Miss Delaney to meet him, which she ignored. She was very cross!'[38] Women on their own were still considered fair game, even with a baby in their arms.

The feminists of the 1970s and 80s would be caricatured as 'man-haters', who would only work with other women. In reality, their movement did not reinvent female friendship, but rather illuminated the primary role that it had historically played in forging communities, caring for the young and the old, and providing women with love and happiness. Some of Shelagh's own later work would contribute to this. But already by the mid-1960s, she had experienced how women in the two very different worlds she straddled – working-class Salford and London's arts scene – depended on each other to survive and thrive.

It was difficult to choose to be a single parent but Shelagh wasn't alone in thinking marriage more of a burden than motherhood. In 1965, twenty-nine-year-old Hannah Gavron, a married mother of two young children, completed a PhD at the London School of Economics on women's lives in contemporary Britain. She published her thesis as a book called *The*

*Captive Wife*. In between her carefully recorded statistics on how many women married under the age of twenty, and how many had babies by the age of twenty-five, Gavron noted the regrets and ambivalences experienced by women from all kinds of backgrounds. 'It's the dancing I miss,' one working-class young woman told her.[39] Gavron had her own regrets; she'd gone to RADA at sixteen, acting opposite Albert Finney, but she gave up her place to get married in the mid-1950s. In 1965 she left her husband to try and create a new life with her two children that involved work, motherhood, romance and independence.

Around the same time Margaret Drabble's marriage broke down and she found that, though traumatic, it was in one sense a liberation. 'I began to lead a slightly more independent life … the children had started school, and … I was doing exactly what I wanted which was writing novels.'[40] Women's lives were changing. By the mid-1960s many of those who'd found *A Taste of Honey* outrageous now judged it run-of-the-mill. Alan Dunsmore, the theatre critic who had dismissed *Honey* as 'sin' in Scotland's *People's Journal*, was somewhat embarrassed when, in 1966, Dundee Repertory staged the play and he discovered that 'I am quoted [on the programme] as saying that the show the last time was like "dustbin drama"'. Watching it for a second time, he conceded that 'it was certainly not all that offensive' – though this, he said, only proved that *Honey* was 'a somewhat dated tragedy'.[41]

Critics like Dunsmore acknowledged the world was changing, but they weren't going to give Shelagh any credit for it. It was true that political reformers were partly responsible. In 1964

Harold Wilson's Labour Party brought thirteen years of Conservative rule to an end. Labour was elected on a manifesto which declared that 'No nation in the history of human endeavour was ever inspired to become great with the venal philosophy of "I'm all right, Jack"'. Recognising that poverty and inequality had not been eradicated by the welfare state, Labour promised to replace 'squalid and over-crowded housing', and to abolish the eleven-plus examination.[42] By 1967, the government had asked local authorities to submit plans for comprehensive schools, abolished capital punishment, legalised abortion and decriminalised homosexuality between consenting adults over the age of twenty-one. From 1967 the NHS could prescribe the contraceptive pill to all women (it had been restricted to married women since its introduction in 1961). Forthcoming reforms were being discussed: in 1968 theatre censorship would end and the following year would see the age of majority reduced to eighteen and the introduction of blame-free divorce. Matters on which the state had previously taken a 'moral' stance were being redefined as matters of individual responsibility and choice. The ability to divorce and exert control over their bodies and sex lives clearly had huge implications for women.

The government was responding to change rather than initiating it. Wilson won in 1964, and increased Labour's majority in 1966, by tapping into a popular mood. Writers like Shelagh Delaney, and Tony Warren on *Coronation Street*, had revealed to huge audiences that poverty still existed in the Tories' 'never had it so good' Britain. Shelagh's own work questioned whether 'morality' in such matters as theatre censorship or abortion law wasn't really a smokescreen for snobbery and high-handedness. Away from the newspapers' moralising, increasing numbers of married women were combining motherhood with paid work, and even before the advent of the contraceptive pill they were limiting the size of their families. Two children was becoming the norm, allowing women of Shelagh's generation more time for activities other than childcare. And by the mid-1960s, more women were single mothers, either through choice or circumstance.

All the same, as Sheila Rowbotham observed, 'There are no easy answers to the question of how you live in a world you want to change radically.'[43] How to live independently as a mother posed a dilemma that plagued and even destroyed women's lives. In 1965 Hannah Gavron's PhD supervisor warned her she'd never get an academic job if she published her thesis and its message about women's discontent with marriage and motherhood. In December 1965 she gassed herself. Years later, her son Jeremy drew on friends' and relatives' reminiscences to piece together the reasons for her death. 'Hannah had a clear view of what was wrong with the world from a woman's point of view, what needed to be changed, and had experienced, too, in her work the difficulties of challenging the status quo,' he concluded. '[O]nce she had seen a different way of being, she could not accept living by the old ways'; but she could see no means of escape. 'That she died [was] not despite the life force, the character, that her friends remember, but because of it.'[44]

Life was different for men. In 1965 Albert Finney and Shelagh finally met when Lindsay Anderson showed Albert the script for Shelagh's anticipated sequel to *The White Bus*. By 1966 they were firm friends.[45] Albert had left his wife and child in 1960, telling a journalist that 'home-ties had a claustrophobic effect on him'. His subsequent relationships with women were 'based on my need for somewhere to eat and sleep which I have not wanted to provide for myself'. Shelagh did not want to spend her life providing that for a man. Stephen Frears, who got to know Shelagh in the late 1960s, remembered her as 'rather queenly ... except that she had this great sense of humour ... I seem to always recall her sitting or lying on sofas ... hysterical that these middle-class people were running around getting her cups of tea.'[46] She enjoyed being taken seriously as an artist and did not want to dissipate her energies caring for a man.

She wanted what Finney wanted for himself: 'to live my life alone, joining up occasionally with someone to share a particular experience. But it needn't be the same person all the time.'[47] By 1967, Shelagh and Albert were occasionally 'joining up' with each other. They took Charlotte on new charter flights whisking car workers, clerks, telephonists and engineers off on package holidays to Corfu and Mallorca. Shelagh and Albert escaped the crowds by renting villas in secluded villages; they spent their days swimming and sunbathing and their evenings gorging on olives, lamb and red wine. Shelagh loved the sheer difference and exoticism of Harvey Orkin: 'Americans are alien to me,' she said once; 'I like travelling in America because I feel like an alien. I don't like places where I feel at home.'[48] But Albert understood her past and this had attractions too. Like her, he'd left Salford at a young age and experienced fame quickly; they were both uneasy with being classified as angry young working-class artists (Albert was forever telling journalists that his father being a bookmaker made him practically middle class), and they were both, by the mid-1960s, trying to work out how to make a living outside the boxes that the media tried to fit them into.

In 1967, Shelagh suggested that they make a film based on their shared experiences. She showed Albert the outline of a script that she had hoped might be used in the second or third part of *Red, White and Blue*. '[I]t was really an outline, a document of about sixty pages,' Albert recalled. 'I responded very much to the character and situation; I felt I wanted to act it.' Shelagh's story followed a successful writer called Charlie on a weekend visit home to Manchester. Albert decided that not only did he want to act in this film, he would also direct it – a first for him, but 'I felt very strongly about the way the film should be treated'.[49] They called the film *Charlie Bubbles*.

Stephen Frears, who was Albert's assistant on the film, soon realised that it was 'a sort of joint autobiography'. Charlie personified the tensions that Shelagh and Albert knew so well. 'Are you still working, sir, or do you just do the writing now?' a waiter, an old friend of Charlie's father, asks Charlie as he serves him breakfast in his Manchester hotel room. Whether writing is 'proper' work clearly worries Charlie too – he isn't sure he deserves the good fortune it's brought him, and fears his luck will run out. Then there are the barriers that fame and fortune can create, epitomised by the airless private box from which Charlie and his son watch Manchester United, removed from the raucous terraces below. 'Shelagh Delaney and I have each had a period where that sort of isolation ... has happened to us,' Albert Finney told the *Guardian*.[50] But unlike John Braine's Joe Lampton, Charlie is not full of angst – he's out to have fun. He relishes being able to afford a swanky car, annoys the po-faced members of a private London club by initiating a food fight, and spends his money on a glamorous young secretary (played by Liza Minnelli) and every up-to-date gadget he can think of, including CCTV throughout his home. He has no idea what the future will bring, but he's got no interest in romanticising the past.

Shelagh hugely enjoyed the project. She and Albert quickly put together the cast and crew, and headed to Manchester to film much of it on location with Stephen Frears. All three of them were 'learning the trade, so to speak', and Shelagh proved invaluable in identifying the best locations and shots. Frears thought 'she was an artist ... sometimes, if you want to get a very tall building in [to a shot] you have to go a long way back. And I can remember her saying, "Oh, what you want is to turn the screen on its side."'[51] The effect was of buildings towering over people; a reminder that even fortunate people like Charlie found themselves in circumstances they could not fully control. Shelagh would use this visual aide repeatedly in later work like *Find Me First*, a 1979 television play which opened with two middle-aged women chasing each other around central Manchester, 'dwarfed by the massive office blocks and hotels that have ruined the city centre'.[52]

Although *Charlie Bubbles* drew on some of the experiences Shelagh shared with Finney, it also pointed to stark differences between the lives of women and men in the so-called 'swinging' sixties. For Charlie, being modern means having the latest consumer goods, but he's using his wealth to establish a traditional set-up. He wants to be the breadwinner and adventurer, keeping a wife and child in a country cottage, and employing a dolly bird secretary-cum-mistress. He's disconcerted when the women in his life want something different. Liza Minnelli's character has no intention of remaining a male fantasy: when Charlie gets her into bed, he discovers that her long black hair is a wig, which she removes as she pleases. She's got ambitions too: her work with Charlie is all fuel for her university dissertation.

Lottie, Charlie's estranged wife, played by Billie Whitelaw, is an even more radical character, who is thoroughly dissatisfied with domesticity. 'The back door was wide open,' Charlie remonstrates with her. 'You might have got a sex maniac.' 'Not with my luck,' Lottie replies. Desperate for a creative outlet she fills the kitchen cupboards with more home-made jam than anyone could ever eat. But she sees this as a poor second-best to having a real life; she's a devoted mother, but it isn't enough to fulfil her. She was, wrote Renata Adler, reviewing the film for the *New York Times*, 'one of the few warm, exhausted, believable women on screen'.[53]

Charlie eventually solves his dilemma over where he belongs by fleeing in a hot-air balloon (we're aware that Lottie, busy looking after their son, has no such escape route). It was an ending that baffled Film Finance's John Croydon, although he recommended that the company underwrite the film. 'It resolves nothing,' he said, and found Shelagh's directions incomprehensible. 'What do the last two sentences [of the script] mean? ... "general ballooning experiences" ... "appreciation of the silence"?'[54]

But she wasn't alone in finding endings difficult to write. The reviewer who'd once described *The Lion in Love* as 'completely formless, almost completely plotless'[55] had also complained that the hero of *Billy Liar* was 'allowed to dwindle into nothing more than a sad-eyed funny man', who fails to follow his dreams to London.[56] Few of the northern writers who'd found publishers in the past decade were able to resolve their work into neat and tidy conclusions. 'Formlessness is the great weakness of the New Trend,' commented T. C. Worsley (the same Worsley who'd suggested, in 1959, that there were quite enough working-class writers already without Shelagh Delaney).[57]

Worsley and his sympathisers missed the point. These writers were documenting an unprecedented generational change. The post-war children who wanted more than their working-class parents, but weren't prepared to settle for an office job and a suburban house, weren't sure what the future held. Sometimes they wondered whether they had a future at all. Albert Finney admitted that he and Shelagh had considered killing Charlie off, but '[t]he fact that Shelagh and I were writing about our experiences showed that there must be some possibility of survival … when Shelagh said, "I think he should go away in a balloon" it felt absolutely right for no known reason … the only answer to his dilemma is time'.[58] As the *New York Times* concluded, 'if the story is not to continue into infinity, there is simply no other way out'. The newspaper ranked it one of the top ten films of 1968, and the British Writers' Guild awarded Shelagh screenplay of the year.[59]

Shelagh was due to travel to the Cannes Film Festival to see how *Charlie Bubbles* fared, but the festival was cancelled due to the 'May Events' in France – general strikes and university occupations demanding an end to capitalism brought the country to a halt and almost toppled the government. In Britain, *Charlie Bubbles* spoke to the dilemma in which many young people found themselves in the late 1960s: upwardly mobile, unsure where they belonged, and feeling life should offer more than a mortgage, car and a nine-to-five job. Some of these young adults watched events in France with sympathetic excitement. They, too, began asserting that the ruling elite should meet their needs and desires, rather than expecting them to fit into the established order. University students – many of them the first in their families to enjoy higher education – protested for self-government on Britain's campuses. Factory workers went on strike for better pay and more control over their workplaces. Nurses, teachers and local government workers – the occupations in which many of the upwardly mobile found a niche – were rapidly unionising. Their demands for change extended beyond their home towns – in cities around the country thousands of students and workers marched against the Vietnam War. But their aims did not yet stretch to equality for women. In kitchens across Britain, mothers sat nursing babies, wives stood with their arms in the sink, and like Lottie Bubbles they wondered, in the words of Maureen Duffy's Paddy: what the hell do I do now?

# 10

# Dance with a Stranger

As the 1960s drew to a close, *A Taste of Honey* was back in the limelight. From being a precocious, immoral playwright, an angry young woman or washed-up writer, Shelagh now offered a standard against which other writers were judged. Penelope Gilliatt, theatre critic for the *Observer*, ridiculed the 'concocted' stereotypes into which most drama placed women. 'No wonder it is such an effort to remember the name of a single woman character in a modern English play since Jo in Shelagh Delaney's *A Taste of Honey*,' she complained.[1] When Studs Terkel, writing in the *New York Times*, wanted to praise Tony Parker's *People of the Streets* – a study of street life in contemporary London – he did so by likening one of his characters to 'Shelagh Delaney's heroine' Jo.[2]

By the late 1960s, the notion that women's lives deserved serious consideration by broadcasters and politicians was no longer groundbreaking. Ken Loach's 1966 *Wednesday Play*, *Cathy Come Home*, followed a homeless woman's struggle to keep her children out of care. He gave a name, a face and a voice to poverty – and made clear that women often bore the brunt of its hardships and indignities. But *Cathy Come Home* also asserted, as *A Taste of Honey* had done, that women were neither to blame for their circumstances nor passive victims of them. Cathy fought for her children, and was angry about her situation. Viewers recognised the truth in this. *Cathy Come Home* was watched by 12 million people, a quarter of Britain's population. After it was broadcast, the BBC switchboard was jammed with calls from people asking how they could help.

Women asserted their desire for more control over their lives. In 1968, female sewing machinists at the Ford Motor Company's Dagenham plant went on strike over the grading of their work, demanding their employer recognise their labour as skilled. Told their work was less valuable than that of men, they showed that without them the factory had to close down production. During their three weeks on the picket line, the Ford workers came to regard their grievances as caused by the sexism of their employers. Women at Ford and elsewhere began to advocate equal pay for men and women at a time when only teachers and civil servants were entitled to this. They had lived through a long period of near-full employment; women's trade union membership was higher than ever before; and more women were staying in work after marriage, and returning after having children. They demanded an equal share to negotiation and to the profits of their labour.

The Ford workers' dispute ended with the intervention of Barbara Castle, Secretary of State for Employment and Productivity, and was one of the causes of the 1970 Equal Pay Act. It also galvanised women trade unionists to found the National Joint Action Campaign Committee for Women's Equal

Rights in 1969. The thousands of women who attended the committee's first rally at Trafalgar Square that year were making history. Their demonstration would become known as the birth of the modern women's movement in Britain.

Many middle-class women were also taking stock of their lives. Among those who attended the rally at Trafalgar Square was Sheila Rowbotham, the twenty-six-year-old Oxford graduate, who was already active in socialist politics. 'Something is stirring,' she wrote in the left-wing newspaper *Black Dwarf,* 'something which has been silent for a long time.' She began attending one of the women's liberation groups that were mushrooming across the country – by the end of 1969 there were more than seventy in London alone. These groups of mainly middle-class women emphasised 'consciousness-raising'. Rowbotham's group 'spent several weeks talking about our personal experiences in childhood and adolescence', trying to make collective sense of the messages, morals and slights that had led so many of them to believe they were inferior to men, at the same time that they were being told they lived at a time of unprecedented opportunity.[3]

In 1970 the two strands of the women's movement came together for a conference in Oxford. The hundreds of women present agreed on four demands: equal pay, equal education and opportunity, twenty-four-hour nurseries, and free contraception and abortion on demand. The word 'demand' was crucial, making clear that they were not going to act like good girls, grateful for whatever men or the state bestowed upon them.

Working-class women who became involved in the women's movement were provoked by personal experience and their mothers' lives, but novels and plays often also played a role.

One of those who was inspired to join a women's group was Dee Johnson, born to millworkers in Oldham in 1948. In 1967 she had gone to teacher training college in Bradford. 'I wasn't confident academically. But then we studied Arnold Wesker's *Chicken Soup with Barley*, about working-class life in the 1930s … I knew about that … And I got an A.' For Dee, 'that was the turning point', when she began to feel entitled to critique the world in which she lived. Cultural influences like Wesker, and later *A Taste of Honey*, were vital; so too were older novels. 'I read *The Grapes of Wrath* … I remember crying with rage … I think my politics until then had been from a very emotional place. That was when I started thinking about governments, banks, structures and how all those things impact on ordinary people's lives, and how you had to organise to beat that.'

These cultural influences prompted Dee to examine her own and her mother's circumstances. 'My dad was very easy-going and happy with his lot. And I think my mum had more ambition … she had huge common sense but she'd never been able to get an education.' Dee knew that 'my life was full of opportunities they'd never had' but she was aware, too, that women were still circumscribed by their sex as well as their class; there'd been few options open to her other than teaching, and the encouragement she received from her college principal – 'a real feminist' – to take advantage of the newly available contraceptive pill was radical and brave. When she became a teacher in Oldham in the early 1970s, Dee joined 'a sort of feminist consciousness-raising group' – a reminder that the women's movement stretched far beyond north London. 'So many of the things we discussed in that group really chimed with me.' She came to believe, as Shelagh did, that 'the feminist movement has just as much to offer men as it has women, because men were locked in those roles, just like we were locked in those roles'.[4]

Most women, however, did not participate in the women's movement. And as the 1970s wore on, the movement itself became fragmented. But the demands which emerged at the 1970 Women's Liberation Conference sought to address problems that were very widely shared. Shelagh explored these problems in her work – though she remained more interested in how women struggled with them than in suggesting solutions. She was still one of very few writers to concern herself with ordinary women's lives, including their bodies, fantasies and sex lives. Her old friend Shirley Evans, now settled in Australia, read Germaine Greer's *The Female Eunuch* published in 1970. 'It reminded me of Shelagh,' she said. 'I think she was an early Germaine Greer.'[5]

By now, Shelagh was reaching a wider audience than she'd been able to before. In 1973 ITV invited her to write one of a series of plays with the overall title *The Seven Faces of Woman*. Hers, *St Martin's Summer*, was broadcast in 1974; it presented Nellie, a middle-aged television actress struggling to maintain her independence as she copes with divorce and being passed over in auditions for younger women. While Shelagh's main character was a woman, she made male prejudice her focus for the first time.

Meanwhile, *A Taste of Honey* was enjoying a new lease of life. Theatres were opening across Britain, benefiting from extra arts funding that had been injected by Wilson's Labour government in the late 1960s. Sheffield's Crucible opened in 1968, Leeds

Playhouse and the Newcastle Playhouse in 1970. Although Labour was defeated by Edward Heath's Conservatives in the general election of 1970, the Arts Council remained more receptive to provincial and experimental arts initiatives. Both commercial and community theatre groups sought to foster local talent and bring drama to a wider audience. Feminist theatre groups sprang up, determined to encourage new writing by women and bring existing work into the limelight. *A Taste of Honey* was in demand. When Glasgow Citizens' Theatre produced the play in 1970, the audience included a large party from the National Federation of Business and Professional Women's Clubs.[6] Shelagh's first play still spoke to the concerns of women from a wide range of backgrounds, trying to make their way in a changing world.

*A Taste of Honey* also reached a new generation of school students. Teachers had long recognised the play's capacity to appeal to working-class pupils. In the early 1960s, Eva Fulleylove taught English at a technical college to a class of 'mainly ex-secondary modern teenagers – average age sixteen'. In an attempt to banish their 'sense of academic inferiority, and a feeling of unimportance', Fulleylove encouraged them to undertake 'improvised scenes and acted play readings ... *The Diary of Anne Frank* and *A Taste of Honey* have been the most successful, and have provided food for discussion which lasted weeks.' She thought both girls and boys could relate to the play and its dialogue: 'the idiom is their own'.[7] By the early 1970s *A Taste of Honey* was a set text in many of the new comprehensive schools. Its performance at Glasgow Citizens' Theatre was watched by students from Albert Secondary

School, which served a working-class area of Glasgow, and eighty students from Dundee College of Commerce, who were studying the play in their English lessons.[8]

Shelagh was inundated with requests to appear in public, visit schools, and speak to the press. She declined almost all of them, being preoccupied with a personal life that was turbulent and sometimes traumatic. Charlotte was growing up to be a rebel – she'd inherited her mother's dislike of authority, though Shelagh allowed her a great deal of freedom. Her version of parenting mirrored the liberal practices advocated by the child-care expert Benjamin Spock, whose ideas about child-centred learning were becoming very popular with a certain section of the middle class. But Shelagh saw herself as simply giving her daughter the independence her own parents had granted her, albeit with more money and comfort. Daily life was more chaotic than it had been at Duchy Road, though: there were no set mealtimes or bedtimes because Shelagh found routine a bore. Her attitudes were riven with contradictions. While she hated structure in her domestic and working life, she thought schools should provide it. She removed Charlotte from the local primary school when she was ten and sent her to a private school where she hoped her daughter would learn more grammar and spelling – despite having previously told journalists that her own most inspiring teacher had been one who 'didn't harp so much as others on rigid English'.[9] Charlotte, however, hated school, even when Shelagh let her move to the local comprehensive her friends attended. Shelagh, who had herself played truant, sympathised with her daughter, and eventually gave up trying to persuade her to attend.

In 1975, Harvey Orkin died from brain cancer. He had moved back to New York in the late 1960s, but the bond between him and Shelagh remained strong. They continued to meet when she visited the States, and she kept him up to date with Charlotte in regular letters. But Shelagh's relationship with him was a closely guarded secret from his own family. They in turn had kept his diagnosis private, so news of his death was an immense shock to her. She felt acutely all the disadvantages of being the 'other' woman. In 1976, in a rare interview with the *Guardian*, she indicated that the preceding year had been hard for her: 'she doesn't want to talk about her private life beyond saying she's getting happier'.[10]

Shortly after Orkin's death, she agreed to write a six-part television series for the BBC, *The House That Jack Built*. The series dealt with a topic that Shelagh would return to over the next few years: how marriage and motherhood shaped a woman's life in a world where they apparently had unlimited choice about how to live. *A Taste of Honey* had dealt with unmarried motherhood at a time when single mothers were stigmatised and abortion illegal. In *The Lion in Love* she had focused on a marriage in trouble at a time when divorce was still difficult to obtain. Now women could get a divorce, decide not to have children, and increasing numbers of them were choosing to live outside marriage, singly, with friends, or cohabiting. Shelagh's television and radio plays of the late 1970s and early 1980s scrutinised how women made these choices and then lived with the consequences, often with humour and panache, like the childless Isobel in *Find Me First* (1979), or the eponymous heroine of *Don't Worry About*

*Mathilda* (1983), who despite being single and unemployed is far happier than her harassed, respectably married and mortgaged brother.

But in her first, and, as it turned out, only, television series, Shelagh dealt with married life. *The House That Jack Built* was broadcast in thirty-minute episodes on BBC1 in 1977. Shelagh then adapted it for the stage, at the request of Will Macadam, who had remained a fan of *A Taste of Honey* and was by now an established actor and director. His production appeared at New York's Cubiculo Theatre in 1979.

*The House That Jack Built* follows Jack and Lu through their first ten years of marriage, from their first day as newly-weds in a terraced house in a northern town to parenthood on a suburban estate. Describing Jack and Lu as 'a cowboy and a madonna', Shelagh made clear that she thought marriage necessitated sacrifices by both men and women. Whether these were worth it was a question she left her audience to answer. She based Jack on her younger brother, Joe. 'My brother in Manchester is a cowboy' – he was married and a father by now, but had never adjusted to domesticity and monogamy, and she thought many men didn't. Women, on whom the pressure to adjust was greater, also had the more difficult time. 'Aren't all women madonnas if they are married and have children?' she rhetorically asked an interviewer. She was making the point that living outside marriage was still hard for women, in a society that saw marriage and motherhood as the pinnacle of feminine fulfilment.[11] But the 'madonna' figure was also ironic – as Lu shows, wives were judged harshly if they didn't conform to the self-abnegation demanded of them.

Shelagh's men were fantasists who achieved little, while her female characters were realists who wanted to change the world. She'd explored that in her early work, but now she went further, by suggesting that domestic comforts blunted men's capacity to act. Her brother Joe had aspirations to be a writer; his letters to her were long and funny, and he'd written at least one play, as June, his wife, told Shelagh: 'I had nothing to do last night so I knitted a white cardigan for Charlotte ... Joe's been typing a letter to you for about two hours. I typed a play on Monday for him – that doesn't mean he'll send it to you. He said it's not quite long enough – still, I am glad he's trying.'[12] Shelagh never saw his play and neither did anyone else.

Women, still bearing the brunt of the chores, had fewer but more urgent hopes. '[T]here's the difference between us,' Lu tells Jack. 'You have these exciting notions and dreams but when it comes to the crunch you never actually do anything about them ... I admit my visions are a bit thin on the ground but when something does take my fancy I like to see it develop.'[13]

Shelagh also made clear that class shaped women's lives quite as much as their sex. When Lu leaves Jack she can only afford to move back in with her mother. She eventually returns to him, 'out of pity' for his inability to look after himself, and because she's realised that she can't keep herself and her children.[14]

Three radio plays; a stage play; a handful of television broadcasts. Some thought Shelagh should have produced more since *Charlie Bubbles*, that the 1970s could have been her decade. 'I tend to be lazy,' she'd told a journalist in 1960. Ten years later, Lindsay Anderson concurred. 'I think she is a beautiful writer, very poetic and personal,' he wrote to the playwright Alan Brown, 'but she finds it difficult to turn the stuff out (apart from anything else, she is very lazy).'[15] She never worked unless she had to. Feminists demanded equal opportunities for work, but Shelagh wanted leisure, too. It had, after all, been the privilege of the upper class for generations; now it was the turn of those whose parents had worked so hard in the 1930s, then fought and died in the war. As Albert Finney said of his decision to spend a year seeing the world in 1965, 'I didn't want to go on being *supposed* to do things, *obliged* to do things.'[16] This was their riposte to all those who'd suggested in their youth that they must be endlessly grateful for every chance, and work tirelessly hard to show themselves worthy of their opportunities.

Shelagh relished spending time in the United States – the perfect country for leisure as far as she was concerned. She and Charlotte spent entire summers at the summer house that Gerry Feil and his wife Hila had bought near the town of Wellfleet on Cape Cod. 'We would write in the mornings, then we'd take off for the beach in the afternoons,' recalled Hila Feil, also a writer. 'At least that was the plan!' Often, Shelagh was tempted away from work to play with Charlotte, read the American magazines she loved, or drive to the local Dairy Queen – an ice-cream and fast-food diner – in the big American car she bought.[17] In the afternoons, she and Charlotte would join Hila for a few hours at Long Pond, the tree-lined lake bordered by a sandy beach where Wellfleet's children and mothers whiled away the summer. 'Shelagh and I made up an entire screenplay on that beach, based on a female private eye called Melon Smoothy,' said Hila. 'We both loved making up names, and

Melon Smoothy I suppose was resonant of those milkshakes that Shelagh would consume in the Dairy Queen.'[18]

In 1975, Hila's novel for children, *The Ghost Garden*, drew evocatively on those summers on the Cape. '[I]f you were to imagine a perfect New England town, you would have imagined ... Wellfleet,' observes the story's young heroine, Jessica, though she quickly realises it is one inhabited by 'hippies' and candle shops. Her first day in town includes a trip to Long Pond. 'A crowd of people filled the tiny beach ... Whatever space they didn't occupy themselves was taken up with beach chairs, blankets, plastic rafts, large inflatable toys, umbrellas and picnic baskets ... Slightly apart from everyone else were two very tall women. As Jessica passed, one of them was saying, "I think the heroine of our movie should be called Melon Smoothy."'[19] In a rare interview in 1976 Shelagh reported that she was spending 'the summer in New England, writing a commissioned novel ... But I don't know if I'll be seduced by the fleshpots of Cape Cod away from my Parker pen.'[20] The novel never appeared.

But her love of leisure wasn't the only explanation of her working routine – or lack of it. 'One of the reasons that Shelagh didn't work more is that she was being a mother,' said Will Macadam, who got to know her well in the 1970s. 'With film, and with the stage, you give it a hundred per cent. You've only got a certain amount of concentrated time to bring a production together. Shelagh could only allow herself to do that every so often.' She was determined to bring up her child herself and the bond she forged with Charlotte was to lead to a lifelong, loving relationship that was precious to both of them. But being a single mother took time and energy. In 1976, a journalist turned up at Gerrard Road only to be cajoled into chauffeuring Shelagh to collect twelve-year-old Charlotte, who had 'run off by herself from Islington to Crayford, Essex, to see a boyfriend … Mum runs the gamut of parental concern … "How could she go off without telling me? I'll throttle her." Then, "Poor little thing. She'll be scared to come home by herself."'[21] She was, says her daughter 'very aware of being the only parent; having to do everything. She couldn't ever really be the bad cop because she had to be the loving one, always; there was no one else.'[22]

Friends provided essential support. Long letters passed between Shelagh and the Feils during the winter months. 'We miss you! Any chance of your coming over soon?' they wrote to her at Christmas 1970.[23] Una Collins remained close to Shelagh, though she had accepted a post at Iceland's National Theatre in the late 1960s, and by the mid-1970s was living in Wales. Her daughter, Sophie, was a regular visitor to Gerrard Road. So too was Christine Hargreaves. In 1978 she took the lead in Jim Allen's television play *Spongers* about a single mother's struggle with welfare cuts. Shelagh also had long-term lodgers, often female friends from Theatre Workshop days like the actress Myfanwy Jenn.

While most of Shelagh's neighbours in Gerrard Road were still the working-class families she'd got to know when she first moved in, her domestic set-up was no longer as unusual as it had been ten years earlier. '[T]he majority of the hundreds of women I encountered … lived in some form of shared housing,' wrote Lynne Segal of the 1970s. A feminist university lecturer, Segal was living in her own shared house just a few streets away from Shelagh. '[C]ollective living was … not just a more economical arrangement … but one which could encourage more open, supportive and creatively shared forms of companionship, domesticity, childcare, political work and community engagement.'[24]

For some women like Segal, collective living was a refreshing alternative to the conservative, middle-class nuclear families in which they'd been brought up. But for Shelagh, this way of life sustained the kind of community she'd enjoyed as a young child, and which, by the 1960s, her mother had re-established at Duchy Road. 'When we visited Salford, there were kids everywhere, knocking at the door asking if I'd come out to play; neighbours might pop in, or you'd stop to chat with them when you went shopping,' recalled Charlotte. 'Having that kind of community was always important to her' – though she relished being able to shut herself away from everyone in her study or her bedroom. In her later work, Shelagh would repeatedly return to the strength and importance of women's friendship; those who lacked this, like Ruth Ellis in *Dance with a Stranger*, were always incredibly vulnerable, whether or not they had a man on their arm.

Her daughter and her friends were the mainstay of her everyday life, but romance was her escape from it. She wanted lovers to woo her with flowers, chocolates and telegrams; to whisk her off on weekends abroad, and to make her laugh. His ability to do all these things sustained the long relationship she enjoyed with the architect Cedric Price, to whom she was particularly close during the 1970s. She'd met Price through Joan Littlewood – he designed Joan's 'Fun Palace', which combined an arts centre, amusement park and an open university. Never built, Price's design did influence the Georges Pompidou Centre in Paris. Like Shelagh, Cedric thought education and culture were unjustifiably restricted in post-war Britain. 'Education, if it is to be a continuous human service run by the community[,] must be provided with the same lack of peculiarity as the supply of drinking water or free teeth,' he'd declared in 1964.[25] He shared Shelagh's dislike of the middle-class gentrifiers moving into Islington in growing numbers, determined to 'conserve' their Georgian houses against council plans to replace them with flats for the borough's overcrowded residents. But he was also impatient with the grim functionalism that Shelagh had despaired of in Salford; he thought communities should be designed around parks, open spaces, playgrounds – and fun. He was practical and happy to help – in 1974 he designed a modish basement conversion for Shelagh. To Charlotte 'he was the nearest I had to a father figure', taking her on architectural tours of London and sending her cartoons and postcards, and invariably adding 'love to C also *of course*' on the back of his letters to Shelagh.[26] But it was his love of spontaneity – whisking Shelagh off for a weekend in Paris; sending her telegrams proposing an imminent rendezvous for dinner, drinks or sex – that most appealed. So did his absolute acceptance that she was a serious writer and deservedly famous. 'Last evening I was in Mr Thomas' Famous Chop House and this barmaid was humming [the Beatles' song] "A Taste of Honey",' he wrote to her in 1973, 'and it seemed daft for me to be alone in Manchester and not having seen you for so long.'[27]

This kind of relationship had its strains. Cedric had two other commitments on his time: he was a workaholic, and lived with someone else. He would disappear for days into his domestic life, or vanish on a work trip for weeks at a time. Clearly this distressed Shelagh: 'as I've said before, I'll never desert you', he wrote to her in the early 1970s; 'I'm sorry I'm such a shit.'[28] And he did not like it if Shelagh reciprocated in kind. If she buried herself in work, or took a short holiday without telling him, she'd provoke a spate of telegrams, demanding she contact him – sometimes she enjoyed the attention but often she felt smothered and aggrieved. Every now and then one of them would break it off. 'I must make up my mind what I want to do as I seem to be causing you a half-life while wallowing in [a whole] one myself,' Cedric wrote to her on one occasion.[29] But a week later he was writing 'happiness is hearing from you – however undeserved'.[30] Shelagh's own frustration and jealousy were kept at bay by her conviction that marriage, even monogamy, could kill the passion and excitement she wanted from her relationships. She rebelled against the conservative fifties; but she was also entranced by the fifties dream of being swept off your feet by romance. She and Cedric went on exchanging Valentines until the end of his life in 2003.[31]

In 1978 Shelagh turned forty. She still relished her independence, but she was reflective about the loneliness and difficulties that this could cause women as they grew older. Mary Ingham, a graduate journalist from a middle-class background, turned thirty in the same year. She'd spent her twenties living in squats and shared houses, experimenting with women-only living spaces and activist groups, taking work she enjoyed or that fitted her politics. Then, 'my brother and I helped my parents move into a tiny flat in a modern communal block. Later, in my brother's car, I confided that it had shaken me to the core. I'd gaily discarded mortgages and security because in the back of my mind I was still in my father's protection ... there was still the home which reminded me of all the comforting protectiveness I'd grown up with and from which I'd felt free to roam.'[32]

Shelagh's life was very different to Mary Ingham's. She had been financially independent from an early age and she was ten years older. But like Ingham, she felt the late 1970s marked the beginning of a different life stage. And yet again, she was entering uncharted territory for an independent woman of her generation. In 1979 her radio play *So Said the Nightingale* explored the choices and regrets that faced older women keen to broaden their horizons. Alice, a middle-aged woman who has spent twenty years looking after her father, receives a proposal of marriage after his death. She's tempted to accept her suitor, Joe, who has courted her since they met at a dance years earlier: 'We could shake a leg together for the next twenty years if you were only willing,' he says. 'It's a high price to pay for a dance,' Alice replies.[33] In the end, she splurges her small inheritance on travelling the world.

When *The House That Jack Built* appeared on the New York stage in 1979, Shelagh was there to see it. The production brought her to the attention of a new generation of American feminists, who were, like their British counterparts, questioning whether monogamy, and even heterosexuality, could fulfil women. Shelagh had had no interest in women's consciousness-raising groups back home, many of which were located in the gentrified London neighbourhoods she disliked. But in New

York, Hila Feil observed that 'she got some new friends around this time'. They were radical feminists, some of them lesbians, who were involved in street protests and squats.

This group made an impression on Shelagh. On her return to London, she mused over whether she was bisexual. In the early 1980s she made friends with Zdena Tomin, who was now a dissident writer living in London. They were introduced by a television producer, a woman, with whom Zdena believed Shelagh 'was having some sort of relationship for a while'.[34] 'She was always sexually attracted to men,' says Charlotte, 'but she found women sensual and sympathetic.' Her conversations about such matters were limited to a few close women friends and, later, to her daughter. Unlike the members of London's consciousness-raising groups, or her American feminist friends, Shelagh did not think explicit talk of sex was liberating. 'She was fiercely private,' thought Zdena, and other friends agreed. She had grown up knowing that women's sex lives, while rarely openly talked about, were a matter for public censoriousness and titivation – evidenced by the media's treatment of her, quite as much as by Salford's unmarried mothers' homes and brothels. The ability to keep her sex life private was a sign of progress. And, as a romantic, she also wondered if long discussions mightn't extinguish the spontaneity and passion she valued so much in her love affairs.

In 1980 came one of the biggest challenges in her career, with a chance to reflect on what had changed in women's lives since her debut as a playwright – and what had not. The film producer Roger Randall-Cutler asked her to write a screenplay based on the life of Ruth Ellis, who in 1955 had murdered her sometime lover, David Blakely, and became the last woman to be executed in Britain. 'I was not immediately seduced by this idea,' she wrote in the *New York Times*, 'but I listened to what he had to say, and a bottle of whisky later I left his office carrying a large, glossy red folder ... I was just being polite ... It wasn't my style. It was too difficult. And it was dangerous. After all, Ruth Ellis was real and hitherto I had only dealt, professionally at least, with figments of my imagination.'[35]

But when she read the file Randall-Cutler had handed her she was gripped. She discovered that Ruth Ellis was a working-class woman from Wales who, at seventeen, had given birth to an illegitimate son, Andy. That was in 1945. At war's end, she had decided to take her chance in London, and there she became a nightclub hostess. After a short-lived marriage to a dentist who turned out to be a violent alcoholic, she became manager of the Little Club. It was there she met David Blakely, a motor-racing driver who became her lover. He turned out to be 'a promiscuous, alcoholic woman beater'. At the same time, Ruth was having an affair with Desmond Cussen, a prosperous businessman, who offered a home to her and her son. But she was obsessed with David, who oscillated between being violently possessive and breaking off their relationship. In April 1955 he beat her up, causing her to miscarry. Blakely's friends urged him to throw Ruth over, believing she 'tried to force her way into a higher class of society than she was fit for'.[36] In May 1955 Ruth sought out Blakely at a pub where he drank with his upper-class friends, and shot him dead. She was executed two months later.

Ruth Ellis's story appealed to Shelagh. She was a reminder of a society that 'couldn't take her feelings seriously. She was the kind of woman who "got what she deserved," "asked for it," "should have known better" or would always "land on her feet and come up smiling".'[37] Exactly how some of Shelagh's critics had interpreted Helen in *A Taste of Honey*.

In 1985, Shelagh's riposte to this version of the 1950s had particular resonance. Margaret Thatcher's Conservative Party had won the election of 1979, and had increased their majority in 1983. Britain's first female prime minister proudly called herself the nation's housewife, and her government championed family, the monarchy, hierarchy and tradition over the vulnerable and needy – just as its predecessors had done in Shelagh's youth. Mike Newell, who directed *Dance with a Stranger*, agreed with Shelagh's interpretation. 'Things ought to have been better after the war but they weren't and this led to a pre-war morality and the age of the Ideal Home Exhibition,' he said. '[H]ere was this woman flaunting her sexuality at a time when you did not do that kind of thing.'[38]

The project was, Shelagh told Charlotte, 'the hardest and most worthwhile writing I've ever done'. Although Ruth Ellis's life appeared to be far less like Shelagh's than some of the female characters she had created over the years, this was the project that felt most autobiographical to her. Shelagh 'looked for [Ruth] within myself and other people as relentlessly as she looked for David Blakely the Easter weekend she killed him'. Ruth's oscillation between her desire for passion and excitement, and her wish to give herself, and her son, peace and security, was a dilemma Shelagh understood well. She represented Ruth Ellis as a woman who could not settle for Desmond Cussen, despite his love for her and desire to help, because to do so would be to relinquish her independence of spirit. 'You'll kill me with kindness,' Ruth tells him in Shelagh's script (presciently, since he gives her the gun with which she murders Blakely). Although Blakely rashly proposes to Ruth more than once, Ruth is unsure about relinquishing her independence for him, too. She is continually drawn back to Blakely because their relationship arouses a 'love and ambition' that she hopes could be the foundation for a new life – but she has no way of working out what form that life might take, or making it happen.[39] Like Hannah Gavron, the young academic who committed suicide in 1965, Ruth realises that, having glimpsed a different life, she cannot settle for marriage with Desmond Cussen, or David Blakely, or anyone else. The tragedy, as Shelagh demonstrates, is that she is powerless to create a happy ending for herself. And, without the friendship or love that Jo and Helen in *Honey* or Kit in *Lion* are able to grasp, she is also unable to survive.

Shelagh had to grapple with how best to portray Ruth Ellis, at a time when Ellis and Blakely still had living relatives and friends, and in a story that centred on sexual passion. Intensely private herself, she found writing about sex particularly hard. 'There were times when I thought that the sex should be much tougher, more highly coloured,' recalled Mike Newell. 'I remember one scene ... quite late on. Ruth brings David back one evening when Desmond is out ... they then have sex on the floor in Desmond's flat. We needed a last line. And I said, "Well, what she should say is, 'Come on then if you're going to.'" And I looked up and Shelagh had blushed.'

She told the *New York Times* that the story 'aroused my fear. I didn't think I could write about these people and the lost domain they'd inhabited – postwar London, drinking clubs, motor racing.'[40] Despite the oft-repeated claim – made by Shelagh as well as others – that she was lazy, she was always scrupulous and exacting in her treatment of her characters, fictional or otherwise. She determined that her story of Ruth Ellis would be fairer than the myth of a neurotic social climber, but doing so meant meticulous preparation. Charlotte, who helped Shelagh with typing and research, recalled that 'she did an enormous amount of research, on the music, the newspaper coverage of the case, Soho, motor racing. It exhausted her.' Once again her flair for dialogue was her key strength. 'What I noticed about it was that she had an ear, she really heard things,' said Newell of her first draft. 'Much of what she wrote in that draft made it into the final version ... The most important thing was what Ruth sounded like and Shelagh had that right from the beginning ... that head tossing, pert, confrontational creature whose sexuality was right on the surface.'

Shelagh showed Ruth to be a woman trapped by circumstances. One of the few choices she could make was to 'reject the other career options ... open to her – i.e., shop, office or factory floor' in search of a new life 'in the night clubs and drinking clubs that were booming in postwar Britain'. For Shelagh, this aspect of Ruth's story had a great deal of personal resonance. In 1984 her oldest friend, Christine Hargreaves, died of a brain haemorrhage. They had had to defy notions of 'respectable' behaviour to achieve their dreams, just as Ruth Ellis did. Shelagh learned that at Ruth's trial the prosecution had implied she was a cheap tart – reminiscent of some of Shelagh's treatment at the hands of the press. Shelagh showed how blonde hair dye, designer clothes, the latest records and her ability to dance were the only tools Ruth had to fashion a life of adventure and love. She traced Ruth's struggle to create a new life for herself, only to be sneered at for trying to do so by David Blakely and his friends, and ultimately treated by the press and the courts as a scarlet woman who'd got her just deserts. 'The story is about the ordinariness of ordinary people,' Shelagh wrote, 'and that in itself can be an extraordinary thing.'[41]

*Dance with a Stranger* was an immediate hit that seemed destined to open up new opportunities for Shelagh. Amanda Schiff, who was working for the National Film Development Foundation, which helped to secure funding for the film, thought it 'didn't feel like a British film, it had that great continental, European quality, because it's about passion and folly'.[42] The *New York Times* praised her 'tough, lean' writing.[43] In 1985 she was elected a Fellow of the Royal Society of Literature – 'That's the award that means most to me,' she told her daughter. She finally felt that she was accepted as a professional writer.

Shelagh and her work were being discovered by a new generation. Mike Newell was stunned to see 'young women out and about around London, looking like Miranda [Richardson] done up as Ruth ... Boots brought out a range of cosmetics to cater for them.' By the time the film appeared she was already becoming familiar to the teenagers and students listening to a new band who'd come out of Manchester. Their singer-songwriter Morrissey said they were called the Smiths because 'it was the most ordinary name and I thought it was time that the ordinary folk of the world showed their faces'.[44] Thatcherite

Relaxing by the fire at Duchy Road, where Shelagh continued to live despite the lure of London

Rita Tushingham as Jo and Murray Melvin as Geoff in Tony Richardson's film adaptation of *A Taste of Honey* (1961)

Celebrating her twenty-first birthday in Salford, 25 November 1959. She was thrilled to finally come of age: 'I've never liked being told what to do'

Shelagh at a Campaign for Nuclear Disarmament demonstration in Trafalgar Square, London, 17 November 1961, talking to actress Vanessa Redgrave. In front of them is the playwright John Osborne. They marched under the Royal Court Theatre's banner

Shelagh at the sit-down protest against nuclear weapons in Trafalgar Square, 17 November 1961, next to jazz musician George Melly and Vanessa Redgrave, and behind John Osborne and the writer Doris Lessing

Shelagh in London *c.*1962, shortly after returning from one of her increasingly frequent trips to the United States

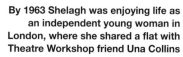

By 1963 Shelagh was enjoying life as an independent young woman in London, where she shared a flat with Theatre Workshop friend Una Collins

Shelagh with producer and ally Wolf Mankowitz prior to the Manchester première of her new play, *The Lion in Love*, September 1963

Shelagh in April 1963, shortly before the publication of her collection of short stories, *Sweetly Sings the Donkey*, which the *New York Times* praised for their 'startling clarity and direct appeal'

Shelagh warily comes to the door of her London flat in 1964, just weeks after the birth of her daughter, Charlotte, which provoked a press furore

Shelagh wrote the screenplay for *Charlie Bubbles* (1968), the only film directed by her friend Albert Finney, who starred in the film alongside Liza Minnelli

Shelagh and Charlotte *c*.1966

Shelagh and her daughter Charlotte, *c*.1970, in a photo booth in London. She brought Charlotte up to relish freedom, having won this for herself with *A Taste of Honey*

Rupert Everett and Miranda Richardson in *Dance with a Stranger* (1985), for which Shelagh wrote the screenplay: 'The hardest and most worthwhile writing I've ever done'

Many summers in the late 1960s and throughout the 1970s were spent on Cape Cod, where writing proved far less tempting than soaking up the sun or going to a drive-in movie

Shelagh writing at home in Gerrard Road, Islington, c.1988. She always did things her way – and avoided photographs for most of her adult life. Being doorstepped by the press in her teens and early twenties meant she fiercely guarded her privacy

politicians castigated single mothers for their irresponsibility, dole claimants for being dependent on the state, and the striking miners of 1984 as the enemy within. At the end of 1984, the Smiths' record 'Reel Around the Fountain', which borrowed heavily from *A Taste of Honey*, quickly became a hit. In 1986, Morrissey, himself from Stretford, just a few miles from Salford, told the *New Musical Express* that 'at least 50 percent of my reason for writing can be blamed on Shelagh Delaney'.[45] His lyrics continued to borrow from, and be inspired by, dialogue and characters in *A Taste of Honey* and *The Lion in Love*.

Shelagh herself was ready for a new challenge: 'after this', she wrote of *Dance with a Stranger*, 'anything will be easy'.[46] But circumstances were against her. Aside from soap operas, which had never appealed to Shelagh, working-class women had never been a popular subject for television, and in the 1980s they faded into the background. On TV and in the cinema, costume dramas became popular, Merchant Ivory's nostalgic take on a past peopled entirely by the upper and middle classes setting the tone. Television dramas like *Boys from the Blackstuff* and *Auf Wiedersehen, Pet* offered refreshing ripostes, but they almost always focused on working-class men.

Those invitations to write that Shelagh did receive tended to fall apart. The Conservative governments of the 1980s and 90s slashed arts budgets, and declared that artists would, like everyone else, have to adopt a more commercial outlook. Gone were the days of Film Finance, when Albert Finney and Shelagh could make a risky film like *Charlie Bubbles*. Shelagh couldn't tolerate tailoring her scripts to appeal to corporate sponsors – 'She walked out of at least one project because she was expected

to go to a marketing meeting before the script was even written,'
Charlotte recalled. Writers were increasingly expected to help
pitch the idea of a film by writing a treatment or synopsis.
'Many writers disliked doing that ... but Shelagh just couldn't,'
remembered Amanda Schiff. 'She would need to inhabit the
project before [she wrote a treatment] ... she probably would
have felt it was dishonest to write it [beforehand].' Zdena Tomin
thought this was too sharp a contrast from Shelagh's early
experiences in film. 'She had been used to being feted, in her
youth, and now she was asked to justify her ideas by writing
synopses. And she wouldn't do it.'

In 1988 she turned fifty. Charlotte was grown up, and Shelagh
had more freedom; but the world had changed in ways that
she found difficult to negotiate. Women were no longer expected
to choose between marriage and a career. In 1987 Charlotte
had become a single mother. Her son attended a nursery where
lone parents, and working mothers, were not exceptional. But
Thatcherite Britain had also corroded the promise of Shelagh's
early adulthood. Women were told by the media and by politicians that they could 'have it all' – which meant juggling long
hours in work with caring for their children. The debates among
feminists of the 1970s about how to share out childcare and
work more equitably, by supporting more cooperative ways of
living and working, seemed to belong to a different era. Shelagh's
relaxed admission that she only worked when she needed to,
that she enjoyed her leisure, were out of place in the frenetic
1980s, where those lucky enough to have a job were expected
to work ever harder to keep it, while the government cut away
the welfare safety net. The arts were a luxury.

With no projects in train, Shelagh found herself short of money. It wasn't a good time to feel the pinch: she was sharing her home with Charlotte and Max, her grandson; the house badly needed repair, and the days when she'd been able to find a plumber or decorator among her neighbours were dwindling. Shelagh's eclectic community in Islington had always included cleaners and bricklayers, market traders and actors down on their luck, musicians passing through and Londoners who'd lived there for generations. But now 'Islington was becoming full of yuppies, making money in finance, and Shelagh hated it', Zdena recalled. She'd also had one of her intermittent fall-outs with her agent, Tessa Sayle, which meant that she'd had to take charge of her own financial affairs. Shelagh's idea of accounting was to shove unopened bills and receipts into a drawer. Increasingly urgent letters from the Inland Revenue arrived at Gerrard Road.

Shelagh responded as she always did in a crisis. She escaped, determined to find peace and fun elsewhere. In 1988 she bought a tiny two-up two-down cottage in Muston, a village on the outskirts of Filey in Yorkshire. 'It is a bit like the Blackpool of my youth,' she wrote to Hila Feil.[47] Leaving Charlotte to look after her London home, she began to spend long periods there. Like many older women, she wanted to live independently, but with the support of family and friends when she needed them. 'Gerrard Road was a bit too much for her,' said Zdena, to whom she grew close in these years. 'She loved young people, but she had to have her own space.'

By the 1990s, London was also too expensive for her dwindling savings. A few new projects came her way – most notably when Roger Randall-Cutler asked her to adapt Jennifer Jones's novel *The Railway Station Man* into a television film. Broadcast in 1992, it starred Julie Christie and Donald Sutherland – 'I thought I would melt, even before he opened his mouth,' Shelagh told Charlotte after meeting Sutherland for dinner.[48] The timing was excellent from a personal point of view, since it allowed her to be in London while Charlotte prepared for the arrival of her second child, Gable, in 1992. But other invitations she accepted – a film adaptation of Margaret Forster's novel *The Battle for Christabel*, and a screenplay based on Jessica Mitford's autobiography *Hons and Rebels* – failed to turn into paid work, as film and television producers struggled to secure funding in the recession of the 1990s.

In her late fifties, without any new projects to bring her to London, she spent most of her time in Muston. She told Zdena that 'she found winter evenings hard', but new friendships helped. Her friends in Filey, Shelagh wrote shortly after her sixtieth birthday, were, like her, intent on growing older disgracefully. 'We are united by the fellowship of the bottle as we are all fond of a tipple or two,' she said of her next-door neighbours, Wilf and Sheila Wade.[49] She was recreating the kind of community she remembered from Ordsall, and had fostered in Gerrard Road.

These neighbours, like her friend Kath Wilkie who hailed from Manchester, and Zdena Tomin, weren't just the same age as Shelagh, but came from provincial working-class or lower-middle-class backgrounds. Wilf and Sheila were from Leeds; Zdena had grown up in post-war Czechoslovakia 'but the parallels were there. We swapped stories and discovered how terribly similar our countries were, even though [Czechoslovakia] was a Communist country ... The grinding poverty; the desire to get out of it. We both laughed at how we finally became middle class without ever wanting to. But you just had to get out of it.' The ability to share childhood memories and jokes without needing to explain herself was vital to Shelagh, and not something she could ever completely find among the London theatre set. Kath and Shelagh would share 'fish and chips on the front at Filey, straight from the newspaper, and giggle about stuff we'd found funny in our childhood – the comic characters, the songs we'd sing'. That kind of companionship was increasingly important as some of those closest to her died in the early 2000s: her mother, her brother Joe and Una Collins. 'They are so kind,' wrote Shelagh of Wilf, Sheila and Kath.[50]

They were also loyal, and she knew she did not need to worry that they'd pass on her whereabouts or her memories to the journalists who still sporadically tried to find her. She liked knowing she'd lived a colourful life, but it was private. 'I'd have enjoyed having a few secrets in my life,' says Nina in Shelagh's radio play *Baloney Said Salome*. 'No illegitimate children. No perverted sexual habits. I've never even smoked.'[51] Shelagh, meanwhile, was sampling marijuana for the first time in years.[52] Unshockable, she was adored by her three grandchildren, Max, Gable and Rosa – born in 2001. But she also liked spending time alone, as long as she knew she had her friends nearby; she wrote in the evenings and then listened to late-night chat shows on the local radio station; her love of dialogue, and her fascination with people's stories, endured.[53] The ties to the past made Muston feel like home, but she was deeply interested in the present.

In the late 1990s she was presented with a new line of work. Polly Thomas, a BBC Radio producer, contacted Shelagh to ask if she might be interested in adapting *Sweetly Sings the Donkey* for radio. Shelagh agreed. Polly 'was totally overexcited, because I'd read *Taste of Honey* years ago, and I just thought it was one of the most breathtaking plays I'd ever read'. She and Shelagh got on well: 'she was lovely, very down to earth, very pragmatic'.[54] Between 1997 and 2010, Shelagh wrote five plays. They included a trilogy that spanned the lives of women of her generation: *Sweetly Sings the Donkey* (2000), set in a children's convalescent home in the 1950s; *Tell Me a Film* (2002), which reunites the women at sixty, and *Baloney Said Salome* (2004) when the women are sixty-five. 'She was very quirky about the leaps that she made in their lives,' said Barbara Marten, who acted in the latter two plays.[55] Just as in 1963 Shelagh had chosen to take an episodic approach to autobiography, so she did again in these plays. Her selection suggested that the conventional milestones in women's lives – marriage, motherhood – were not the only ones. In her plays, childhood and older age allow women a freedom and perspective denied to them in the frenetic round of work and childcare that occupies younger women and the middle-aged.

'Radio is the best fun as far as I am concerned,' Shelagh told Hila Feil by email – she finally mastered the art in 2000 to keep in contact with her old American friends. There was more certainty that what you wrote would actually be broadcast, and once in the studio 'you have the minimum time to do it' – helpful for a woman who got bored quickly and needed strict deadlines.[56] Music, always important in her work, took on a new significance in the radio plays; Shelagh drew on her own youth of rock and roll and jazz, but also brought in more recent music including garage and funk. 'The music always got a really strong, positive audience response,' recalled Polly Thomas. 'I was like, "Shelagh, how do you know this stuff?" She said, "Well, I'm an insomniac, and I just listen to anything." Her musical knowledge was phenomenal.' She wanted to keep up to date, and try her hand at new projects. At one point the BBC asked her if she would write a modern-day *Taste of Honey*. '"I can't,"' she told Polly. '"I wouldn't know what those people would say now." And yet it would've been so easy for her to just have turned that out. She was always being asked that. But she ... wouldn't ... because it wasn't honest.'[57]

Her plays were once again forging a feminist perspective on a subject neglected by both politicians and the media: in this case, ageing women. Shelagh drew on her personal experience to explore the transition faced by many older women from being the carer to the cared for. In her early sixties Shelagh had a mild stroke. She grew frail, and in 2004 she found a lump in her breast. 'She didn't tell anyone about it for months,' said Charlotte, who began to suspect something was badly wrong when Shelagh arrived to stay with her for a few weeks and took to bed, 'getting sicker and sicker but assuring me she was just a bit depressed'. Eventually, against Shelagh's wishes, Charlotte took her to hospital – and doctors diagnosed breast cancer. 'She confessed that she "had taken off her glasses" – metaphorically – "and ignored the lump".'[58] Shelagh had a mastectomy. 'She told me she felt sorry for the cancer because it was only doing its job,' said Charlotte. 'I think that attitude helped her to keep going.' Still, 'a lot of the time she didn't feel a hundred per cent', recalled Kath Wilkie. 'It was really important to her to go on working, because she didn't want to be a has-been. It was important to her self-worth.' But as her eyesight failed, writing became harder. When Zdena Tomin visited Shelagh in 2003 she found that 'she had to have the lettering so large on the computer screen that she could only see a few words, and [because of the stroke] her right arm would just slide away from the keyboard. She was very distressed.'

The sadness involved in giving up her independence infused her radio play *Baloney Said Salome*. Nina is dying and must rely on friends to look after her. The group of women she assembles are widows, divorcees or unmarried – their friendship with each other is far more important and enduring than any ties to men. Shelagh was thankful to have her own set of good friends, and, even more precious, the companionship and unwavering support of her daughter. She eventually sold the Gerrard Road house with its many steps and crumbling walls to buy a more accessible and inexpensive house for the whole family on the Suffolk coast. Shelagh was worried about the future. She confided in Zdena that she no longer enjoyed life in Muston. 'She liked the cottage. She loved the neighbours next door and they took care of her, bless them. But the rest of them – gossiping Tories.' At the same time, 'she was unhappy about having to rely on Charlotte; she did not want to be a burden, and of course she was effectively saying a whole period of her life was over'.[58] She stayed regularly in Southwold, but resisted moving there permanently. 'After a while she'd go quiet. Or maybe we'd have a row,' Charlotte recalled. 'And she'd say, "I'd like to go home now please." So I'd drive her all the way back to Filey.' Polly Thomas appreciated Shelagh's ability to enjoy her own company, and her honesty about needing it. 'She always said she wanted to come and visit Hebden Bridge, where I lived. So she came over. We had a cup of tea in a cafe. We went for a walk at the park, and it started drizzling. I was ill, I'd just had flu. She said, "I'm gonna go home, actually." It was mad. All the way back to Filey. But it wasn't rude at all. I was feeling really ill. It was raining. She wanted to go home.'

Shelagh and her contemporaries, brought up on wartime rations, post-war school milk and the National Health Service, were living longer than any previous generation. She mused with friends on the paradox of getting older while often feeling and behaving as she had done fifty years earlier. 'She was a binger,' recalled Zdena. 'She took food and drink and cigarettes like she took life: it was there, and you just took it in binges ... I'd bring a meat pie or pork pie or fish and chips and she'd wolf it down. Red wine.' It was reminiscent of the newspaper interviews she'd given in London cafes in the wake of *Honey*'s success. Back then, she had hidden from the press her insecurities about her appearance, but fifty years later they were still with her. In the years after her mastectomy she told Charlotte that 'she wished she'd had both breasts off because the remaining one used to get on her nerves'. But this bothered her less than her old self-consciousness about being tall. 'She was apprehensive about her height,' said Zdena. 'Once she stormed out of a supermarket in Filey because she thought that the shop assistants were saying, "Oh, look at the size of her." I doubt they said it. But she stormed out and never walked in that supermarket again.'

In Shelagh's work she'd often explored how young and middle-aged women could be attracted by the glamour of femininity, while simultaneously feeling impatient with it or even oppressed by its demands. Now she realised older women were not immune to this dilemma. She enjoyed having no one to look after and being able to dress as scruffily as she liked, but 'she was vain about her looks and spent a lot of money on creams and stuff', Zdena recalled. She read women's magazines avidly, and would periodically direct Charlotte 'to stock up on the latest health foods or anti-ageing beauty miracle treatments', before once more reverting to the comfort of woolly jumpers and unbrushed hair.

*Baloney Said Salome* captures the frustration of increasing frailty while one's mind is still alert and the urge to dance and sing still strong. But it also expresses the joy of companionship, the comfort of knowing that, when needed, relatives, friends and the NHS are all there to help. The play's openness about older women's bodies, loves, resilience and anger – and about cancer, a taboo illness when Shelagh's own father had died of it in the 1950s – signalled how much society had changed, a process to which Shelagh's work had contributed.

She remained very private, keen to avoid a fuss and to ignore any frailties. By the summer of 2011, Charlotte suspected that her mother was seriously ill, but Shelagh refused to see a doctor. 'She was afraid of what they'd say. She'd seen her dad die of cancer. Better just not to talk about it and hope it would go away.' In September, on a visit to Southwold, she fell over and was unable to get up. As Charlotte drove her to hospital, 'she did admit to me that she'd found another lump [in her breast]'.

By 29 September doctors had confirmed that she had terminal cancer.

Faced with the finality of this judgement, Shelagh accepted it. At the beginning of November, she rang Kath Wilkie. 'I'd been trying to get hold of her for weeks. And she called and said: "I'm dying, Kath." She was – well, you always hope you'll have longer than you get, don't you? But she came straight out with it, honest as ever.' Later that month, Zdena visited her. 'She couldn't walk any more but we chatted. And she was still worried about how she looked. And I said, "Shelagh, you're beautiful." She was ever so pleased.' In *Baloney Said Salome* she'd suggested that a good death meant being at home, in bed, surrounded by your dearest friends or relatives having 'a chat and a laugh' and a sing-song, fortified by memories and 'a bottle each' of champagne.[60] On the evening of 20 November 2011, five days before her seventy-third birthday, Shelagh died peacefully at home in Southwold, holding her daughter's hand, her grandchildren next to the bed. Charlotte sang 'You Are My Sunshine'.

# 11

# Shelagh, Take a Bow

Shelagh Delaney's obituaries inevitably focused on *A Taste of Honey*. It was, she knew, 'my masterpiece'.[1] That didn't mean she thought it was her best work – good writing often becomes a masterpiece by the accident of time and place. In her case, that meant writing at a time when radical, socialist theatre had sufficient influence to ensure that her voice was heard more widely. Shelagh expressed a growing impatience at political hypocrisy; anger at the way working-class people were treated; boredom with the status quo; and – less obviously, but beginning to crystallise – frustration at women's lot. She suggested that ordinary people had the potential to change the post-war world for the better, rather than simply being the grateful recipients of whatever was bestowed upon them.

Those critics who wanted *A Taste of Honey* to be suppressed were, by the mid-1960s, sneering at Shelagh as out of date. A decade before the May Events in Paris of 1968, and twelve years before the British Women's Liberation Movement held its first national conference, *Honey* asserted women's right to be heard. Shelagh's refusal to be silenced after the play's debut rammed her point home: working-class women like her weren't content with recreating Richard Hoggart's childhood, but nor did they want to become middle-class ladies. *Honey* didn't provide any easy answers about what they did want or how they might get there, but it did suggest those questions were worth exploring. Shelagh herself never offered any solutions, but she spent the rest of her life pursuing love and creativity. Her work illuminated how women who did likewise were condemned as feckless or crazy, while showing that in fact it was those who lived within the code of respectability who ended up exhausted by hard work, frustrated at their narrow lives, or consumed by self-importance.

*A Taste of Honey* enthused, excited and enraged audiences around the world. Many of its fans were young women. Some of them, in turn, introduced it to later generations, through their work as teachers in the expanding further education colleges of the 1960s and the new comprehensives of the 1970s and 80s, or as lecturers in the departments of theatre, cultural studies and women's studies that they fought to establish in British universities and polytechnics. Others did so as participants in the agitprop feminist and socialist theatres that mushroomed across Europe and America in the 1970s.

In the 1970s and early 1980s, *A Taste of Honey* and its author almost became respectable. '[I]t holds up better than most plays of England's look-back-in-anger period,' commented the *New York Times* on a revival of *Honey* in 1981. 'There's a clear-eyed, unsentimental nobility about Miss Delaney's writing that recalls the spirit of Samuel Beckett.'[2] No longer a women's play or a working-class drama, it was simply compelling theatre.

It's no coincidence that this was the era when Shelagh's offers of attractive work increased. Her plays for radio and television and her screenplay for *Dance with a Stranger* testified to an acceptance by some within the arts establishment that ordinary lives mattered. Her success also signalled that feminism was influencing the mainstream – not only thanks to the activism of the Women's Liberation Movement, but also to Shelagh's writing, and the work of writers who came after her, who illuminated the hopes and frustrations of ordinary women. Feminism owed as much to Ordsall's residents as it did to Oxford graduates.

To some of those who came to *Honey* in this era, it was a memorial to a lost world – a reminder of how far women in particular had come. Kirk Bridges, born in the 1960s, studied the play at his comprehensive school in Little Hulton, a former mining community between Salford and Bolton. Kirk 'wasn't very studious at school, just wanted to get out there and work' and see life. He thought *A Taste of Honey* was 'very raw'. Shelagh Delaney's Salford was a more illiberal place than Kirk grew up in – 'you had to be married – it was the early sixties, wasn't it?' – where a girl could be 'ostracised for having a relationship with a black boy'. Her portrayal of inner-city life, though, raised doubts about whether all the changes had been progress. Kirk's own family had 'lived near the docks originally – when it was the docks. Trafford Road. There's a story in that on its own, isn't there?' His parents were among hundreds of Ordsall families rehoused at Little Hulton when Salford Council pulled their old homes down – 'they called them slum areas at the time. But people were living there success-fully.' *Honey* told the story of these vanished streets; one of 'hard-ship', but also one of working-class people who lived and worked in the city they'd built and hadn't yet been obliged to move to its margins, out of policymakers' sight.[3]

Others found in Shelagh's work an echo of their own frustrations. Steven Morrissey, born the year after *Honey*'s premiere, spent the early 1970s hating his Catholic secondary modern in Stretford, where desultory lessons were punctuated by beatings and meagre school dinners. 'The condition of England supported the predicament of taking whatever is dished out, whether this be food or violence. In order for there to be winners there needed to be losers, and the winners were already seated at fully heated Stretford Grammar.'[4] Beacons of hope were reading and music, but, frustrated by the 'dribble' of pop lyrics, 'I am caught by what *could* be and *should* be, as the sagging-roof poetry of Shelagh Delaney's rag-and-bone plays say *something* to me about my life'.[5] Morrissey repeatedly returned to her work in the years that followed, as he left school and entered a world where the threat of nuclear war loomed as large as it had in Shelagh's youth, but where unemployment was rising and politicians were dismantling the welfare state.

In 1980, a year after Britain elected Margaret Thatcher's Conservative government, one of Morrissey's contemporaries found a platform for her frustrations. Andrea Dunbar, born to a working-class family in Bradford in 1961, was a teenage single mother living in a women's refuge when one of the workers there showed her play, *The Arbor*, to a contact at London's Royal Court. Max Stafford Clark, the Court's artistic director, decided to stage her story of a working-class teenage girl dealing with an unplanned pregnancy. Dunbar – who read *Honey* while redrafting *The Arbor* – shared Shelagh's strength for dialogue.

Unlike Shelagh, she enjoyed even greater success with her second play, *Rita, Sue and Bob Too*, performed in 1982 also at the Royal Court. In 1987, this story of two teenage girls living on a northern housing estate, who begin a relationship with an older man to escape the callous reality of unemployment, substandard housing and a state that doesn't care, became a hit film.

Dunbar found fame at a moment in the early 1980s when working-class women's voices were finding space on theatre stages and television. But her experience indicates just how fragile and brief a moment this proved to be. Most of the right-wing press denounced her plays just as they had done *Honey*, the *Daily Express* calling Dunbar 'immoral'. It was left to Philip French at the *Observer* – Ken Tynan's old stamping ground – to point out in a review of the film adaptation of *Rita, Sue and Bob Too* 'the fortitude of Rita and Sue. The strength afforded by their friendship helps them survive in a desolate world of permanent unemployment that is destroying those around them and will eventually get them too.'[6]

As French suggested, there was no hint of a hopeful future in Dunbar's work, unlike in *Honey* or even in Shelagh's bleaker second play *The Lion in Love*. Shelagh had grown up at a time when the world held the promise of better times to come. The welfare state wasn't perfect, but education and the arts were expanding, driven by Labour's conviction that everyone should benefit from these. Andrea Dunbar, growing up a generation later, spent her early life on the Buttershaw estate, several miles and a long bus journey from the centre of Bradford. Like Duchy Road, Buttershaw had been conceived as a desirable place to live, offering security and comfort – but by the 1980s public spending cuts and unemployment meant it was a 'sink' estate.

The arts scene had changed, too. Unlike Dunbar, Shelagh had had the support network of a radical, socialist, theatre scene. This centred on Theatre Workshop but encompassed the Royal Court and Woodfall Films. When she fell out with Joan Littlewood, she had other supporters. Although Andrea Dunbar credited teachers at her comprehensive with encouraging her to write – the converse of Shelagh's experience at grammar school – she had to rely exclusively on Max Stafford Clark's patronage to survive in the theatre world. When he found fresh talent she had nowhere to turn. Community and radical theatres were collapsing as the Conservatives cut funding to the arts, and the BBC and most London theatres showed little interest in supporting working-class writers. Unlike Shelagh Delaney, Andrea Dunbar was unable to conceive not only of a happy ending, but of survival. Having glimpsed a different future, she turned to drink, and died in 1990 from a brain haemorrhage after collapsing in a local pub. 'I am convinced,' says her biographer, Adelle Stripe, 'that the political and social times in which she lived were what killed her.'[7]

This was the world in which Steven Morrissey formed the Smiths, whose lyrics introduced millions of fans to Shelagh Delaney's work. Like Shelagh, Morrissey attacked the media and political establishment for claiming that 'they have an understanding of the working classes and their fascinations, which they patently do not'. Morrissey, again like Shelagh, identified with those people the government dismissed as marginal – militant strikers, dole claimants and 'deviant' homosexuals. 'I'm very interested in what emerges from the ashes of poverty,' Morrissey explained; 'to see what people are capable of in extremes.'[8]

Morrissey positioned the Smiths as champions of working-class culture for a new generation – 'the most realistic and lyrical voice of the 1980s', he later claimed.[9] Their fame coincided with the apparent collapse of older working-class institutions, epitomised by the miners' strike of 1984–5, defeated by Thatcher's government while the increasingly right-wing Labour leadership stood silently by. As mainstream politicians and the media focused on royal weddings and London yuppies, Morrissey, like Shelagh before him, fought to expose a different truth. 'I don't want to sing about football results or importune people to dance,' he said.[10] The Smiths' record covers created a gallery of working-class icons, many of them female: Shelagh Delaney was placed alongside Viv Nicholson (the Yorkshire miner's wife who, on winning the pools in 1961, famously declared 'I'm going to spend, spend, spend!') and Pat Phoenix. Morrissey regularly talked about the inspiration he gained from *Honey* and other 'kitchen sink' creations like Sillitoe's *Saturday Night and Sunday Morning*: 'for the very first time people were allowed regional accents and were allowed to be truthful and honest about their situation'.[11] But it was Shelagh's work that he plundered most regularly for lines and ideas that studded his songs. 'I dreamt about you last night. Fell out of bed twice' appeared in 'Reel Around the Fountain' and 'I'll probably never see you again' – from *Honey* and *The Lion in Love* – in 'Hand in Glove'. The band's 1985 hit 'This Night has Opened My Eyes' retold the story of *A Taste of Honey*, appropriating lines like 'the dream's gone but the baby's real enough'.

The Smiths turned Shelagh Delaney into an icon of working-class culture. For Michael Calderbank, growing up in a working-class family in 1980s Preston, 'the north felt depressed and neglected', a place where boys like him could only hope to find joy in 'birds, booze and football'. For bookish Michael, the Smiths were 'a badge of pride because they'd come from this'. Morrissey not only suggested that 'it was all right to be introverted, to be into books and films', but that in doing so you could connect with a forgotten working-class culture.[12] For Maxine Peake, born in 1976 to a working-class family in Lancashire, 'The Smiths opened up this whole world, including *A Taste of Honey*, and so suddenly you realise it all links up.'[13] Michael's search 'for all Morrissey's references' – one being feverishly conducted in bedrooms and fanzines across the country – took him to Shelagh Delaney, 'who I think played a similar role for Morrissey that Morrissey played for me'. Discovering that she was a writer 'was like, "Wow, somebody like me can write things and people can take them seriously."' Michael went to university, read English, and became one of the editors of *Red Pepper* magazine. Shelagh Delaney and Morrissey were links that connected Smiths fans with a working-class tradition of artistic innovation.

Those who encountered Shelagh Delaney's work in the 1980s were often attracted by her language rather than her storylines. In the 1960s and 1970s *Honey*'s story had still been hard-hitting, but Michael Calderbank was one of many late-twentieth-century viewers who thought it 'melodramatic' – it was 'the quality of the dialogue' that impressed him. Her language resonated with many of those growing up in the

1980s. Among them were budding actors, writers and directors from working- and lower-middle-class backgrounds. They included Sean O'Connor, born in 1968, who grew up on the Wirral. Sean's mother and father were keen for him and his siblings to 'climb the ladder, basically. Particularly me and my brother – they moved house so that we would go to a good grammar school, assuming we passed the eleven-plus, which we did.' Sean was a keen classicist and expected to study the subject at university, but meanwhile he developed other interests. 'On a Saturday my parents would go shopping in Birkenhead, where my grandmother lived, and I'd stay with her. We'd eat scouse and watch old films. That was how I saw *A Taste of Honey.*' As a teenager, Sean and a female friend discovered they shared a love of Shelagh's first play, one enhanced by the Smiths. 'It wasn't so much what happened, or who the characters were,' said Sean, 'they were just a vehicle for her dialogue, for the language. It was the language that really drew us in, we'd repeat lines to each other. They spoke to us.' Once enrolled at University College London, Sean swapped classics for English and set his sights on a career in the theatre. 'I went back to *Honey* and then I found *Lion* ... Her voice was authentic, it was northern, which was rare then and still is now ... and her writing had passion.' In his subsequent career as a director, Sean would seek out these qualities in other writers.

Shelagh's foregrounding of working-class women struck a chord with those whose class or sexuality marginalised them in Thatcher's Britain. 'She was writing about women's disappointments, and I could see that in my mother,' said Sean. 'A woman who was bright, who could have done so much, but wrong class, wrong time, wrong place.' Sean, growing up gay in a provincial town, could identify with this sense of being in the wrong place at the wrong time. So could Sarah Frankcom. Born in 1968, she came from 'a quite ordinary, northern, working background' in Sheffield. Bored and alienated at the private school she'd won a scholarship to attend, she joined the Sheffield Crucible's youth theatre and this inspired her to study English and drama at university. She almost dropped out in her first year because the writers she read 'didn't represent anything that I knew about … it didn't feel like my DNA was in those plays'. Then 'a brilliant drama lecturer told me to go to the Royal Court, and gave me *A Taste of Honey* to read'. Like Shelagh Delaney, Sarah was just as incensed by the lack of working-class people in the plays she was reading and seeing as she was by the 'unreal' women. 'I read *Honey*; I was like, "I get this."'[14] In 2008, she became artistic director of Manchester's Royal Exchange Theatre.

Sarah, privately educated, did not encounter Shelagh Delaney until university; Sean O'Connor, educated at a grammar school, found her independently through his own love of film. Those who attended comprehensive schools were more likely to come across *Honey* and its author during their early teens. Maxine Peake was introduced to Shelagh's work by a drama teacher at her Bolton comprehensive in the late 1980s. 'I really distinctly remember one day the teacher saying, "We're going to watch a film." And … everyone sat and was quiet. That really struck me. And then we read it. And that's the first time I'd ever made that connection … because it was up the road, you're going, "There's this happening in Salford."' It wasn't only the familiarity that appealed, but also the sense that ordinary people were, as Jo says, unique: 'I don't know what it tapped into, but you just went, "Oh, right, yeah, I can do that."'

For working-class women wanting a career in the arts, Shelagh Delaney was, in Jeanette Winterson's words, 'like a lighthouse – pointing the way and warning about the rocks underneath'.[15] She became an inspiration to Maxine Peake who began to think seriously about an acting career. 'I was at [sixth-form] college when I learned how old Shelagh Delaney was when she wrote it, and that's inspiring: you can be a working-class girl and you can do something with yourself – because it isn't easy – and if you want to be an actor, which I did, you're thinking, "Well, maybe I'll get a part serving behind the bar on *Coronation Street* if I'm lucky." And then reading her plays, there are parts there for you.' Maxine determined to go to drama school, eventually entering RADA on her third attempt.

By the time Maxine Peake was at her sixth-form college, performances of Shelagh Delaney's plays were confined to smaller theatres and community drama groups. In 1992, Interact, a theatre group in Oldham which brought disabled and able-bodied people together, staged *The Lion in Love*, much to Shelagh's delight; she told the group she thought it had been entirely forgotten.[16] Performances of *A Taste of Honey* now emphasised its contemporary relevance as 'powerful working-class drama' that 'with hard-nosed intensity ... addresses strong issues of friendship, parenthood and survival for a single mother in an apparently harsh and unsympathetic society'.[17] Shelagh's work was welcomed by people who increasingly felt their lives and interests were ignored by politicians and the media. But, just as in the late 1950s, few theatre managers thought it could reach beyond those whose daily lives were reflected onstage. This kind of 'relevance' wasn't demanded of plays about middle-class and upper-class people. Their lifestyles were depicted as inherently cultured – whereas the representation of working-class life needed a more sociological justification.

Shelagh Delaney's legitimacy in both the theatre and in the school curriculum increasingly relied on her being a writer of working-class dramas. But her feminist perspective was either ignored or treated as controversial. As political times changed, so children studying *A Taste of Honey* were encouraged to view its main characters with greater disapproval. In the 1980s, examination guides presented both Helen and Jo sympathetically: 'Helen … is by turns selfish, immature, crude and cruel,' stated the *Penguin Passnotes* for *A Taste of Honey*. 'At the same time we probably find her a sympathetic character, and it is certainly quite difficult to blame her completely for what she does.'[18] By the early twenty-first century, though, students were encouraged to blame Helen in particular for fecklessness. The Learning and Teaching Scotland guide to *Honey*, published in 2006, described Helen as 'a bully … by the standards of the time, immoral in her sexual behaviour … racist … Homophobic … she blames society for her poverty when, in fact, it is due to the flaws in her own character'. Jo 'has inherited many of her mother's weaknesses: she has a tendency to drift, rather than make a determined effort to achieve something; she has little ambition'; her redeeming feature was that 'she has a higher standard of personal morality'.[19] In 2017, the BBC's *Bitesize* series for GCSE students judged Helen 'a very selfish mother [who] has thought nothing of leaving Jo alone even at Christmas in order to enjoy the company of a variety of different men'.[20] Within education, politics and the theatre, the right of working-class women to self-expression was regarded with greater suspicion in the twenty-first century than it had been in the 1970s.

In her later life, Shelagh was dispirited by continual requests to rewrite *A Taste of Honey* for a new generation. She refused because she didn't want to be defined by her first play, but also due to her dislike of the way that working-class people were represented in the arts and politics in the early twenty-first century. Critics on right and left romanced the past. From the right, Ferdinand Mount argued that the 'underclass' were culturally 'impoverished … in relation to their parents and grandparents'.[21] Meanwhile Andrew O'Hagan, like a latter-day Richard Hoggart, lamented that working-class people were 'docile and careless', in thrall to 'celebrity culture and credit cards'.[22] The media and politicians simultaneously regretted working-class people's 'social exclusion', while suggesting this was due to their lack of hard work and aspiration.

At the same time, the 1950s were revived as a Cath Kidston decade in which everyone's problems were solved by baking and happiness came in the form of a flowered tablecloth. In this romantic haze, Shelagh Delaney's success was selectively remembered as a sign of what had been possible in the post-war decade, when people somehow both knew their place and yet also rose out of it.[23] She wanted no part in this.

In 2014, three years after her death, the National Theatre staged a new production of *A Taste of Honey*. It was favourably reviewed, but two of Shelagh's most trusted colleagues and collaborators, Sean O'Connor and Polly Thomas, had reservations. Sean judged it 'like *Call the Midwife* – sweet, anodyne, a totally antiseptic version of the fifties'. Polly agreed and thought 'it presented this version of Shelagh as a teenager who did this in 1958, hadn't done anything since, and the whole thing is preserved in aspic'. As Rachel Creaser, reviewing *Honey* for the teachers' publication *Teaching Drama*, put it, 'I'm not sure what this production is trying to say in 2014 … there's something missing from the original spark that would have been found at Theatre Royal Stratford East.'[24] That spark was Shelagh's anger at the way ordinary people were treated, and her defiant claim to a different world.

It was her defiance – and particularly her refusal to accept that women should primarily be wives and mothers – that drew a new generation to her. For some women growing up in the 1990s and the 2000s, Shelagh Delaney's work and her image – stylised by the Smiths – became important ripostes to the political status quo and to the media and music industry's rebranding of feminism as 'girl power', embodied by celebrities who suggested women could achieve whatever they wanted if they tried hard enough – and looked glamorous. A series of Conservative governments blamed single mothers for causing poverty and delinquency, a theme picked up by the New Labour government of 1997 which immediately cut welfare benefits to lone parents.

Elsewhere in Europe, a similar conservatism prevailed. Valeria Scialbini grew up in a small town in Italy, where she was taught to aspire to Catholic motherhood. From an early age 'I knew

I wanted to get away. I used to say I was going to live in London.' When she came across the Smiths as a teenager in the 1990s the band 'opened up a new world for me ... the angry young men, the kitchen sink dramas'. Valeria was entranced by the image of Shelagh on the cover of *Louder Than Bombs*. 'I thought she looked a bit scruffy. I imagined that because it was the fifties, and because she was successful, that she would be really polished. And I thought, "That's good. We can all be scruffy and do well in life."' Reading *A Taste of Honey*, and learning more about Shelagh Delaney, provided Valeria with signposts to a life different from the conformity and femininity she felt defined women's lives in Italy 'where everyone wears the same shoes ... and Italian TV shows have half-naked women in them, literally doing anything'.

For Valeria, as for Ahuva Weisbaum decades earlier, Shelagh Delaney provided one inspiration to forge an independent life overseas. Like Ahuva, Valeria focused her dreams on England's north-west; Shelagh Delaney's experience and writing convinced her this was a place where independent women might thrive. 'Some people would dream of going to America, I was dreaming of coming to Manchester', a move she eventually made in the 2000s. Life there is far from perfect – Valeria is 'a lot more creative than my job entails', but she has to prioritise making ends meet, and she is unsure what Brexit will mean for her future. But she didn't expect to find a utopia, simply a place she could be relatively free of the family and societal bonds that she'd found so claustrophobic in her youth. She continues to enjoy watching the film of *Honey*, and has read the play 'four or five times. I love it. I always find something new in it ... It feels real.'[25] For Valeria, Shelagh's assertion that women want more than marriage and motherhood, and her simultaneous acknowledgement that their role as actual or potential mothers shapes their lives, continues to resonate. And Shelagh's own story of challenging the moral and political 'common sense' of the 1950s in order to create an independent life for herself, is as attractive and hopeful to Valeria today as it was to Ahuva Weisbaum in the 1960s.

Throughout her life, Shelagh resisted the stereotypes to which women were meant to conform. She did this not least as a lone parent who was able both to enjoy motherhood and write about the losses it brought, as a lover determined to maintain her independence, and in her celebration of women's friendship. She was also clear that a woman should not be defined by a single event, whether passing the eleven-plus, writing a play, walking down the aisle or having a baby. Her work asserted that while most women had few options, those who exploited or committed violence against women, or sat in judgement over them, always had a choice. 'What was so amazing about *Dance with a Stranger*,' said Amanda Schiff, 'was that although you knew what the end had to be, Shelagh's script made you think it might not be a foregone conclusion; that Ruth might get off.' By creating imperfect, flawed female characters, she suggested that women should be allowed to be *good enough* mothers, wives and workers, not expected to become madonnas or 'have it all' career women. She explored with searing honesty the ambivalences and contradictions with which ordinary women grappled: the resentment and fierce love inspired by motherhood; the passion and frustration of sexual relationships; the allure of romance and the desire for independence.

Social movements and pioneering individuals are, at best, considered ahead of their time, but they're more usually dismissed as eccentric or mad. The considerable achievements of the women's movement in promoting nursery care, equal opportunities legislation, and also in exploring ways of living outside the nuclear family without stigma or reproach, are often ignored. So too is Shelagh Delaney's contribution to cultural change. Never active in a political organisation after her stint with CND, nor a member of a feminist group, nor very prominent in the media after 1964, she's a reminder that what goes on in the wings explains everything that happens centre stage. If her later plays were considered less shocking than *A Taste of Honey*, that was because of a transformation she'd helped to initiate. When she enjoyed success with the screenplay of *Dance with a Stranger*, the media claimed they'd known she was a great writer all along. It was more palatable to peddle this myth than to admit that women like Shelagh had changed the world.

Over the past decade, some of those inspired by Shelagh's work, whether influenced by schoolteachers or Smiths lyrics, have begun to argue for a revival and reconsideration of her legacy. Notably, the greatest enthusiasm for her work is found away from London's theatres. With her daughter's permission, the Guinness Partnership – a provider of affordable housing – has named a Salford tower block after her. The official opening included a performance of a play by MaD Theatre Company, a self-described 'working-class theatre company' that operates in Greater Manchester. MaD's director, Rob Lees, is a working-class

Mancunian who 'wants to make theatre something that is as affordable and entertaining as football'. He and his co-director, Jill Hughes, were keen to celebrate Shelagh because 'yes, her work is about ordinary people, and she recognises that ordinary life makes art. But that last point's the most important – it is art. It isn't just a mirror held up to everyday life, but more than that. It's entertaining, it's a particularly rich slice of life, showing what people have the potential to do – experience strong emotions and take the piss out of the powerful. That's what working-class culture has always been about.'[26]

Shelagh's focus on women's lives has also resonated in her home town. Since 2014, local people in Salford have organised an annual Shelagh Delaney Day to commemorate her as both an excellent playwright and an icon of working-class culture. Founder Louise Woodward Styles believes remembering 'her legacy is vital to inspire this generation and generations to come to reach their potential'.[27] Roni Ellis, one of the contributors to Shelagh Delaney Day, believes that this is particularly important for young women. Born in 1972 to a working-class Salford family, Roni is now director of the Salford Arts Theatre, situated within a working-class neighbourhood of the city. Her theatre's youth group is full of young women who 'have been given the same careers advice at school that I was given: "Why don't you get a trade, do hairdressing or make-up, you're not going to be able to be a dancer or an actor."' Shelagh's work and life provided inspiration for the group to write and perform their own monologues about growing up in Salford. 'I'd been listening to interviews of Shelagh Delaney talking about young people in Salford being like tethered horses [on the BBC's *Monitor* programme of 1960] and it rang true for me, and for some of the group,' recalled Roni.[28] Like Shelagh, many of these young women crave self-expression and creativity. They don't aspire to a career in the arts because they want celebrity, but because they have something to say.

The problem, according to Roni Ellis and Rob Lees, is not a lack of aspiration or talent among young women – it is the obstacles they face in achieving their ambitions. Sporadic media debates about how to find Shelagh Delaneys are focusing on the wrong question. There are already countless young working-class actors and writers. But, as Rob Lees points out, they're more likely to find a voice in community theatre than in the larger commercial theatres. 'We've been performing for more than ten years, we have sell-out shows, but no Manchester or London theatre has ever come and asked how we might work together – we've had to do it all on our own.' Far from despairing at the state of working-class culture, MaD's members, like Roni Ellis, see themselves as the inheritors of a long, radical, working-class tradition centred on Salford and Manchester. 'You've got Ewan MacColl, Shelagh Delaney, the Working Class Movement Library – there's all these connections,' says Roni. In 2017 MaD staged two performances of Shelagh Delaney's *Sweetly Sings the Donkey* trilogy of plays at Salford's Lowry Theatre – Charlotte Delaney, herself a writer, adapted them from her mother's radio scripts. The actors hailed from Salford and north Manchester – areas among the most socio-economically deprived in Britain. Both performances sold out. There are working-class women writing and acting, and there is an audience for their work.

The question is not how to find new Shelagh Delaneys, but how to break down the barriers they face. Recently, Shelagh's story has been used as a sign of how far we've come – 'if we now think there is nothing freakish or unusual about women dramatists making a mark in their teens or coming from a working-class background, we have Shelagh Delaney to thank for it', wrote Michael Billington in the *Guardian* in 2011.[29] But we have very few women dramatists, let alone from working class backgrounds. Maxine Peake, who wrote and directed her first play in 2012, thinks working-class women's presence in the arts remains precarious. 'If you've got a regional accent it's hard, *really* hard to be taken seriously; and if you're actually working class, well, you've got to prove yourself. It isn't as basic as people being surprised you can actually write, but it isn't far off. Yes, there are a few roles [for northern working-class women], but are you going to settle for being typecast all your life? There's very few who break through, who are taken seriously for other roles.'

Sean O'Connor agrees. His experience, like Maxine Peake's, suggests that while poor careers advice, a lack of contacts and money help explain why young working-class people find it hard to break into acting, directing and writing, there's a bigger problem – and it's one that primarily affects women. Sean believes that 'most parts, in the theatre, in television, are written for men, by men ... white, middle-class men writing about and producing things about themselves. As a result, there is no room for working-class women.' Even when interest grew in *A Taste of Honey*, 'there was no means of capitalising on that, extending it to say something more significant about Shelagh and her work. I'd wanted to do *Lion* for a long time. I said to the National, how about considering two plays: *Lion* and *Honey*. But Nick Hytner [artistic director of the National Theatre at the time] would not have two women's plays; it was hard enough to get him to allow one.' The notion that women are allowed a token appearance is one that Roni Ellis recognises and is keen to eschew at her theatre: 'You have to think about how to use Shelagh Delaney and all of her work as an inspiration, see it as part of a tradition, not just keep returning to *Honey*.' Shelagh's work consistently asks why women – especially working-class women – are confined to certain roles and considered incapable of playing a full part in public life. Far from suggesting that we need to raise these women's aspirations, or broaden their minds, her work indicates that we should be more concerned with confronting the inequalities that consign the majority of the population to the cheap seats, while a privileged few dominate the stage.

'Young people are slipping out of the auditorium to make their own music,' said E. P. Thompson of the late fifties, 'but the Show must go on.'[30] Shelagh Delaney banged the door behind her and demanded that the audience become the actors and take centre stage. *A Taste of Honey* showed that it is possible to grow up in a conservative society and question its justifications, challenge convention, and change the world. Over the next decade she found acceptance in a new milieu of artists and writers who, regardless of background, shared her belief that anyone could create art, given the means to do so. It seemed possible that the world she'd depicted in *A Taste of Honey* might be consigned to the past. She benefited from the chances that a welfare state and education gave to her generation, and used them to demand more for everyone. Times changed, and from the 1980s it was harder to find directors and funders willing to back her ideas, or producers who wanted to hear about the state of contemporary women's lives. Yet she continued to write, and in doing so to show that those often considered marginal to political debate and artistic endeavour – working-class people, and especially women and children – are the majority of the human race. More, they are worth listening to. 'I write as people speak,' said Shelagh. How dangerous. How inspiring.

# Acknowledgements

The idea for a biography of Shelagh Delaney began as a conversation with my husband, Andrew Davies, who in the intervening years has offered unflagging enthusiasm, astute advice, forensic knowledge of Manchester and Salford, and vital domestic support. He bears no resemblance to any of the husbands created by Shelagh Delaney, for which I am deeply grateful.

My agent Rachel Calder made this book possible, first by introducing me to Shelagh's daughter, Charlotte, and then through her unshakeable conviction that it would find a publisher. As ever, Rachel combined compassion and criticism throughout our discussions and her reading of my manuscript. She also helped to persuade Becky Hardie, my editor at Chatto, of its merits. At our very first meeting Becky turned my brain inside out to find the wider significance of Shelagh Delaney's story; I have benefited from her rigour and perception ever since. Thanks to all at Chatto & Windus who helped to produce this book.

The unstinting support of Shelagh's daughter was essential. I cannot thank Charlotte enough for entrusting me with the role of biographer. As well as allowing me full access to her mother's private papers, Charlotte has been immensely generous with her insights, observations and address book. It is thanks to her powers of persuasion that so many of Shelagh Delaney's friends agreed to speak to me. Charlotte revisited painful memories as well as happy times with a rare honesty and clarity. As a fellow writer, she also helped me to navigate the process of turning a colourful and complex personality into prose. Most importantly, she insisted on injecting fun into every stage of the research and writing. I hope she feels I've captured something of her mother's spirit.

Shelagh Delaney habitually burned or threw away personal papers and photographs – partly because she was so protective of her privacy, and partly because she found grand gestures cathartic after falling out with relatives, friends or lovers. Writing this book would therefore have been impossible without the cooperation of her family, friends and colleagues and I am deeply grateful to those who agreed to talk to me. Some are quoted in this book, but many more offered me memories and observations that enriched my understanding of her life and her work.

I have also benefited from the help and insights of fellow admirers of Shelagh Delaney, some of whom are quoted in the book. Special mention is due to the biographer John Harding, author of *Sweetly Sings Delaney: a study of Shelagh Delaney's work 1958–68*, who has been exceptionally generous with his time, research material and contacts.

Many librarians and archivists helped my research immeasurably. They are too numerous to mention here, but each archival citation in the notes owes much to their efforts and often their ingenuity. Special thanks to Katie Ankers at the BBC

Written Archives in Caversham, whose imagination and generosity saved me a huge amount of time, and Lynette Cawthra at the Working Class Movement Library in Salford, who, together with the library's volunteers, offered introductions to interviewees, research tips and excellent biscuits.

Funding from the British Academy, the Oxford University Fell Fund, the Arts Council (reference 27927134) and the Arts and Humanities Research Council (reference AH/N00986X/1) enabled the research and writing, and allowed me to work with MaD Theatre Company (thanks to Jill Hughes and Rob Lees), Charlotte Delaney and the Guinness Housing Partnership (thanks to Karen Harford and Paul Heaton) to bring some of Shelagh's radio plays to the stage – a venture that introduced me to several interviewees and informs the final chapter of this book. The linchpin of that project was the brilliant Dr Andrea Thomson, who also carried out some of the interviews that appear in these pages, and took care of the paperwork that, as Shelagh Delaney knew, can badly encroach on writing time. I am indebted to her for her practical help, energy and enthusiasm.

My warm thanks go to the Fellows and staff of St Hilda's College and to my colleagues in the History Faculty at Oxford University for supporting my research leave, especially to Ms Aileen Mooney, Dr Hannah Smith and Dr Ruth Percy. I owe a huge debt of gratitude to Professor Senia Paseta for taking over the Oxford University Women in Humanities network that we co-direct and allowing WiH to host this project. Thanks to my doctoral students for tolerating long-distance supervision and for discussions about post-war women and feminism that have influenced this book.

# Acknowledgements

This book is dedicated to two feminists who have regularly reminded me why writing about women's lives matters. The period during which I have written this book has been one of constant attacks on women's rights. I've been acutely conscious that my ability to write and publish, without anything like the struggles Shelagh Delaney faced, is due to feminism. Her assertion that women's experience – our socialisation, our actual and potential role as mothers, and the discrimination we face as a result of our sex – should be central to politics and culture is as relevant today as it was in 1958. Thank you to Ruth Conlock, Cathy Devine, Jayne Egerton, Rosa Freedman, Lin Harwood, Jane Clare Jones, Kathleen Stock, Ruth Todd, Beth Vennart and all the other feminists who go on insisting that a woman's place is centre stage.

# List of Illustrations

**Plate Section I**

1. (Clockwise from top left): Shelagh Delaney (standing) with Jackie Shaw (mid-1940s); Shelagh in school photo with classmates (© The Delaneys); Shelagh and Micky, the Delaneys' dog, outside Duchy Road, Salford (© The Delaneys); Pendleton High School Building (1924) (held at Salford Museum Local History Library).
2. Letter from Shelagh Delaney to Joan Littlewood sending the script of *A Taste of Honey* (1958) (pen & ink on paper, English School, twentieth century / British Library, London) (© British Library Board. All Rights Reserved / Bridgeman Images).
3. *A Taste of Honey*, Original Manuscript (1958) (ink on paper, English School, twentieth century / British Library, London (© British Library Board. All Rights Reserved / Bridgeman Images).
4. Shelagh at her typewriter at Duchy Road (1959) (© Trinity Mirror / Mirrorpix / Alamy Stock Photo).
5. (Clockwise from top): Shelagh backstage with cast members from the premiere of her play *A Taste of Honey*, Theatre Royal, Stratford, London (1958) (©Howell Evans / Stringer); Shelagh with mother Elsie at Wyndham's Theatre, London (1959) (© Trinity Mirror / Mirrorpix / Alamy Stock Photo); Shelagh with Joan Littlewood (1959) (© Daily Mail /Shutterstock).
6. Shelagh outside her house on Duchy Road, Salford (1959) (© estate of Daniel Farson / National Portrait Gallery, London).
7. Shelagh smoking a cigarette whilst being interviewed in a pub, London (1959) (© Howell Evans / Stringer); Shelagh holding a copy of Elvis's album *King Creole* in Stratford, London (1958) (© Howell Evans / Stringer).

8. Shelagh sporting her beatnik look (1959) (© Associated Newspapers/ Shutterstock).

## Plate Section II

9. Shelagh relaxing at home in Salford (1958) (© Associated Newspapers/Shutterstock).

10. Rita Tushingham and Murray Melvin in the 1961 film adaptation of *A Taste of Honey*, directed by Tony Richardson (© Granger Historical Picture Archive / Alamy Stock Photo); Shelagh opening twenty-first birthday cards at her home in Salford (© Trinity Mirror / Mirrorpix / Alamy Stock Photo).

11. Shelagh with John Osborne and Vanessa Redgrave amongst the crowd in Trafalgar Square, for a Ban the Bomb sit-down demonstration, London (1961) (© Fox Photos / Stringer); Shelagh with Doris Lessing, John Osborne, George Melly and Vanessa Redgrave at the sit-down demonstration in Trafalgar Square, London. They were all later arrested (1961) (© Keystone Press / Alamy Stock Photo).

12. Shelagh in London after returning from one of her trips to the United States (*c.* 1962) (© The Delaneys).

13. (Clockwise from top left): Shelagh with Wolf Mankowitz before the opening of her play *The Lion In Love* at the Palace Theatre, Manchester (1963) (© Trinity Mirror / Mirrorpix / Alamy Stock Photo); Shelagh smiling with cigarette (1963) (© The Delaneys); Shelagh in 1963 (© L Forde/Daily Mail/Shutterstock).

14. Shelagh a few days after giving birth to her daughter Charlotte (1964) (© Terry Disney/Daily Express/Hulton Archive/Getty Images); *Charlie Bubbles* (1968) (© Everett Collection, Inc. / Alamy Stock Photo).

15. Shelagh and Charlotte in a photo booth in London (*c.* 1970) (© The Delaneys); Shelagh and Charlotte (*c.*1966) (© The Delaneys); Rupert Everett and Miranda Richardson in *Dance with a Stranger* (1985) (© United Archives GmbH / Alamy Stock Photo).

16. Shelagh in Cape Cod, Massachusetts, United States (© The Delaneys); Shelagh writing at home in Gerrard Road, Islington, London (*c.* 1988) (© The Delaneys).

*Every effort has been made by the publishers to trace the holders of copyright. Any inadvertent omissions of acknowledgement or permission can be rectified in future editions.*

# Note on Sources

All written sources, including unpublished manuscripts, are from Shelagh Delaney's private papers, unless noted otherwise. These are in the possession of Charlotte Delaney and are reproduced here with her permission.

All interviews were conducted by the author between 2014 and 2018, unless noted otherwise. To avoid cluttering the text with notes, these interviewees are cited in the endnotes when they are first mentioned and subsequently only where required for clarification. The interviewees are:

Michael Calderbank
Sophie Collins
Charlotte Delaney
Roni Ellis (interviewed by Andrea Thomson)
Shirley Evans (née Gray)
Sarah Frankcom
Stephen Frears
Bill Gray
Carol Greitzer
Valerie Ivison (interviewed by Andrea Thomson)
Hugh Karraker

Dee Johnson (interviewed by Andrea Thomson)
Rob Lees
Will Macadam
Barbara Marten
Murray Melvin
Kirk Morris (pseudonym)
Mike Newell
Sean O'Connor
Jenna Orkin
Kevin Palmer
Maxine Peake
Harold Riley
Amanda Schiff
Valeria Scialbini (interviewed by Andrea Thomson)
Polly Thomas
Zdena Tomin
Rita Tushingham
Beryl Twemlow
Sheila Wade
Wilf Wade
Ahuva Weisbaum
Jean Whur
Kath Wilkie

# Notes

## Chapter 1: Curtain Up

1 Letter from Shelagh Delaney to Joan Littlewood, April 1958, Joan Littlewood Archive, Production Correspondence: Shelagh Delaney and A Taste of Honey – First Production, British Library.

2 'An ear for dialogue', *Listener*, 21 August 1958, p. 291.

3 Interview with Stephen Frears.

4 Shelagh Delaney, *A Taste of Honey*, Bloomsbury, 2014, Act 2, Scene 1, p. 55.

5 Quoted in interview with Murray Melvin.

6 Denis Constanduros, 'Television Drama Report on *A Taste of Honey*', BBC drama department, 5 June 1958, T48/201/1 Monitor TX 25/09/1960, BBC Written Archives.

7 Interview with Norman Rimmell, Theatre Archive Project, British Library Sound Archive.

8 Quoted in Kay Mellor, *A Taste of Honey by Shelagh Delaney – the Legacy*, BBC Radio 4, 22 May 2008.

9 Alan Brien, 'First and Last Things', *Spectator*, 5 June 1958, p. 13.

10 See for example: Leonore Davidoff, *Worlds Between: Historical Perspectives on Gender and Class*, Cambridge, 1995, p. 12; Sheila Rowbotham, *Promise of a Dream: Remembering the Sixties*, Penguin, 2000, p. 4.

11 Angela Carter, 'Truly it felt like Year One', in Sara Maitland (ed.), *Very Heaven: Looking Back at the 1960s*, Virago, 1988, p. 210.

12 Jean Floud, *Social Class and Educational Opportunity*, Heinemann, 1956.

13 Mary Evans, *A Good School: Life at a Girls' Grammar School in the 1950s*, Women's Press, 1991, p. 36.

14 Rowbotham, *Promise of a Dream*, p. 61.

15 Carter, 'Truly it felt like Year One', p. 210.

16 Richard Hoggart, *The Uses of Literacy*, Penguin, 1957, pp. 99–101.

17 'Whatever Happened to Shelagh Delaney?', *Financial Times,* 26 July 1963, p. 8.

18 Jeanette Winterson, 'My hero: Shelagh Delaney', *Guardian*, 18 Sept 2010, https://www.theguardian.com/books/2010/sep/18/jeanette-winterson-my-hero-shelagh-delaney, consulted 2 May 2017.

19 Interview with Zdena Tomin.

## Chapter 2: Becoming Shelagh

1 Quoted in Laurence Kitchin, *Mid-Century Drama*, Faber, 1960, p. 167.

2 Sheila Rowbotham, *Promise of a Dream: Remembering the Sixties*, Penguin, 2000, p. 54.

3 Quoted in Kitchin, *Mid-Century Drama*, p. 167.

4 Unpublished MS by Elsie Delaney, *c.*1975.

5 Alexander Thomas Sadler, 'Socioeconomic Determinants of Tuberculosis', PhD Thesis, York, 2013, table 1.3, p. 72.

6 Charles Webster, 'Healthy or Hungry Thirties?', *History Workshop Journal*, vol. 13, no. 1, 1982, pp. 116–17.

7 Shelagh Delaney, *Sweetly Sings the Donkey*, Penguin, 1968, p. 53.

8 Note from Joseph Delaney to Elsie Delaney, 20 November 1939.

9 'Shelagh Delaney's Salford', *Monitor*, dir. Ken Russell, BBC, 1960.

10 Manchester and District Regional Survey Society, *Report on a Survey of Housing Conditions in a Salford Area*, Manchester, 1930, pp. 5 and 12.

11 Richard Hoggart, *The Uses of Literacy*, Penguin, 1957, pp. 35–6.

12 'Shelagh Delaney's Salford', *Monitor*.

13 Interview with anon (DG is a pseudonym), NWSA 2002. 0755a, Manchester Archives, Manchester Central Library.

14 Hoggart, *The Uses of Literacy*, p. 37.

15 Anon, in I. Brotherston and C. Windmill (eds), *Bridging the Years: A History of Trafford Park and Salford Docks as Remembered by Those who Lived and Worked in the Area*, Salford Quays Heritage Centre, 1992, p. 13.

16 Ibid., p. 25.

17 Hoggart, *The Uses of Literacy*, p. 22.

18 Interview with Charlotte Delaney; interview with Beryl Twemlow.

19 Hoggart, *The Uses of Literacy*, p. 29.

20  Interview with Charlotte Delaney; unpublished MS by Elsie Delaney, *c.*1975.

21  Sue Lane quoted in *Bridging the Years*, p. 13.

22  Shelagh Delaney, 'Never Underestimate 18-Year-Old Girls', *New York Times Magazine*, 28 May 1961, p. 31.

23  Interview with Charlotte Delaney.

24  Quoted in Kitchin, *Mid-Century Drama*, p. 167.

25  Carol Dix (ed.), *Say I'm Sorry to Mother*, Pan, 1978, p. 15.

26  Quoted in 'An Artist's View', *Salford City Reporter*, 8 September 1961, p. 5.

27  Salford Education Committee, *Salford Education Committee Report 1943–1953*, Salford Council, p. 35.

28  John Berger, *About Looking*, London, 1980, p. 88.

29  Interview with Charlotte Delaney.

30  Interview with Jean Whur.

31  'Housing Displaced Tenants', *Salford City Reporter*, 26 February 1936, p. 6.

32  'Salford Council and Its Officials', *Manchester Guardian*, 5 December 1935, p. 7.

33  On Salford's housing policy, see Salford City Housing Committee, minutes and reports from the 1940s, held at Salford City Archives and Local History Centre (no accession number).

34  'Shelagh Delaney's Salford'.

35  Interview with Jean Whur.

36  Hoggart, *The Uses of Literacy*, p. 37.

37  Interview with Charlotte Delaney.

38  Alva Myrdal and Viola Klein, *Women's Two Roles: Work and Home*, Routledge & Kegan Paul, 1956.

39 Interview with Shirley Evans; interview with Jean Whur.

40 Carolyn Steedman, *Landscape for a Good Woman*, Virago, 1986, p. 72.

41 Delaney, *Sweetly Sings the Donkey*, p. 37.

42 Ibid., p. 71.

43 Interview with Charlotte Delaney.

44 'Treatment of Osteomyelitis', *Lancet*, 27 October 1945, p. 532.

45 Quoted in http://www.patient.co.uk/forums/discuss/56-years-of-living-with-osteomyelitis-and-its-after-effects-part-1–38001, consulted 12 September 2015.

46 Quoted in *Playbill: a weekly magazine for theatregoers*, 4 October 1960, p. 31.

47 'Convalescent Homes', *Lancet*, 6 September 1947, pp. 359–60.

48 Annette Kuhn, *Family Secrets: Acts of Memory and Imagination*, Verso, 1995, p. 75.

49 Delaney, *Sweetly Sings the Donkey*, p. 38.

50 Ibid., p. 12.

51 Ibid., p. 42.

52 Ibid., pp. 50–1.

53 For example A. S. Byatt, 'The Pleasure of Reading', in Antonia Fraser (ed.), *The Pleasure of Reading*, pp. 136–43; Lorna Sage, *Bad Blood,* Fourth Estate, 2000, p. 110.

54 Delaney, *Sweetly Sings the Donkey*, p. 14.

55 Quoted in Joan Littlewood, *Joan's Book: The Autobiography of Joan Littlewood*, Methuen, 2003, p. 376.

56 Delaney, *Sweetly Sings the Donkey*; interview with Harold Riley.

57 Interview with Harold Riley.

58 Rowbotham, *Promise of a Dream*, p. 12.

59 Quoted in Kitchin, *Mid-Century Drama*, p. 166.

60 Delaney, *Sweetly Sings the Donkey*, p. 14.

61 Ibid., p. 38.

62 Steedman, *Landscape for a Good Woman*, p. 93.

63 Ibid., p. 82.

64 Margaret Forster, *Hidden Lives: A Family Memoir*, Penguin, 1996, p. 177.

## Chapter 3: Borderline Girl

1 Draft script for 'Shelagh Delaney's Salford', T32/982/1 Monitor TX 25/09/1960, BBC Written Archives.

2 Interview with Jean Whur.

3 L. Moss, *Education and the People*, HMSO, 1945, p. 2.

4 'Shelagh Delaney's Salford', *Monitor*, dir. Ken Russell, BBC, 1960.

5 Interview with Jean Whur.

6 'Shelagh Delaney's Salford'; 'School Entrance', *Manchester Guardian*, 16 May 1950, p. 6; A. Moon, 'Educational guidance and the borderline child', *Educational Review*, 1 June 1957, vol. 9, no. 3, pp. 190–6.

7 'Shelagh Delaney's Salford'.

8 Annette Kuhn, *Family Secrets: Acts of Memory and Imagination*, Verso, 1995, p. 104.

9 E. P. Thompson, 'Outside the Whale', originally published 1960; reprinted in *The Poverty of Theory and Other Essays*, Merlin Press, 1978, p. 19.

10 Kuhn, *Family Secrets*, p. 104.

11 Interview with Valerie Ivison.

12 Ministry of Education, *The New Secondary Education*, HMSO, 1947, pp. 30–1.

13 Report of HM Inspectors on Broughton County Modern Secondary School (Girls' Department), Salford, 20, 21 and 22 May 1947, The National Archives (TNA), ED 109/8925, p. 2.

14 'The History Club', *Broughton School Magazine*, July 1952, p. 3.

15 Quoted in Laurence Kitchin, *Mid-Century Drama*, Faber, 1960, p. 168.

16 John Mapplebeck, 'Playwright on Probation', *Guardian*, 20 September 1960, p. 9.

17 Quoted in Kitchin, *Mid-Century Drama*, p. 168.

18 Sheila Delaney, 'The Vagabond', *Broughton School Magazine*, July 1952, p. 4.

19 Salford Education Committee, *Salford Education Committee Report 1943–1953*, Salford Council, p. 28.

20 Interview with Valerie Ivison.

21 Salford Education Committee, *Salford Education Committee Report*, pp. 26–7.

22 'A Playwright's Education', *Manchester Guardian*, 12 December 1958, p. 4.

23 Pendleton High School for Girls School Register 1953, held at Salford Local History and Archives Centre (no accession number).

24 'Shelagh Delaney's Salford'.

25 Salford Education Committee, *Salford Education Committee Report 1943–1953*, p. 46; The National Archives (TNA):

ED 109/8925, Report of HM Inspectors on Pendleton High School for Girls, Salford, 6, 7, 8 and 9 October 1953, p. 3.

26 Draft script for 'Shelagh Delaney's Salford'.

27 Report by HM Inspectors on Pendleton High School for Girls, pp. 6 and 15.

28 Interview with Jean Whur.

29 Report by HM Inspectors on Pendleton High School for Girls, p. 6.

30 Mary Evans, *A Good School: Life at a Girls' Grammar School in the 1950s*, Women's Press, 1991, p. 31.

31 Ethel Rogers, 'House Report', *Pendleton High School Magazine*, April 1954, p. 5.

32 Jean Pearson, 'Memories', *Pendleton High School*, Salford Council, 1967, p. 10.

33 John Newsom, *The Education of Girls*, Faber, 1948, p. 147.

34 1951 Conservative Party Manifesto, http://www.conservativemanifesto.com/1951/1951-conservative-manifesto.shtml, consulted 1 November 2016.

35 E. P. Thompson, 'Outside the Whale', originally published 1960; reprinted in *The Poverty of Theory and Other Essays*, Merlin Press, 1978, p. 23.

36 Quoted in Report by HM Inspectors on Pendleton High School for Girls, p. 3.

37 Interview with Jean Whur.

38 HM Inspectors of Schools, Notes of Meeting with the Governing Body of Pendleton High School for Girls, 16 October 1953.

39 Norma Rowles, quoted on www.francisfrith.com/salford, consulted 15 April 2014.

40  Pammy1241 on https://services.salford.gov.uk/forum/forum-posts.asp?forum=20&id=133091, 11 December 2011, consulted 15 July 2015.

41  'Shelagh Delaney's Salford'.

42  Interview with Jean Whur.

43  'That Salford Film … This Reader Says "Bravo"', *Salford City Reporter*, 18 September 1960, p. 4.

44  Carolyn Steedman, *Landscape for a Good Woman*, Virago, 1986, p. 122.

45  Letter from Jessie Hargreaves and letter from Elsie Delaney, *Salford City Reporter*, 27 February 1959, p. 3.

46  Interview with Harold Riley.

47  Interview with Shirley Evans.

48  Interview with Beryl Twemlow.

49  Sheila Delaney, 'Learning to Ride a Bicycle', *Pendleton High School Magazine*, July 1954, p. 3.

50  The title of Vivian Mercier's review in the *Irish Times*, 18 February 1956, p. 12.

51  Samuel Beckett, *Worstward Ho*, Calder, 1983, p. 89.

52  Lorna Sage, *Bad Blood*, Fourth Estate, 2000, p. 130; L. F. Moore, *Going Comprehensive, or Unspoken Thoughts of a Deputy Head*, WPS, 2009, p. 108.

53  Shelagh Delaney, *Dance with a Stranger*, MS, Working Title Productions, 1985, pp. 13 and 61.

54  'Mothers Out at Work', *The Times*, 2 June 1958.

55  Email from Shelagh Delaney to Hila Feil, 26 May 2003; interview with Harold Riley; interview with Beryl Twemlow.

56  Interview with Albert Finney in Hal Burton (ed.), *Acting in the Sixties*, BBC, 1970, p. 66.

57  Kitchin, *Mid-Century Drama*, p. 167. Describing her jobs after leaving school, Shelagh says 'instead of training to be a teacher', implying that her teachers had expected this of her.

58  'A Playwright's Education', letter from F. A. J. Rivett, *Manchester Guardian*, 20 December 1958, p. 6.

59  'A Playwright's Education', letter from Shelagh Delaney, *Manchester Guardian*, 12 December 1958, p. 4.

60  'Teacher Was Wrong About These Two!', *TV Times*, 10–16 June 1962, p. 22.

61  'A Playwright's Education', *Manchester Guardian*, 12 December 1958, p. 4.

62  Kuhn, *Family Secrets*, p. 108.

## Chapter 4: 'I Write As People Talk'

1  Quoted in Laurence Kitchin, *Mid-Century Drama*, Faber, 1960, p. 168.

2  Salford Youth Service, *Report for 1953–1957*, Salford City Council, p. 70.

3  'Who's a Square?', *Daily Mirror*, 9 May 1958, p. 11.

4  Letter from Shirley Hynd, *Pendleton High School Magazine*, p. 43.

5  Interview with Beryl Twemlow.

6  Draft script for 'Shelagh Delaney's Salford', T32/982/1 Monitor TX 25/09/1960, BBC Written Archives.

7  Shelagh summarises her employment history in Kitchin, *Mid-Century Drama*, Faber, 1960, p. 167.

8  Monica Edwards, *Joan Goes Farming*, Bodley Head, 1954, p. 20.

9  Interview with Murray Melvin.

10 Edward Shils and Michael Young, 'The Meaning of the Coronation', *Sociological Review*, vol. 1, no. 2, December 1953, p. 63.

11 Conservative Party 1955 Manifesto, http://www.conservativemanifesto.com/1955/1955-conservative-manifesto.shtml, consulted 14 April 2017.

12 'Problem Families a Menace', *The Times*, 28 September 1953, p. 3.

13 Interview with Valerie Ivison.

14 Draft script for 'Shelagh Delaney's Salford'.

15 Interview with Charlotte Delaney.

16 Draft script for 'Shelagh Delaney's Salford'.

17 Shelagh Delaney, 'Never Underestimate 18-year-old Girls', *New York Times Magazine*, 28 May 1961, p. 32.

18 Report of the Committee on Homosexual Offences and Prostitution (The Wolfenden Report), HMSO, 1957.

19 Interview with Kath Wilkie.

20 Alan Sillitoe, *Life Without Armour: An Autobiography*, HarperCollins, 1995, p. 235.

21 Kenneth Tynan, 'Summing Up: 1959', in Kenneth Tynan (ed.), *Curtains: Selections from the Drama Criticism and Related Writings*, Longmans, 1961, p. 232.

22 Kenneth Tynan, 'Backwards and Forwards', *Observer*, 30 December 1956, p. 8.

23 Kenneth Tynan, *A View of the English Stage 1944–65*, Methuen, 1975, p. 178.

24 Quoted in Charles Marowitz and Simon Trussler (eds), *Theatre at Work: Playwrights and Production in the Modern British Theatre. A collection of interviews and essays*, Methuen, 1967, p. 83.

25 Draft script for 'Shelagh Delaney's Salford'.

26 Interview with Bill Gray.

27 Lilian Barker, https://services.salford.gov.uk/forum/forum-posts.asp?=132092, consulted 5 March 2016.

28 Quoted in Carol Dix (ed.), *Say I'm Sorry to Mother*, Pan, 1978, p. 30.

29 Interview with Jean Whur.

30 Labour Party, *Let Us Face the Future*, Labour Party Manifesto, Labour Party 1945, p. 2.

31 Keynes quoted in Christopher Frayling, *The only trustworthy book … Arts and Public Value*, Arts Council of England, 2005, p. 31.

32 Theatre Union Manifesto, 1936, http://wcml.org.uk/maccoll/maccoll/theatre/theatre-union/, consulted 10 April 2017.

33 N. Rowland and Manchester City Council, *City of Manchester Plan*, Jarrold, 1945, p. 104.

34 Library Theatre Company, https://homemcr.org/about/history/library-theatre-company/, consulted 29 May 2016.

35 'New Writer', *Newsweek*, 26 September 1960, p. 44.

36 Interview with Murray Melvin; information from Ann Knowles and Harold Riley.

37 Ewan MacColl, *Journeyman: An Autobiography*, Sidgwick & Jackson, 1990, p. 244.

38 Irving Wardle, *Theatre Criticism*, Routledge, 1992, p. 4.

39 Interview with Charlotte Delaney; Charlotte Delaney, 'Shelagh Delaney – a true rebel', National Theatre Blog, http://national-theatre.tumblr.com/post/77804985203/shelagh-delaney-a-true-rebel-by-charlotte, consulted 3 September 2015.

40 Quoted in Kitchin, *Mid-Century Drama*, p. 168.

41 Interview with Charlotte Delaney.

42 Quoted in Kitchin, *Mid-Century Drama*, p. 168.

43 Phyllis Bentley, *O Dreams, O Destinations*, Gollancz, 1962, pp. 266–7.

44 Richard Hoggart, *The Uses of Literacy*, Penguin, 1957.

45 Annette Kuhn, *Family Secrets: Acts of Memory and Imagination*, Verso, 1995, pp. 118–19.

46 Tom Courtenay, *Dear Tom: Letters from Home*, Black Swan, 2001, p. 189.

47 Stan Barstow, *In My Own Good Time*, Smith Settle, 2001, p. 85.

48 Carolyn Steedman, *Landscape for a Good Woman*, Virago, 1986, p. 15.

49 Draft script for 'Shelagh Delaney's Salford'.

50 Quoted in Kitchin, *Mid-Century Drama*, p. 168.

51 Sillitoe, *Life Without Armour*, pp. 221–2.

52 Quoted in Harry Ritchie, *Success Stories: Literature and the Media in England, 1950–1959*, Faber, 1988, p.189.

53 Shelagh Delaney, *A Taste of Honey*, Bloomsbury, 2014, Act 2, Scene 2, p. 72.

54 Interview with Stephen Frears, and also interviews with Mike Newell and Sean O'Connor.

55 Interview with Kath Wilkie.

56 Hoggart, *The Uses of Literacy*, pp. 50–1.

57 Shelagh Delaney, *Baloney Said Salome*, MS, n.d., c.2004, p. 3.

58 Shelagh Delaney, *Dance with a Stranger*, MS, Working Title Productions, 1985, p. 36.

59 *The Youth Service in England and Wales. Report of the Committee appointed by the Minister of Education in November 1958*, London, 1960, p. 29.

60 Delaney, *Dance with a Stranger*, p. 32.

61 'Shelagh Delaney's Salford'.

62 Interview with Harold Riley.

63 Interview with Charlotte Delaney.

64 Sillitoe, *Life Without Armour*, p. 39.

65 Shelagh Delaney, *So Said the Nightingale*, MS, *c.*1979; *Tell Me a Film*, MS, *c.*2003.

66 Interviews with Murray Melvin and Harold Riley.

67 Quoted in Kitchin, *Mid-Century Drama*, p. 168. See also 'New Writer', *Newsweek*, 26 September 1960, p. 44.

68 'Shelagh Delaney's Salford'.

## Chapter 5: A Taste Of Honey

1 Letter from Shelagh Delaney to Joan Littlewood, April 1958, Joan Littlewood Archive, Production Correspondence: Shelagh Delaney and A Taste of Honey – First Production, British Library.

2 Ewan MacColl, *Journeyman: An Autobiography*, Sidgwick & Jackson, 1990, p. 255.

3 Nadine Holdsworth, '"They'd Have Pissed on My Grave": the Arts Council and Theatre Workshop', *New Quarterly*, vol. 15, no. 1, 1999, pp. 3–4.

4 Kenneth Tynan, 'Debit Account', *Manchester Guardian*, 13 October 1957, p. 16.

5 'Lines not approved by Lord: Fines on members of Theatre Workshop company', *Manchester Guardian*, 17 April 1958, p. 6.

6  Laurence Kitchin, *Mid-Century Drama*, Faber, 1960, p. 168.

7  Interview with Shelagh Delaney, *ITN News*, February 1959, uploaded by *Channel 4 News*, https://www.youtube.com/watch?v=SM22loR53TQ, consulted 15 February 2017.

8  For an account of Theatre Workshop's history see Howard Goorney, *The Theatre Workshop Story*, Methuen, 1981.

9  Interview with Murray Melvin.

10  Press release, T32/982/1 Monitor TX 25/09/1960, BBC Written Archives.

11  Irving Wardle, 'All the World's a Workshop', *Independent*, 2 April 1994, http://www.independent.co.uk/arts-entertainment/theatre-all-the-worlds-a-workshop-joan-littlewood-revolutionised-the-stage-irving-wardle-reviews-her-1367588.html, consulted 19 April 2017; interview with Peter Rankin, Theatre Archive Project, British Library Sound Archive.

12  Oscar Lewenstein, *Kicking Against the Pricks: A Theatre Producer Looks Back*, Nick Hern Books, 1994, p.90.

13  Interview with Murray Melvin.

14  Shelagh Delaney, *A Taste of Honey*, Bloomsbury, 2014, Act 2, Scene 1, p. 47.

15  Ibid., Act 1, Scene 2, p. 26.

16  Quoted in Goorney, *The Theatre Workshop Story*, p. 109.

17  Ibid.

18  Ibid.

19  Interview with Murray Melvin.

20  Shelagh Delaney, blurb for TV listing of *A Taste of Honey*, *Radio Times*, 24 September 1987, p. 81.

21 Delaney, *A Taste of Honey*, Act 1, Scene 1, p. 13.

22 Ibid., Act 1, Scene 1, p. 15.

23 Colin MacInnes, 'A Taste of Reality', *Encounter*, no. 67, April 1959, pp. 70–1.

24 Delaney, *A Taste of Honey*, Act 1, Scene 2, p. 25.

25 Ibid., Act 2, Scene 1, pp. 48 and 50.

26 Shelagh Delaney, unpublished script of *A Taste of Honey*, with Joan Littlewood's notes, March 1958, Add MS 89164/8/75, British Library. All subsequent quotations from Delaney's script or Joan's amendments are taken from this source.

27 Quoted in John Harding, *Sweetly Sings Delaney: A Study of Shelagh Delaney's Work 1958–68*, Greenwich Exchange, 2014, p. 64.

28 Delaney, *A Taste of Honey*, Act 2, Scene 1, p. 63.

29 Interview with Sean O'Connor.

30 Quoted in Harding, *Sweetly Sings Delaney*, p. 65.

31 Reader's Report, 5 May 1958, Stage Play Submitted for Licence, A Taste of Honey, 1958/1017, Lord Chamberlain's Papers, British Library.

32 Letter from Brigadier Gwatkin to E. L. Norton Esq, 2 February 1959, A Taste of Honey, 1958/1017, Lord Chamberlain's Papers, British Library.

33 Letter from Brigadier Gwatkin to Gerry Raffles, 8 May 1958, 1958/1017, Lord Chamberlain's Papers, British Library.

34 Kenneth Tynan, 'At the Theatre', *Observer*, 6 June 1958, p. 15.

35 Doris Lessing, 'At the Theatre', *Observer*, 23 November 1958, p. 17.

36 'An ear for dialogue', *Listener*, 21 August 1958, p. 291.

37 Interview with Shelagh Delaney, *ITN News*, February 1959.

38 'Honey? It's more like marmalade', *Daily Mail*, 28 May 1958, p. 3.

39 Quoted in Alan Sinfield, *Literature, Politics and Culture in Postwar Britain*, Blackwell, 1989, p. 233. Maugham made the remark in the *Sunday Times* in December 1955.

40 Alan Brien, 'First and Last Things', *Spectator*, 5 June 1958, p. 13.

41 'Honey? It's more like marmalade', *Daily Mail*, 28 May 1958, p. 3.

42 Quoted in John Mapplebeck, 'Playwright on Probation', *Guardian*, 20 September 1960, p. 9.

43 E. P. Thompson, *The Making of the English Working Class*, Penguin, 1968, 2nd edn, pp. 8–12.

44 'Shelagh Has the Right Idea', *Salford City Reporter*, 9 May 1958, p. 3.

45 Editorial, *Salford City Reporter*, 20 June 1958, p. 1.

46 '*A Taste of Honey* Has Bitter Flavour', *Salford City Reporter*, 23 January 1959, p. 3.

47 Ann Oakley, *Taking it like a woman*, Cape, 1984.

48 Carolyn Steedman, *Landscape for a Good Woman*, Virago, 1986, p. 79.

49 Interview with Zdena Tomin. A similar view was given by Stephen Frears.

50 Correspondence between Shelagh Delaney and Mollie Lee, July 1958, Shelagh Delaney, File 1 1958–1962, Personal Files, BBC Written Archives.

## Chapter 6: The Lucretia Borgia of Salford

1 Information from Gerry Feil.

2 'My Clothes and I', *Observer*, 19 April 1959, p. 15.

3 'The Lucretia Borgia of Salford, Lancs', *Daily Mail*, 9 February 1959, p. 6.

4 *Playbill*, 4 October 1960, p. 31.

5 Interview with Charlotte Delaney; interview with Murray Melvin; interview with Kevin Palmer.

6 *Playbill*, 4 October 1960, p. 31.

7 'Miss Delaney gets her own taste of honey', *Manchester Guardian*, 5 December 1958, p. 5.

8 Ibid.

9 'New Writer', *Newsweek*, 26 September 1960, p. 44.

10 Ibid.

11 Tom Courtenay, *Dear Tom: Letters from Home*, Black Swan, 2001, p. 190.

12 'Miss Delaney gets her own taste of honey', p. 5.

13 Quoted in John Harding, *Sweetly Sings Delaney: A Study of Shelagh Delaney's Work 1958–68,* Greenwich Exchange, 2014, pp. 64–5.

14 Interview with Polly Thomas.

15 Letter from E. L. Norton Esq to Lord Chamberlain, 29 January 1959, *A Taste of Honey*, 1958/1017, Lord Chamberlain's Papers, British Library.

16 '*A Taste of Honey* Has Bitter Flavour', *Salford City Reporter*, 23 January 1959, p. 5.

17 Interview with Shirley Evans.

18 Letter from Mrs Crewe of Pendleton, *Salford City Reporter*, 27 February 1959, p. 3.

19  Letter from Yvonne Carter, *Salford City Reporter,* 27 February 1959, p. 3.

20  Richard Hoggart, *The Uses of Literacy,* Penguin, 1957, p. 22.

21  Quoted in Courtenay, *Dear Tom,* p. 183.

22  Alan Sillitoe, *Life Without Armour: An Autobiography,* HarperCollins, 1995, p. 252.

23  M. A. Cohen, 'Plays for the People?', *Marxism Today,* July 1959, p. 213.

24  'A Honey of a Play by the Ex-usherette', *Daily Herald,* 12 February 1959, p. 7.

25  Thomas C. Worsley, 'The Sweet Smell', *New Statesman,* 21 February 1959, vol. LVII, no. 1458, p. 252.

26  Quoted in Irving Wardle, 'Introduction', in Charles Marowitz and Simon Trussler (eds), *Theatre at Work: Playwrights and Production in the Modern British Theatre. A collection of interviews and essays,* Methuen, 1967, p. 11.

27  'Playwright on Probation', *Guardian,* 20 September 1960, p. 9.

28  Letter from G. Hodcroft, *Salford City Reporter,* 5 March 1959, p. 3.

29  'Shelagh Annoyed', *Salford City Reporter,* 29 October 1959, p. 3.

30  'A Taste of Cash for Shelagh but a kick in the teeth for Salford', *Salford City Reporter,* 13 February 1959, p. 9.

31  Alan Dunsmore, 'Theatre', *People's Journal,* 15 September 1962, p. 6.

32  Quoted in Kay Mellor, *A Taste of Honey by Shelagh Delaney – the Legacy,* BBC Radio 4, 22 May 2008. On middle-class

attitudes to sex, see Geoffrey Gorer, *Exploring English Character*, Cressett Press, 1955, p. 95.

33  'Shelagh Says ... ', *Daily Mirror*, 12 February 1959, p. 2.

34  Keith Waterhouse, *City Lights and Streets Ahead*, British Library, 2013, pp. 228 and 230.

35  Sally Alexander, in Michelene Wandor (ed.), *Once a Feminist: Stories of a Generation*, Virago, 1990, p. 83.

36  Interview with Shelagh Delaney, *ITN News*, February 1959, uploaded by *Channel 4 News*, https://www.youtube.com/watch?v=SM22loR53TQ, consulted 15 February 2017.

37  Quoted in Carol Dix (ed.), *Say I'm Sorry to Mother*, Pan, 1978, p. 34.

38  Elizabeth Wilson, *Mirror Writing: An Autobiography*, Virago, 1982, p. 71.

39  'The Lucretia Borgia of Salford, Lancs', *Daily Mail*, 9 February 1959, p. 6.

40  Dix, *Say I'm Sorry to Mother*, p. 30.

41  Lorna Sage, *Bad Blood*, Fourth Estate, 2000, p. 99.

42  'It's the Well-Groomed Who Get the Jobs', *Manchester Evening News*, 26 September 1960, p. 3.

43  'Shelagh's Taste of Money', *Daily Mail*, 2 January 1959, p. 3.

44  'The Lucretia Borgia of Salford, Lancs', *Daily Mail*, 9 February 1959, p. 6.

45  Shelagh Delaney, *A Taste of Honey*, Bloomsbury, 2014, Act 2, Scene 1, p. 50.

46  'My Clothes and I', *Observer*, 19 April 1959, p. 15.

47  'Shelagh's Taste of Money', *Daily Mail*, 2 January 1959, p. 3.

48  Shelagh Delaney, 'Never Underestimate 18-Year-Old Girls', *New York Times Magazine*, 28 May 1961, p. 32.

49 'Playwright on Probation', *Guardian*, 20 September 1960, p. 9.

50 'More Theatre Workshop Plays for the West End', *The Times*, 8 December 1958, p. 14.

51 'A Raw Slice of Theatre', *Manchester Guardian*, 18 February 1959, p. 5.

52 'Playwright on Probation', *Guardian*, 20 September 1960, p. 9. See also Laurence Kitchin, *Mid-Century Drama*, Faber, 1960, p. 168.

53 Interview with Murray Melvin.

54 Quoted in Joan Littlewood, *Joan's Book: The Autobiography of Joan Littlewood*, Methuen, 2003, p. 376.

## Chapter 7: Coming of Age

1 *Playbill: a weekly magazine for theatregoers*, 4 October 1960, p. 31.

2 Interview with Murray Melvin.

3 'Playwright on Probation', *Guardian*, 20 September 1960, p. 9.

4 Aesop, *Aesop's Fables*, translated by George Townsend, Gutenberg, 2008, ebook, CIX.

5 Ian Gazeley, *Poverty in Britain 1900–1965*, Palgrave, 2003, pp. 181–2.

6 Debate on the Address, House of Commons Debates, *Hansard*, 30 October 1959, vol. 612, col. 622–3.

7 The National Archives (TNA): HLG 101/297, 'Problem Families', MS, p. 2.

8 B. S. Rowntree and G. R. Lavers, *Poverty and the Welfare State*, Longmans Green, 1951, p. 57.

9 'Mothers Out at Work', *The Times*, 2 June 1958, p. 13.

10 Interview with Sean O'Connor.

11 Shelagh Delaney, *The Lion in Love: a play*, Methuen, 1961, Act 3, p. 101.

12 Ibid., p. 103.

13 Ibid., p. 95.

14 Ibid., p. 96.

15 Ibid., p. 97.

16 From *Joan's Book*, quoted in John Harding, *Sweetly Sings Delaney: A Study of Shelagh Delaney's Work 1958–68*, Greenwich Exchange, 2014, p. 95. Also interview with Murray Melvin.

17 Quoted in Harding, *Sweetly Sings Delaney*, p. 95.

18 Quoted in ibid.

19 Clive Barker, 'A Brief History of Clive Barker', *New Theatre Quarterly*, 23, 2007, p. 295.

20 Memorandum from Betty Willingale, Script Library, to Mr Hugh Stewart, Drama Producer, Birmingham, 23 August 1960, and Report from Drama Producer, Birmingham, on *The Lion in Love*, to AHD (Television), 7 September 1960, Shelagh Delaney, T48/201/1 1958–1962, Personal Files, BBC Written Archives.

21 Jeremy Brooks, 'Chunks of Life', *New Statesman*, 17 September 1960.

22 'Playwright on Probation', *Guardian*, 20 September 1960, p. 9.

23 John Osborne, *Looking Back: Never Explain, Never Apologise*, Faber, 1999, p. 99.

24 Kenneth Tynan, 'The Lion and the Mange', *Observer*, 1 January 1961, p. 18.

25 'The Lion in Love: Royal Court', *Guardian*, 30 December 1960, p. 5.

26 Richard Findlater (ed.), *At the Royal Court: 25 Years of the English Stage Company*, Ambergate, 1981, p. 101.

27 Email from Arnold Wesker to the author, 24 June 2014.

28 BBC drama department, Report on a meeting with Shelagh Delaney, 1959, Shelagh Delaney, File 1 1958–1962, Personal Files, BBC Written Archives.

29 Draft script for 'Shelagh Delaney's Salford', T32/982/1 Monitor TX 25/09/1960, BBC Written Archives.

30 'Playwright on Probation', *Guardian,* 20 September 1960, p. 9.

31 Quoted in Harding, *Sweetly Sings Delaney*, p. 75.

32 'A Playwright's Education', *Manchester Guardian*, 20 December 1958, p. 6.

33 Draft script for 'Shelagh Delaney's Salford'.

34 'The Pregnant Globe', *Observer*, 2 October 1960, p. 25.

35 'Last night's television', *Guardian*, 26 September 1960, p. 7.

36 'Salford Flays Shelagh's Film', *Salford City Reporter*, 21 September 1960, p. 3.

37 'That Salford Film', *Salford City Reporter*, 23 September 1960, p. 4.

38 'Salford Flays Shelagh's Film', *Salford City Reporter*, 21 September 1960, p. 3.

39 'That Salford Film', *Salford City Reporter*, 23 September 1960, p. 4.

40 Alistair Cooke quoted in E. P. Thompson, 'Outside the Whale', originally published 1960; reprinted in *The Poverty of Theory and Other Essays*, Merlin Press, 1978, p. 1.

41 Thompson, 'Outside the Whale', p. 31.

42 Leila Berg, 'All We Had Was a Voice', in Sara Maitland (ed.), *Very Heaven: Looking Back at the 1960s*, Virago, 1988, p. 60.

43 Shelagh Delaney, 'Never Underestimate 18-Year-Old Girls', *New York Times Magazine*, 28 May 1961, pp. 30–3.

44 'Big Pay-Out Follows the Big Sit-Down', *Daily Mirror*, 19 September 1961, pp. 14–15.

45 Quoted in interview with Philip Hedley, Theatre Archive Project, British Library Sound Archive.

46 An excellent account of the trial is provided in Chris Hilliard, '"Is It a Book That You Would Even Wish Your Wife or Your Servants to Read?" Obscenity Law and the Politics of Reading in Modern England', *American Historical Review*, vol. 118, no. 3, 2013, pp. 653–78. Quote is from this source.

47 Quoted in Robert Hewison, *Too Much: Art and Society in the Sixties 1960–75*, Methuen, 1986, p. 18.

48 Arnold Wesker interviewed by Simon Trussler, in Charles Marowitz and Simon Trussler (eds), *Theatre at Work: Playwrights and Production in the Modern British Theatre. A collection of interviews and essays*, Methuen, 1967, p. 84.

49 *Playbill: a weekly magazine for theatregoers*, 4 October 1960, p. 31.

50 Ibid.

51 'Teacher Was Wrong About These Two!', *TV Times*, 10–16 June 1962, p. 22.

52 Interview with Mike Newell.

53 Tony Warren, *I Was Ena Sharples' Father*, Duckworth, 1969, p. 27.

54 Quotations from 'Salford Rebel Sister Shelagh Delaney', *Salford Star*, 22 November 2011, http://www.salfordstar. com/article.asp?id=1196, consulted 10 November 2017; information from Harold Riley.

55 Interview with Harold Riley.

56 '*A Taste of Honey* Has Bitter Flavour', *Salford City Reporter*, 23 January 1959, p. 5. See also 'Odd Request', *Salford City Reporter*, 5 February 1960, p. 4.

57 '"We Should be Proud of Shelagh" Say Building Workers', *Salford City Reporter*, 29 April 1960, p. 5.

58 'Reasons for wanting to begin a community centre theatre in Salford', MS, *c*.1960, Clive Barker Archive, Rose College Library.

59 Manchester Branch of the Musicians' Union, 'A Post War Plan for the Entertainments Industry', 14 February 1945, MU/4/1/5/7, Musicians' Union Archive, University of Stirling Archives.

60 Manchester and Salford Council of Social Service, *Setting Up House*, MSCS, *c*.1960, p. 19.

61 'Theatre Talk in Shelagh's Home', *Manchester Evening News*, 10 January 1961, p. 7.

62 'Future of the Windsor Theatre', *Salford City Reporter*, 6 October 1961, p. 3.

63 Letter from Jack Goldberg to Clive Barker, 19 June 1962, Clive Barker Archive.

64 Letter from Clive Barker to Jack Goldberg, 23 June 1962, Clive Barker Archive.

65 Keith Waterhouse, *Billy Liar*, Longman, 1966, (first published 1959), p. 70.

## Chapter 8: New Horizons

1 Brendan Behan and Paul Hogarth, *Brendan Behan's New York*, Hutchinson, 1964, p. 50.

2 Quoted in Victor Spinetti, *Up Front: His Strictly Confidential Autobiography*, Robson, 2006, p. 126.

3 Oscar Lewenstein, *Kicking Against the Pricks: A Theatre Producer Looks Back*, Nick Hern Books, 1994, p. 104.

4 Interview with Murray Melvin; interview with Zdena Tomin.

5 'My Clothes and I', *Observer*, 19 April 1959, p. 15.

6 'The Salford Madonna', *Guardian*, 4 August 1976, p. 10. Information on Shelagh's activities in New York from interviews with Will Macadam and Murray Melvin.

7 Interview with Carol Greitzer.

8 '48 Playwrights in Apartheid Protest', *The Times*, 26 June 1963, p. 12; interview with Charlotte Delaney.

9 Interview with Will Macadam.

10 Carol Greitzer, letter in *New York Times,* 27 December 1959, p. X3.

11 'Theatre without illusion', *New York Times*, 5 October 1960, p. 46.

12 'Dead End Kids', *Time*, vol. 82 no. 9, 30 August 1963, p. 28.

13 Shelagh Delaney, 'Never Underestimate 18-Year-Old Girls', *New York Times Magazine,* 28 May 1961, pp. 30–3.

14 Letter in *New York Times*, 27 December 1959, p. X3.

15 Interview with Carol Greitzer.

16 Letter in *New York Times*, 27 December 1959, p. X3.

17 Shelagh Delaney, 'Never Underestimate 18-Year-Old Girls', *New York Times Magazine*, 28 May 1961, p. 31.

18 Interview with Carol Greitzer.

19 Carol Greitzer, 'We won the battle for the square, but now are we at risk of losing it again?', *The Villager*, 17 October 2013, http://thevillager.com/2013/10/17/we-won-the-battle-for-the-square-but-now-are-we-at-risk-of-losing-it-again/, consulted 31 March 2017.

20 Betty Friedan, *The Feminine Mystique*, W. W. Norton, 1963.

21 Letter from John Croydon to R. E. F. Garrett Esquire, Film Finance, 30 May 1960, File: A Taste of Honey, 310 K42C294F16, Film Finance Archive.

22 Interview with Rita Tushingham.

23 Ibid.

24 Pat Phoenix, *All My Burning Bridges*, Star Books, 1976, p. 70.

25 Interview with Rita Tushingham.

26 'It's a Busy Life for Shelagh', *Salford City Reporter*, 17 March 1961, p. 3.

27 Lavinia Brydon, 'Shelagh Delaney (1938–2011), in Jill Nelmes and Jule Selbo (eds), *Women Screenwriters: An International Guide*, Palgrave Macmillan, 2015, p. 654; letter from John Croydon to R. E. F. Garrett.

28 Interview with Rita Tushingham.

29 'Rita's No Honey – but this film tastes of success', *Daily Mirror*, 15 September 1961, p. 19.

30 Interview with Zdena Tomin; also interview with Charlotte Delaney.

31 Letter from John Croydon to R. E. F. Garrett.

32 'It's a Busy Life for Shelagh', *Salford City Reporter*, 17 March 1961, p. 3.

33 Terry Lovell, 'Landscapes and stories in British realism', *Screen*, vol. 31, no. 4, 1990, pp. 357–76.

34 Interview with Rita Tushingam.

35 Interview with Julie Christie, in Sara Maitland (ed.), *Very Heaven: Looking Back at the 1960s*, Virago, 1988, p. 170.

36 'Rita's No Honey – but this film tastes of success', *Daily Mirror*, 15 September 1961, p. 19.

37 Interview with Shirley Evans.

38 Interview with Charlotte Delaney.

39 Interview with Zdena Tomin.

40 Interview with Ahuva Weisbaum.

41 Jenna Orkin, 'Against the Dying of the Light', https://alzheimersdementiaresidence.wordpress.com, consulted 10 October 2018.

42 Neil Simon, *Rewrites: A Memoir*, Simon & Schuster, 1996, p. 121.

43 Jenna Orkin, 'Who Was Harvey Orkin?', https://harveyorkintvmoviescomedy.wordpress.com, consulted 10 October 2018, and interview with Jenna Orkin; Jenna Orkin, 'Against the Dying of the Light'.

44 Email from Shelagh Delaney to Hila Feil, 5 March 2002.

45 Shelagh Delaney, *Dance with a Stranger*, MS, Working Title Productions, 1985, p. 1.

46 'A Taste for Life', *New York Times*, 15 September 1963, p. 357.

47 Shelagh Delaney, *Sweetly Sings the Donkey*, Penguin, 1968, pp. 95–9.

48 Lorna Sage, *Bad Blood,* Fourth Estate, 2000, p. 234.

49 Peter Eckersley, 'Piercing Cries', *Guardian,* 20 March 1964, p. 22.

50 'A Taste for Life', *New York Times,* 15 September 1963, p. 357.

51 Quoted in Sage, *Bad Blood,* p. 234.

52 'Dead End Kids', *Time,* 30 August 1963, p. 28.

53 Ann Oakley, *Taking It Like a Woman,* Flamingo, 1985, pp. 2, 4.

54 Carol Dix (ed.), *Say I'm Sorry to Mother,* Pan, 1978, p. 10.

55 Carolyn Steedman, *Landscape for a Good Woman,* Virago, 1986, p. 6.

56 Interview with Sophie Collins.

57 Interview with Zdena Tomin.

58 Information from Gerry Feil.

59 Information from Gerry Feil; interview with Kevin Palmer.

## Chapter 9: Happy Ever After

1 'Shelagh Delaney Declares she is Mother of Baby Girl', *New York Times,* 2 April 1964, p. 27.

2 'Shelagh reveals "I had a baby"', *Daily Mirror,* 2 April 1964, p. 1.

3 Interview with Harold Riley.

4 Interview with Kevin Palmer.

5 'How Imagination Retraced a Murder', *New York Times,* 4 August 1985, p. H15.

6 Pat Thane and Tanya Evans, *Sinners? Scroungers? Saints?: Unmarried Motherhood in Twentieth-Century England,* Oxford University Press, 2012, p. 83.

7 Maureen Duffy, Preface, *That's How It Was,* Virago, 1983 (originally published 1962), p. xi.

8 Lorna Sage, *Bad Blood,* Fourth Estate, 2000, p. 237.

9 Interview with Shirley Evans.

10 Such marriages are examined in Thane and Evans, *Sinners?,* p. 82.

11 Sage, *Bad Blood,* p. 232.

12 Letter from Elsie Delaney to Mr Ken Russell, 4 October 1960, T32/982/1 Monitor TX 25/09/1960, BBC Written Archives.

13 Interview with Will Macadam; interview with Harold Riley.

14 'Shelagh Delaney's Book', *Salford City Reporter,* 3 September 1964, p. 3.

15 'What You Can See On That "See Your City" Tour', *Salford City Reporter,* 12 July 1962, pp. 4–5.

16 Shelagh Delaney, 'The White Bus', *Sweetly Sings the Donkey,* Penguin, 1968, pp. 128–9.

17 Lindsay Anderson, Programme note for *The White Bus,* 1979, LA 1/4/5/1, Lindsay Anderson Archive, University of Stirling Archives.

18 Lindsay Anderson, *The Diaries: Lindsay Anderson,* edited by Paul Sutton, Methuen, p. 105.

19 Telegram from Harry Moore to Shelagh Delaney, 8 July 1965, T32/982/1 Monitor TX 25/09/1960, BBC Written Archives.

20 Quoted in John Harding, *Sweetly Sings Delaney: A Study of Shelagh Delaney's Work 1958–68,* Greenwich Exchange, 2014, p. 150.

21 Interview with Harold Riley.

22 Interview with Shirley Evans.

23  Press cuttings file: The White Bus, 1/4/6/1/3, Lindsay Anderson Archive, University of Stirling Archives.

24  'Screen', *New York Times*, 21 December 1979, p. C14.

25  'Give Me Back My Yo-Yo', *New York Times*, 30 March 1969, p. D35.

26  Interview with Zdena Tomin.

27  John Ferris, *Participation in Urban Planning – the Barnsbury Case: a study of environmental improvement in London*, Bell, 1972, p. 48.

28  Sylvia Tunstall, *Experiencing Childbirth: A survey of 40 Islington Women. For Islington Community Health Council*, Islington CHC, 1978, p. 7.

29  Ferris, *Participation in Urban Planning*, p. 23.

30  Ibid., p. 44.

31  Interview with Stephen Frears.

32  Email from Shelagh Delaney to Hila Feil, 25 June 2002.

33  Interview with Will Macadam.

34  Interview with Stephen Frears.

35  Neil Simon, *Rewrites: A Memoir*, Simon & Schuster, 1996, p. 122.

36  Interview with Charlotte Delaney.

37  Interview with Zdena Tomin.

38  Letter from Jane Noak to Charlotte Delaney, *c*.2012, Charlotte Delaney's private papers.

39  Hannah Gavron, *The Captive Wife*, Penguin, 1968, p. 65.

40  Iris Rozencwajg, 'Interview with Margaret Drabble', *Women's Studies: An interdisciplinary journal*, Vol. 6, no. 3, 1979, p. 347.

41  Alan Dunsmore, 'Theatre', *People's Journal*, 12 November 1966, p. 5.

42  Labour Party, 'New Britain. Manifesto for 1964', http://labourmanifesto.com/1964/1964-labour-manifesto.shtml, consulted 5 May 2017.

43  Quoted in Jeremy Gavron, *A Woman on the Edge of Time: A son's search for his mother*, Scribe, 2015, p. 256.

44  Ibid., pp. 256–7. All details of Gavron's life are taken from this source.

45  Harding, *Sweetly Sings Delaney*, p. 160.

46  Interview with Stephen Frears.

47  'The philosophy of Finney', *London Evening Standard*, n.d., Scottish Theatre Archive Press Cuttings, File no. 16, 1960–61, Scottish Theatre Archive, Special Collections, Glasgow University Library.

48  'The Salford Madonna', *Guardian*, 4 August 1976, p. 9.

49  'Indentikit Finney', *Guardian*, 12 February 1969, p. 6. *Charlie Bubbles* was the only film Finney directed.

50  Shelagh Delaney, *Charlie Bubbles*, MS, *c.*1968; ibid.

51  Interview with Stephen Frears.

52  Shelagh Delaney, *Find Me First*, MS, *c.*1979.

53  'The Ten Best Films of '68', *New York Times*, 22 December 1968, p. D3.

54  Charlie Bubbles, 422 K42C400F16, pp. 3 and 5, Film Finance Archive.

55  'Chunks of Life', *New Statesman*, 17 September 1960, p. 378.

56  Ibid.

57  'Not What It Used to Be: Writers of the New Trend Transform the West End', *New York Times*, 29 January 1961, p. X3.

58  'Indentikit Finney', *Guardian*, 12 February 1969, p. 6.

59  'Ten Best Films of '68', *New York Times*, 22 December 1968, p. D3.

## Chapter 10: Dance With a Stranger

1  'Our cardboard women', *Observer*, 10 January 1965, p. 25.

2  'On the rich turf of London streets', *New York Times*, 19 May 1968, p. BR18.

3  Sheila Rowbotham, *Promise of a Dream: Remembering the Sixties*, Penguin, 2000, pp. 236 and 243.

4  Interview with Dee Johnson.

5  Interview with Shirley Evans.

6  A Taste of Honey production file, Glasgow Citizens' Theatre, 1970, Eq 8/12, Scottish Theatre Archive, Special Collections, Glasgow University Library.

7  'Teenagers taped', *Guardian*, 30 January 1963, p. 6.

8  A Taste of Honey production file, Glasgow Citizens' Theatre.

9  Quoted in Laurence Kitchin, *Mid-Century Drama*, Faber, 1960, p. 168.

10  'The Salford Madonna', *Guardian*, 4 August 1976, p. 10.

11  Ibid.

12  Letter from June Delaney to Shelagh Delaney, 16 March 1967.

13  Shelagh Delaney, *The House That Jack Built*, stage play MS, 1979, Act 1, Scene 2, pp. 12–13.

14  Ibid., Act 2, Scene 3, p. 25.

15  Letter from Lindsay Anderson to Alan Brown, 28 August 1975, p. 2, LA/5/01/1/4/120, Lindsay Anderson Archive, University of Stirling Archives.

16  Interview with Albert Finney, in Hal Burton (ed.), *Acting in the Sixties*, BBC, 1970, p. 66.

17  Information from Hila Feil; interview with Charlotte Delaney.

18  Information from Hila Feil.

19  Hila Feil, *The Ghost Garden*, Macmillan, 1975, pp. 16–17 and 27.

20  'The Salford Madonna', *Guardian*, 4 August 1976, p. 10.

21  Ibid.

22  Interview with Charlotte Delaney.

23  Postcard from Gerry and Hila Feil to Shelagh Delaney, 21 December 1970.

24  Lynne Segal, *Making Trouble: Life and Politics*, Serpent's Tail, 2007, p. 75.

25  'Cedric Price: obituary', *Guardian*, 15 August 2003, https://www.theguardian.com/society/2003/aug/15/urbandesign.artsobituaries, consulted 18 May 2017.

26  Information from Charlotte Delaney; see for example letter from Cedric Price to Shelagh Delaney, 4 February 1975.

27  Letter from Cedric Price to Shelagh Delaney, 13 September 1973.

28  Letter from Cedric Price to Shelagh Delaney, c.1972.

29  Letter from Cedric Price to Shelagh Delaney, 17 July 1967.

30  Letter from Cedric Price to Shelagh Delaney, 24 July 1967.

31  Information from Charlotte Delaney.

32  Mary Ingham, *Now We Are Thirty*, Methuen, 1982, p. 174.

33  Shelagh Delaney, *So Said the Nightingale,* MS, *c.*1979, p. 48.

34  Interview with Zdena Tomin.

35  'How Imagination Retraced a Murder', *New York Times,* 4 August 1985, p. H15.

36  Ibid.

37  Ibid.

38  Quoted in 'How sensational crime of passion became hit film 30 years later', *Ottowa Citizen,* 16 September 1985, p. B9.

39  Information from Charlotte Delaney; Shelagh Delaney, *Dance with a Stranger,* Working Title Productions, 1985, p. 33; Shelagh quoted in 'How Imagination Retraced a Murder'.

40  'How Imagination Retraced a Murder'.

41  Ibid.; Shelagh Delaney, *in Dance with a Stranger Production Notes,* Working Title Productions, 1985, p. 2.

42  Interview with Amanda Schiff.

43  'Film', *New York Times,* 18 August 1985, p. H15.

44  Quoted in Simon Goddard, *The Smiths,* 2004, p. 20.

45  Quoted in *NME,* 7 June 1986, p. 4.

46  Delaney, in *Dance with a Stranger Production Notes,* p. 2.

47  Email from Shelagh Delaney to Hila Feil, 4 July 2002.

48  Information from Charlotte Delaney.

49  Email from Shelagh Delaney to Hila Feil, 4 July 2002.

50  Interview with Kath Wilkie; Ibid.

51  Shelagh Delaney, *Baloney Said Salome,* MS, n.d., *c.*2004, p. 6.

52  Email from Shelagh Delaney to Hila Feil, 4 July 2002.

53 Interview with Zdena Tomin; interview with Wilf and Sheila Wade.

54 Interview with Polly Thomas.

55 Interview with Barbara Marten.

56 Email from Shelagh Delaney to Hila Feil, 3 June 2002.

57 Interview with Polly Thomas.

58 Information from Charlotte Delaney.

59 Interview with Zdena Tomin.

60 Delaney, *Baloney Said Salome*, p. 29.

## Chapter 11: Shelagh, Take a Bow

1 Interview with Charlotte Delaney.

2 '*Taste of Honey* Revived at Roundabout', *New York Times*, 29 April 1981, p. C19.

3 Interview with Kirk Morris (pseudonym).

4 Morrissey, *Autobiography*, Penguin, 2013, p. 58.

5 Ibid., p. 92.

6 Quoted in Oscar Lewenstein, *Kicking Against the Pricks: A Theatre Producer Looks Back*, Nick Hern Books, 1994, p. 180.

7 Adelle Stripe speaking at the Working Class Movement Library, Salford, June 2017. Other information about Dunbar is from conversations with Adelle Stripe and from Stripe's brilliant *Black Teeth and a Brilliant Smile*, Wrecking Ball Press, 2017.

8 Interview with Morrissey, *A Chance to Shine: A Morrissey fanzine*, no. 12, c.1995, p. 10.

9 Ibid., p. 7.

10 Morrissey, *Morrissey in Quotes*, Babylon Books, 1988, p. 10.

11 Ibid., p. 47.

12  Interview with Michael Calderbank.

13  Interview with Maxine Peake.

14  Interview with Sarah Frankcom.

15  Jeanette Winterson, 'My hero: Shelagh Delaney', *Guardian*, 18 September 2010, https://www.theguardian.com/books/2010/sep/18/jeanette-winterson-my-hero-shelagh-delaney, consulted 2 May 2017.

16  Correspondence between Shelagh Delaney and Margaret Baron, August 1991.

17  A Taste of Honey production file, Glasgow Citizens' Theatre, 1994, Ex 25/21, Scottish Theatre Archive, Special Collections, Glasgow University Library.

18  Susan Quilliam, *Shelagh Delaney: A Taste of Honey, Penguin Passnotes*, Penguin, 1987, p. 61.

19  Charles Barron, *Drama: A Taste of Honey, Learning and Teaching Guide*, Learning and Teaching Scotland, 2006, p. 21.

20  BBC, Bitesize revision series: GCSE English Literature: *A Taste of Honey*, 2017 http://www.bbc.co.uk/education/guides/zcxwmnb/revision/2, consulted 2 May 2017.

21  Ferdinand Mount, *Mind the Gap: the new class divide in Britain*, Short Books, 2004, p. 2.

22  Andrew O'Hagan, 'The Age of Indifference', *Guardian*, 10 January 2009, https://www.theguardian.com/books/2009/jan/10/andrew-ohagan-george-orwell-memoriallecture, consulted 2 August 2012.

23  See for example Dominic Sandbrook, *Never Had It So Good: A History of Britain from Suez to the Beatles*, Little, Brown, 2005, p. 194, and also his contribution to National Theatre,

'A Taste of Honey by Shelagh Delaney: theatre programme', 2014.

24  Rachel Creaser, 'A Taste of Honey', *Teaching Drama*, Summer term 1, 2013–14, p. 36.

25  Interview with Valeria Scialbini.

26  Interview with Rob Lees.

27  Quoted in 'Special plaque unveiled at Salford house where "genius" writer Shelagh Delaney penned A Taste of Honey', *Manchester Evening News*, 3 September 2014, https://www.manchestereveningnews.co.uk/news/greater-manchester-news/special-plaque-unveiled-salford-house-7714996, consulted 9 November 2018.

28  Interview with Roni Ellis.

29  'Shelagh Delaney gave working-class women a taste of what was possible', *Guardian*, 21 November 2011, https://www.theguardian.com/stage/2011/nov/21/shelagh-delaney-working-class-women, consulted 2 May 2017.

30  E. P. Thompson, 'Outside the Whale', originally published 1960; reprinted in *The Poverty of Theory and Other Essays*, Merlin Press, 1978, p. 32.

# INDEX

# Index

marriage and 2–3, 83, 84–5, 87–8, 89, 138, 185, 214

motherhood and 2, 3, 82–3, 84, 85–6, 87, 88, 89–91, 94, 101, 139–40

National Theatre production (2014) 10, 224–5

new lease of life, early 1970s 182–3

New York Drama Critics' Circle Award 136

premiere, Theatre Royal, Stratford East (27 May 1958) 4, 92–3, 109

race and 2, 4, 5, 6, 11, 59, 83, 84, 85–6, 99, 101, 137, 138, 140, 141, 214

radio adaptation 100

rehearsals 79–91, 100

reviews/critics 4, 5, 47, 81, 86–7, 92–4, 99, 100–5, 131, 138, 139, 142, 152, 169, 178, 212, 225

*Salford City Reporter* and 93–4, 100–1, 104, 131, 143–4

Salford Council and 160–1

SD attends rehearsals 79–81

SD obituaries focus on 212

SD sends manuscript to Joan Littlewood 1, 77–8, 79

SD writes 75–6

set text, comprehensive school 10, 183

Smiths and 200, 201

West End transfer (1959) 10, 96, 98–9, 100–3

Woodfall Films acquires film rights to 108, 110, 121

Attlee, Clement 8, 24, 25–6

Baldwin, James 137

*Baloney Said Salome* (radio play) 73, 205, 206, 208, 210, 211

Banks, Lynne Reid: *The L-Shaped Room* 157

Barker, Clive 116–17, 132, 133

Barker, Lilian 64

Barstow, Stan 69, 70

*A Kind of Loving* 70

BBC 7, 62, 72, 94, 102, 105, 123, 162, 166, 207, 217, 223–4

*A Taste of Honey*, asks SD to write a modern-day version 207

*A Taste of Honey* radio adaptation 100

*Cathy Come Home* and 178–9

Joan Littlewood turns down offer to become Head of Features 77

Manchester and 72, 129

SD refuses to join drama department 13, 121, 160

'Shelagh Delaney's Salford' (*Monitor* programme) 45, 56, 58, 123–5, 159, 160

*Sweetly Sings the Donkey* radio plays 206–7

*The House That Jack Built* television series 185, 186–7, 194–5

*The Lion in Love* and 117

'The White Bus' *Wednesday Play* proposal 160–1

*Z Cars*, SD writes for 11, 160

'Beanstalk Generation' 54

Beatles: 'A Taste of Honey' 147, 192

Beckett, Samuel 65, 213

*Waiting for Godot* 50, 66, 75, 76

*Worstward Ho* 50–1

Behan, Brendan 80, 103

*The Hostage* 117, 135

*The Quare Fellow* 79

Belgrade Theatre, Coventry: opens 128

*The Lion in Love* and 116–17, 118, 120, 128

Benson, Jane 168

Benson, Jo 168

Bentley, Phyllis 68

Berg, Leila 125

Berger, John 24

Billington, Michael 231

*Billy Liar* (film) 98, 146–7 *see also* Waterhouse, Keith

*Black Dwarf* 180

Blakely, David 73, 196, 197, 198, 200

Blears, Hazel 144

Booth Theatre, New York 144

Braine, John: *Room at the Top* 2, 67, 83, 92, 143, 173

Brecht, Bertolt 65

281

# Index

Index

# Index

# Index

# Index

# Index

# Index

Labour Party 6, 8, 24, 25–6, 35, 112,
123, 128, 132, 133, 144,
170, 182, 183, 216, 218, 225
Arts Council and 64, 128
Attlee administration 8, 24, 25–6
comprehensive schools and 123
general election (1945) 6, 24
general election (1951) 41–2
general election (1955) 57
general election (1964) 169–70
general election (1966) 170
general election (1970) 183
general election (1979) 197, 215
general election (1983) 197
New Labour 144, 225
post-war political consensus and
34–5
Salford and 57, 132, 133
Thatcher administration and 218
theatre and 64–5, 128, 132, 133,
182–3
welfare state and 3, 6, 7, 29, 34,
35, 46, 68, 84, 93, 112, 139,
170, 215, 216, 225, 233
Lane, Sue 22
Lansbury, Angela 135
Latham, Harry 130
Lawrence, D. H. 105, 126
*Lady Chatterley's Lover* 126–7, 137
'Learning to Ride a Bicycle' (SD
piece submitted to school
magazine, 1954) 50
Lee, Mollie 94, 95
Leeds Playhouse 182–3
Leek, Miss (SD's headmistress) 36–7,
38, 39
Lees, Rob 228–9, 230, 236
Lessing, Doris 92, 127
Lewenstein, Oscar:
*A Taste of Honey* Broadway run and
121, 136
*A Taste of Honey*, on collaborative
nature of original production 81
*A Taste of Honey* film and 142
*A Taste of Honey* West End transfer
and 96, 116
*Look Back in Anger* and 81
proposes trilogy of films to SD
161–2

*The Lion in Love* and 116
Library Theatre, Manchester 66, 72
*Lion in Love, The* (play):
Belgrade Theatre, Coventry
production 116–17, 128
Interact production of 222
Joan Littlewood and 115–16, 126
Morrissey and 201, 218
New York run 13
problems with 117–18, 175–6
reviews 117–18, 175–6
Royal Court Theatre run 118
SD secures support of Wolf
Mankowitz and Oscar
Lewenstein for 116
success of 13, 117–20
themes 112–15, 185, 216
title 111–12
*Listener* 2, 92
Little Club, London 196
Littlewood, Joan 130
asks SD to join Philip Hedley in
running Stratford East as a
playwright-cum-director 126
*A Taste of Honey* as the work of 13,
81, 117
*A Taste of Honey* rehearsals and
edits to original script 79, 82,
85, 86, 88–91, 99–100
Cedric Price and 191–2
David Scase and 66
Ewan MacColl and 64–5, 77
film adaptation of *A Taste of Honey*
and 135, 136, 145
Gerry Raffles and 79
SD adult relationship with 126
SD as creation of the imagination
of 80, 81
SD defers to 97, 164
SD falls out with 79, 217
SD on genius of 91
SD on value to work of relation-
ship with 79
SD presents herself as pliant
protégée to 78, 97, 109, 110
SD sends *A Taste of Honey* manu-
script to 1, 77–8, 79
SD stays at house in Blackheath
81, 96

289

# Index

# Index

# Index

# Index

# Index